W9-BZW-486

Enjoying Your Journey With God

by Daniel A. Brown, PhD

ctw
Commended to The Word

ENJOYING YOUR JOURNEY WITH GOD by Daniel A. Brown, PhD

This book or parts thereof may not be reproduced in any form, stored in a retrieval system or transmitted in any form by any means—electronic, mechanical, photocopy, recording or otherwise—without prior written permission of the publisher, except as provided by United States of America copyright law.

Unless otherwise noted, all Scripture quotations are from the New American Standard Bible. Copyright © 1960, 1962, 1963, 1968, 1971, 1972, 1973, 1975, 1977 by the Lockman Foundation. Used by permission. (www.Lockman.org)

Scripture quotations marked KJV are from the King James Version of the Bible.

Scripture quotations marked NIV are from the Holy Bible, New International Version. Copyright © 1973, 1978, 1984, International Bible Society. Used by permission.

Scripture quotations marked NKJV are from the New King James Version of the Bible. Copyright © 1979, 1980, 1982 by Thomas Nelson, Inc., publishers. Used by permission.

Cover design by Dann Ledwick
Interior design by Koechel Peterson

Copyright © 2001, 2008 by Daniel A. Brown, PhD
All rights reserved

Library of Congress Catalog Card Number: 2001089806
International Standard Book Number: 978-1-4276-3584-6

Published by Commended to The Word
280 State Park Drive
Aptos, CA 95003
ctw.coastlands.org

ctw
Commended to The Word

Printed in the United States of America

CONTENTS

Introduction

SOME THINGS WE CAN NEVER HEAR TOO MANY TIMES. Genuine empathy when a day turns out lousy; assurances that something wasn't our fault, and anyone would have done what we did; compliments on our voice; honest encouragement about our uncertain future; and simple reminders that we are known and loved—such words make life easier and more enjoyable to live. They give us extra oomph, and they settle the turbulent waters rising around us.

Some truths about God can, likewise, never be heard enough. They are the earliest lessons, what some people refer to as the basics, a curriculum for new believers in Jesus. They may be simple understandings, but they have a way of penetrating even the most complicated of life situations so that our life with the Lord is made easier and far more agreeable. God is good. His standing invitation is for us to taste of that goodness, that delight, that deeply satisfying essence. This book will, I hope, help in that process.

Walking with God and enjoying His nearness is supposed to be the most natural activity of our lives. Yet it has been complicated by so many contrary themes—our inability to believe that He truly likes us; distorted requirements that we mistakenly imagine He puts on us; our well-meaning but misplaced zeal; the seemingly inescapable cloud of guilt that dogs our days; our religious, almost superstitious tendencies to try to earn things from or prove things to Him. We keep getting things backwards, and almost always end up mistranslating His language of affection for and delight in us so that it speaks to us instead of burdensome expectation and duty.

That is why I am fond of telling people that I do not believe in the God they struggle with, the one they do not believe in. My God is much different than that.

This book offers you points of understanding, not bits of informative knowledge. There are lessons to be learned, but not for the mere sake of memorization or for being able to pull answers up in your mind for a catechism test. Rather than giving you facts to digest like so many vitamin pills, these chapters present you with a language, a vocabulary to make simple but profound sense out of the experiences you will have as you walk with Jesus day by day.

> God's ways are
> interwoven into
> the fabric of our
> world. No matter
> where you look—
> if you know what
> to look for—you
> will find them.

Throughout your journey with the Lord, you will keep coming across various themes and points of understanding common for all of us who choose to follow Him. His ways are not like our ways, and you will progressively learn, by revelation and by others' testimony, how to grab hold of the manner in which He thinks and acts.

The discovery process is exciting, not because of all the data and doctrines we learn, but because we get to see, in an unfolding manner, so much of what is true of God as a knowable Being. You will discover that His all-encompassing love for us sometimes manifests itself in surprising ways. Learning the truths of His kingdom is not like learning facts from a textbook. It is more like hiking over the rise of a hill and, for the first time, catching a glimpse of a valley where you could gladly spend the rest of your life. With each new element of truth you grasp, you find yourself thinking, *This is the best.* Like a world traveler encountering one city marvel, one delightful culture, after another, you soon become hard-pressed to pick a favorite truth.

His truths form the very foundation of the whole cosmos. His ways are interwoven into the fabric of our world. No matter where you look—if you know what to look for—you will find them. Yet His ways are also so incredibly personal to each of us. Somehow the macro themes God spoke into existence when everything was made are still able to touch each of us in the most familiar and special ways.

God is like the perfect host of an expansive garden party with millions of guests. He has thought of everything and prepared lavishly for it all—orchestrating the big-ticket items certainly and completely, but also adding the little touches like the hand-written name tags and the delicately flowering plants that trim each centerpiece. His workings in the world communicate to each of us that He was thinking personally about us when He chose the songs for the band to play or picked the color themes for the decorations.

Moment after moment, in the midst of a zillion other guests, you feel as though the party were thrown *just for you.* By means of an intimate miracle, God allows you and me poignantly and personally to live out the offer of abundant life He extends to everyone. Over and over again you will find yourself marveling at what He has arranged for your life. You discover that He has gone before you to situate matters perfectly for your growth and for your fulfillment.

You will feel His pleasure in your progress in the way a father delights at a child learning to take those faltering steps from crawling to walking. In fact, you will sometimes find yourself wondering if the reason you are being taught some lesson again is more because it is just one of His favorites to teach, as opposed to something you didn't quite catch the first time around.

That is how it is supposed to be in your walk with the Lord—sensing His delight, His pleasure in being with you. Once you were lost to Him forever and, like a father who has only recently received back his ransomed child from the clutches of a kidnapper, He still has not gotten over the horror of what it was like without you in His life.

Every spiritual lesson you undergo, every truth of the kingdom you come to grasp and all the themes and understandings you encounter in your life with Jesus are incredibly personal and freshly apprehended (by you) as though no one else has ever quite experienced what you have. That is the wonder of serving a living God who knows and loves you. The simple topics in this book will emerge in your life over and over. They are like familiar places to which you will come again and again in times of realization, in hours of need and in moments of worship.

Yet these landmarks and familiar sightings on your journey with Jesus are also places where generations of saints before you have returned. They have been, throughout the ages, the timeless guideposts, the faithful markers by which every child of God has paused, considered, wept and rejoiced. Gathered there beneath the cross, their eyes were opened to behold wonders from His Word.

As you work your way through this "journey" book, you will find many scriptures quoted either in the text or in the sidebars. Others will say "read" followed by a reference. Look these verses up in your own Bible, for they are opportunities for you to become better acquainted with God's Word.

Then use the additional spaces in the sidebar columns to add your own comments and study notes as you progress on your "journey."

May you enjoy a fresh retelling of these ageless truths.

—Daniel Brown

▲ You will feel His
▲ pleasure in your
▲ progress in the
▲ way a father
▲ delights at a child
▲ learning to take
▲ those faltering
▲ steps from
▲ crawling to
▲ walking.

CHAPTER ONE

Getting to Know God Personally

MORE THAN ANYTHING ELSE, GOD DESIRES A RELATIONSHIP WITH YOU. He created the world out of the overflow of His heart, wanting to be with and to share with people like you and me. As incredible as that sounds—*the almighty God who made every single thing on this planet did so with us in mind*—it is the simple truth from which flow all other understandings about God.

We did not happen upon the earth as a result of cosmic coincidence. The beginnings of our race did not unfold in a vacuum of uncertainty or in empty swirls of random particles. Rather, we are the culmination of God's creative and intentional handiwork. His purpose for us has always been the same—to reveal Himself to us and to love us. He longs to have us know Him better and better. And that explains everything else He does.

Though it is somewhat difficult to think of God in human terms—just because He is so much greater in every way than any human being—we cannot adequately grasp His intentions for relationship with us unless we use language that is familiar to our everyday lives.

In fact, one of the most common misconceptions about God is that He only wants to be thought of in grandiose, religious ways. Many people assume that since God is so great and holy, they should stay away from Him! Yet He reveals Himself to us in the Bible as a God who longs to have us by His side. He wants to talk with us, express His love for us and make plans with us. He thinks about us, remembers us and makes promises to us—and He wants us to do the same with Him. He does many of the same things that we do, except one—He never does anything wrong!

God is knowable. He has a distinct character, one so wondrously perfect and magnificent that it seems almost preposterous to imagine that finite humans could ever get to know Him for who He actually is. How we could ever get to know God

> The almighty God who made every single thing on this planet did so with us in mind.

IN THIS CHAPTER YOU WILL DISCOVER THAT GOD . . .

- ▲ Wants to reveal Himself to us.
- ▲ Created the world expressly to have a relationship with us.
- ▲ Prefers to be called "Daddy God" and wants to be intimate with us.
- ▲ Always wants to be with us more than we want to be with Him.
- ▲ Knows everything about us.
- ▲ Thinks about us all the time.

and why He would want to disclose Himself to us are great mysteries—but we can and He does. Before we see how, we first want to focus on God's unique nature.

All gods are not the true God; the Lord does not go by various aliases in different countries in the world. Our God has characteristics and qualities that set Him apart from all other gods. No god is like our God.

Read Psalm 86:8. What does this verse say about the true God, whose name is Jehovah?

There is none like Him, the true Jehovah.

Is it possible that your concept of God has been confused by attributes of other gods?

Could be - depends on what gods we're talking about or attributes that belong to other gods that I don't realize I'm attributing to our God.

Can you think of specific examples?

> God does not want us to know *about* Him, but to actually know Him as Moses did—"face to face, just as a man speaks to his friend."

As you walk with the Lord, you will increasingly learn to distinguish the Lord and His works from all other gods and their activities. There are two lies about the Lord that our culture tends to embrace. Some view Him as a nebulous presence like a low-grade electrical force that can be barely sensed when the conditions are favorable or when particularly sensitive people are present. Others confuse God with all the other gods in the world. He becomes a composite caricature of Thor, Zeus, Vishnu and everyone's ideas about what He is probably like. People's ideas about God can be like idols—false and misleading. Just because something is worshiped does not mean it is the Lord.

God is knowable, and He wants you to get to know Him.

RELIGION OR RELATIONSHIP?

Christianity is the only faith that presents God as a loving Father who wants to have an intimate, personal relationship with His followers. Here's a quick look at how some other religions portray God.

The angry avenger. Some religions teach that God is a cruel judge who spends most of His time punishing His followers when they disobey His orders. He is not a god of love, but a god of violence and hatred.

The mystical spirit. Many people worship a god who is elusive, mysterious and impersonal. They view this being not as loving and personal, but as some kind of energy force that hides its true identity from mankind. Only a few can figure out this god's strange "secret code," so they explore the occult to glimpse him.

The apathetic creator. Some people believe in a Supreme Being who has no intimate interest in individual people. After He created the world He abandoned us to live on our own.

The impotent god-man. Many people in Western cultures have fashioned their own god—in their own image. God is really just like man and tolerant of any and every "sincere" moral code or religion.

KNOWING GOD UP CLOSE

God is much more than a force or a vague power coursing through the universe. He is not just a principle of oneness, an energy of life, a universal understanding or a featureless supreme being. He is the Creator of all things, but He is not diffused throughout all things. He was before all things came into being, but He is not merely a primal energy that gave rise to life and has since faded into the cosmos.

We are invited to know Him not at a distance, but up close. He does not want us to know *about* Him, but to actually know Him as Moses did—"face to face, just as a man speaks to his friend" (Exod. 33:11).

Question: What do you think it means to know God face to face?

_____

_____

Do you feel that you know Him that closely—like a best friend?

_____

What sorts of things do you tell only to a best friend?

_____

_____

Do you feel that you can tell them to the Lord?

I can tell Him more things.

The great day will come for each of us who know the Lord through Jesus Christ, when we will be "face to face" with Him in heaven (1 Cor. 13:12).

For now we see in a mirror dimly, but then face to face.
—1 Corinthians 13:12

In the meantime, we get to become better acquainted with Him each day. God loves all the people of the earth. For those who do not yet know Him personally, glimpses of His nature can be seen by looking at the cosmos—His creation. (Read Romans 1:19–20.)

Read Psalm 19:1–6. God has left His signature in the sky. What impressions have you had about God when you saw a spectacular sunset or gazed out into the vastness of a starry night?

Awesome! Glorious – unbelievable utterly amazing God that could create something like that, and that is even small compared to Him.

Describe how you were moved and how close you felt to Him.

Thankful that I can see His display – that He lets me in on something like that!

Considering the grandeur and majesty of all creation, it is incredible that God would think about mankind. David was a man whose heart was in tune with the Lord's. Yet, he was puzzled by God's attention and affection toward us. Contemplating the vastness and beauty of the night sky, he asks, "What is man that You are mindful of him?" (Ps. 8:4, NKJV). We might well add, "Who am I that God would want to disclose Himself to me on a personal basis?"

We describe the process of getting to know other people as *growing closer and closer to them.* It works the same way with the Lord. The better we get to know Him, the closer we feel to Him. He longs to be near to us, close at hand, so that He can help us in our times of need and be there for us. The nearness of our God— the intimacy with which He relates to us—is one of the most amazing attributes of our relationship with Him, and one that differentiates Him from all other gods. The writer of Deuteronomy put it this way: "For what great nation is there that has a god so near to it as is the LORD our God whenever we call on Him?" (Deut. 4:7). In Jeremiah 23:23, God reminds His people, "Am I a God who is near . . . and not a God far off?" His constant invitation to us throughout our life is, "Come near to Me" (Isa. 48:16).

WHAT GOD IS REALLY LIKE

If God had wanted to be unfair, whimsical, unjust, cruel, spiteful or careless, He could have been. Have you ever stopped to consider what life would be like if God had chosen to be other than how He is? What a horrid cosmos this would be!

We can be glad God is God as God is. His kind intentions are manifest in everything He does. (Read Ephesians 1:3–6.) The more we come to understand His heart and the characteristics of His dealings with people, the better we will come to know Him.

God is gracious. He bends down like a loving parent to do for us what we cannot do for ourselves. "Therefore the Lord longs to be gracious to you, and therefore He waits on high to have compassion on you. For the Lord is a God of justice; how blessed are all those who long for Him" (Isa. 30:18).

God is merciful. He understands us and our frailties, and He eagerly extends forgiveness to us for what we do wrong. "But Thou, O Lord, art a God merciful and gracious, slow to anger and abundant in lovingkindness and truth" (Ps. 86:15).

God is compassionate. He cherishes us the way a mother thinks fondly about the child in her womb. "For the Lord your God is a compassionate God; He will not fail you nor destroy you nor forget the covenant with your fathers which He swore to them" (Deut. 4:31).

God is kind. He unexpectedly takes special interest in us the way that a famous pro football star might greet a young kid. "But love your enemies, and do good, and lend, expecting nothing in return; and your reward will be great, and you will be sons of the Most High; for He Himself is kind to ungrateful and evil men" (Luke 6:35).

God is good. He is bountiful, cheerful, at ease and glad. Well-being and health flow from Him, and He makes everything better. "For Thou, Lord, art good, and ready to forgive, and abundant in lovingkindness to all who call upon Thee" (Ps. 86:5).

God is righteous. Absolutely nothing is wrong with Him. He is always and only the way He should be. He is the absolute standard by which we can set our lives. "The Lord is righteous in all His ways, and kind in all His deeds" (Ps. 145:17).

WHAT GOD REALLY WANTS

The Genesis (Beginnings) account of creation holds some of the most intriguing details about God's intended relationship with us as a people and with us as individuals. In the first place, we were made in God's image to resemble and reflect Him in the most significant ways so that we could relate to Him (Gen. 1:26–27).

Isn't that one of the prerequisites to relationship among people—to have things in common? God made us like Himself so that He would not seem strange to us. We were fashioned to fit in perfectly with Him and to coincide with what is true about Him.

He is not a strange God. In fact, He warns us against allowing any strange god to turn our hearts away from Him (Ps. 81:9).

Though He is majestic and awesome in scope and power, God never intended to be so different from us that we would struggle to relate to Him. What makes it hard for us to have a comfortable relationship with Him is *our wrongness,* not *His strangeness.* We are His offspring, His children. Earthly parents may, at times, wonder how they could have given birth to children who seem so different in looks or behavior. However, it is unimaginable that the Lord

Then God said, "Let Us make man in Our image, according to Our likeness; and let them rule over the fish of the sea and over the birds of the sky and over the cattle and over all the earth, and over every creeping thing that creeps on the earth." And God created man in His own image, in the image of God He created him; male and female He created them.
— Genesis 1:26–27

Let there be no strange god among you; nor shall you worship any foreign god.
— Psalm 81:9

would, in anticipation of future conversation and connection with us, bring forth people who were unlike Himself.

In both image and likeness, we resemble the Lord. While we are not close to being as great as He is or to having His power, our image is like a pale, powder blue to His deep, royal blue. At our core—our spirit—our inner shade is the same basic color as His. Our frame and constitution are limited by physical realities, whereas His composition is not. But in the beginning His nature was impressed into ours. That is why the story of redemption and growth in the Lord can be seen as our restoration back to being like Him.

Each of the following scriptures tell us something specific about God restoring His children in His image—just as He had made us in the beginning. **Read the verse** and then fill in what God said.

Romans 8:29

> For God knew His people in advance, and He chose them to be like His Son, so that His Son would be the firstborn, with many brothers and sisters.

2 Corinthians 3:18

> And all of us have had that veil removed so that we can be mirrors that brightly reflect the glory of the Lord. And as the Spirit of the Lord works in us, we become more and more like Him and reflect His glory even more.

Colossians 3:10

> In the place of evil nature, you have clothed yourselves with a brand new nature that is continually being renewed as you learn more & more about Christ who created this new nature within you.

2 Peter 1:3–4

> As we know Jesus better, His divine power gives us everything we need for living a godly life. He has called us to receive His own glory and goodness! His power...

We were made male and female in the beginning. God saw that it was not good for man to be alone. That was the condition He Himself had been in before He created man. Knowing how full His own heart had been with longing to share His love, He created a companion for Adam, and Eve became the perfect counterpart. Just as God wanted man and woman to be together, to have communion and conversation with one another, so He wants us to be together with Him. In the beginning, before man's wrong choices ruined the profound connection between God and us, He walked and talked with Adam and Eve in the midst of the garden. (Read Genesis 2 and 3.)

That is how He wants to accompany you in your life. Day after day, year by year, you will experience an ongoing disclosure of who He is and what He is like.

Just as God wanted man and woman to be together, to have communion and conversation with one another, so He wants us to be together with Him.

OTHER NAMES OF GOD

Many times in the Scriptures the Lord discloses a new aspect of His character to someone by revealing a new name for Himself. When Moses encountered God in a burning bush, God told Moses that His name was "I AM WHO I AM." (Read Exodus 3:14.) This name for God revealed that He is transcendent, eternal and all-sufficient. God reveals other aspects of His nature with other names like:

"The Lord Will Provide" (Read Genesis 22:14.) — God showed Abraham that He would indeed provide the sacrifice necessary to pay for our sins.

"The Lord Is My Banner" (Read Exodus 17:15.) — God told Moses that He goes before us and fights against what opposes us.

"The God Who Saves Me" (Read Psalm 51:14, NIV.) — The psalmist learned that God preserves us from death and eternal destruction.

God "My Hiding Place" (Read Psalm 32:7.) — David came to understand that he could find safety and comfort in the Lord's mercy.

"Wonderful Counselor" (Read Isaiah 9:6.) — The prophet realized that God listens to our problems, understands our hurts and has great wisdom to resolve our conflicts.

"My Strong Deliverer" (Read Psalm 140:7, NIV.) — The psalmist understood that no matter what difficulty entraps us, even if it is a result of our own sin, God in His mercy will set us free.

"The Good Shepherd" (Read John 10:11.) — Jesus Christ revealed the tender, loving heart of God when He compared His love to that of a shepherd defending his sheep from danger.

GOD'S FAVORITE NAME

Most of us do not have much of a choice about our name. It was given to us, and unless we change it, it is ours for life. But there are a few situations in life when we have the opportunity to tell people what we want to be called—grandparents, sweethearts and close friends can push for nicknames. God has lots of names and titles. He is "I AM," the Eternal One, the Almighty, God the Provider, Maker of the heavens and earth, and many other names.

But the intimacy and tenderness with which God loves us is wrapped up in one of His favorite names, the one His Spirit teaches us to say first, just after we are restored to relationship with Him. This name is *Abba,* which is Hebrew for "Daddy" (Rom. 8:15; Gal. 4:6). He loves to be called "Daddy God."

God has a father's heart. That is why we call Him "God our Father." He is a perfect father who always knows what is best for us

For you have not received a spirit of slavery leading to fear again, but you have received a spirit of adoption as sons by which we cry out, "Abba! Father!"

— Romans 8:15

And because you are sons, God has sent forth the Spirit of His Son into our hearts, crying, "Abba! Father!"

— Galatians 4:6

and who always does what is best for us. Unfortunately, many people end up with a distorted picture of God because their earthly fathers were unable to be everything God wanted them to be for their children. Whereas earthly fathers may be distant or absent, God is always there for us—"a very present help in trouble" (Ps. 46:1). He is "the one who goes with" us anywhere we go (Deut. 31:6). Instead of being impatient or critical as some earthly parents can be, God patiently and compassionately deals with our shortcomings. He is slow to anger, quick to forgive.

OUR EARTHLY FATHER AND DADDY GOD

Even the best parents will say and do things that cause their children lingering grief. Our human failings and weaknesses make us vulnerable to hurting and disappointing the very people we most want to cherish. So it is that moms and dads sometimes choose poorly—and do lasting harm to their kids. This is especially true when a father repeatedly misses the mark in how he relates toward his children. Children whose earthly fathers did not have a positive, intimate relationship with them will carry a measure of mistrust and confusion toward God, their heavenly Father, even into their adult years.

If you had a difficult upbringing and were unable to truly rest in the close presence of your father—for whatever reason—it may explain some of your awkwardness with the Lord. The table below contrasts what you may have come to expect from your earthly father(s) and what you can always count on with your heavenly Father.

Earthly Father(s)	Daddy God	Bible Verses
Distant or absent— Dad was always at work; had a weak personality; dead or divorced; he spent no lingering time with you.	**Close and ever present—** He will never desert or forsake you; He is a near help in times of trouble; One who is near, not far off.	Read Deuteronomy 4:7; 31:8; Psalm 46:1; 73:28; Jeremiah 23:23; Matthew 28:20; Hebrews 10:22.
Selfish or self-serving— family life revolved around his wants and convenience; many confusing rules; kids *"seen, not heard."*	**Compassionate and sacrificial—** He spared not His own Son; God graciously does for us what we cannot do for ourselves.	Read Psalm 86:15; 103:4; Isaiah 30:18; Daniel 9:9; Hosea 2:23; Matthew 9:36; John 3:16; James 5:11.
Conditionally loving— attention was based on accomplishment or behavior; *if or when* were the only paths to affection.	**Unconditionally loving—** based on His promise, not our performance; nothing can separate us from His love; He loved us before we loved Him.	Read Jeremiah 31:3; John 3:16; Romans 8:38–39; 1 John 4:10.

Angry or violent— unpredictable outbursts kept you on edge; you feared for your safety, well-being; you felt that you could do nothing right.	**Patient and encouraging—** slow to anger and abounding in mercy; focused on our well-being; seeks to do us good and give us peace.	Read Nehemiah 9:17; Psalm 145:8; Joel 2:13; Jonah 4:2; 2 Peter 3:9.
Critical or fault finding— his focus was always on what's wrong; you felt "out of favor," never good or right enough.	**Forgiving and gracious—** He covers our faults and trespasses; we are never "too" bad; He cleans us from wrong.	Read Psalm 103:10; Isaiah 43:25; Micah 7:19; Hebrews 8:12; 10:16–17.
Abusive— sexually, emotionally or verbally you were the target; his touch and words shamed you; you felt like discarded leftovers.	**Restorative and redemptive—** He bandages broken hearts and liberates captives of emotional, physical, spiritual and mental abuse.	Read Psalm 69:16–20, 29–33; Isaiah 40:31; 61:1–3, 7; Jeremiah 30:17–18; Joel 2:25; Zechariah 9:12.
Controlling or authoritarian— stern punishment landed on you without love; punishment was harsh and sterile; you were never allowed to explain yourself.	**Loving and attentive—** He draws us to Himself in compassion; disciplines us for our good; gives us choice and free will.	Read Deuteronomy 7:7–9; 30:19; 2 Chronicles 16:9; Isaiah 49:13, 15; Hebrews 12:5–11.

> God is a perfect father who always knows what is best for us and who always does what is best for us.

Question: Which characteristic of earthly fathers in the chart above best describes your earthly father?

_____

Through which of the characteristics of your heavenly Father has God revealed Himself to you?

_____

_____

Which characteristic of your heavenly Father do you feel is the most important way that you need God to reveal Himself to you right now? Why?

_____

_____

For your husband is your Maker, whose name is the LORD of hosts.

—Isaiah 54:5

And I will betroth you to Me forever; yes, I will betroth you to Me in righteousness and in justice, in lovingkindness and in compassion, and I will betroth you to Me in faithfulness. Then you will know the LORD.

—Hosea 2:19–20

As the bridegroom rejoices over the bride, so your God will rejoice over you.

—Isaiah 62:5

A FAITHFUL HUSBAND

Another telling picture of God and how He feels about being in constant relationship with us can be seen when He describes Himself as a Husband who intentionally betroths us to Himself forever in faithfulness, love and tender mercy (Isa. 54:5; Hos. 2:19–20). Just as a bridegroom feels about his bride, so God feels about us—filled with excited anticipation about all the years ahead (Isa. 62:5). He does not want a casual, intermittent relationship with us. He has done everything He can to assure that we can get to know Him and be with Him forever.

How sad that so many people imagine a god who barely puts up with them. They see a god who is put out and perturbed, who must somehow tolerate people for whom he doesn't really care. To them, relationship with God is tenuous at best and based only on their ability to perform adequately. Because they do not understand the family connection God wants to have with them, they feel they have to live up to certain standards in order to remain acceptable to Him. The tragedy is that no one can be good enough to maintain relationship with God on his or her own. People who do not grasp how much God Himself wants to maintain the relationship with us end up feeling resentful toward Him. They feel an angry guilt.

God's love is so powerful, His desire for eternal closeness with us is so compelling, that He was willing to give up everything most valuable to Him in order to reestablish His lost relationship with us.

What a contrast such a viewpoint is to the truth about God. His love is so powerful, His desire for eternal closeness with us is so compelling, that He was willing to give up everything most valuable to Him in order to reestablish His lost relationship with us. What He sacrificed and why He had to restore our broken relationship with Him is really the story of the Bible. We will consider this story from many different angles in this book. But for now, the most important truth to remember is that God always wants a relationship with us more than we want it with Him. He is the initiator and the repairer of the relationship.

You never have to wonder if God wants you around. No matter what, He wants you. Whatever happens, whatever you do, whatever choices you may make, you can be completely assured that God, our heavenly Father, our Husband, our Maker, always wants to have you near Him. And He will use every situation in your life to disclose more of Himself to you.

Since God is God—the One who made all the initial decisions about how reality was to be configured and the One who has the last word about everything—He could be any way He wanted to be. No one could tell Him what He should be like. He had no counselor at creation (Rom. 11:34). If God had wanted to be unfair, whimsical, unjust, cruel, spiteful or careless, He could have been.

GOD KNOWS US

Ultimately, God wants us to see and know Him as fully as He knows us (1 John 3:2). God knows everything about us—inside and out. He knows all the places we go with our feet and with our thoughts. Before we say something, He knows what we are going to say. But He doesn't just know things *about* us such as curious details of our past, all the nicknames we've ever had, how tall we were at age seven and why we have that scar above our right eye. He knows us for *who we are*—distinct from all the other people in the world.

That is because He made us Himself. And the way He made you—or me—is unlike the way He made anyone else.

Read Psalm 139:13–16. The psalmist marvels at how God created each of us so uniquely. What does he say about God's involvement while we were in the womb?

_____

_____

⎯

The expression *wonderfully made* actually means "with differentiating marks and distinctions." The Lord is our designer and manufacturer. What comfort in knowing that He knows us better than we know ourselves. What reassurance in knowing that the One who made us—with our notable uniqueness—is the One who offers to oversee the details of our life circumstances. In effect, day by day and situation by situation, as we place ourselves in His hands we are sending ourselves back to the manufacturer for proper treatment and necessary repairs.

Since He has made each of us different from one another, I do not have to wonder if His plan for my life would be better if it resembled His arrangement for yours. You need not struggle trying to follow His assignment for me. Remember, we are not self-made beings who somehow show up on the planet and present ourselves to God. No one has to remind Him who you are. We are not objects of study or things to be memorized by Him. He already knows you—really knows you. He can pick you out of the crowd at a Rose Bowl game on New Year's Day.

His knowledge and understanding are intensely personal when it comes to things about us. In much the same way that a mother knows her youngest son—his quirky humor, the colors he likes best, the jeans he prefers to wear, the hesitation he feels about ladders and

> For who has known the mind of the Lord, or who became His counselor?
> —Romans 11:34

> Beloved, now we are children of God, and it has not appeared as yet what we shall be. We know that, when He appears, we shall be like Him, because we shall see Him just as He is.
> —1 John 3:2

the teacher he had in fourth grade—God knows us. He has the insider's perspective. He is privy to our innermost sensibilities. He knows us absolutely and loves us absolutely.

Read the following verses, and then write down how God's awareness of and focus on you is described:

2 Chronicles 16:9_____

_____

Matthew 10:30_____

_____

How do these ideas change your picture of how well God knows you?_____

_____

> God's love is so powerful, His desire for eternal closeness with us is so compelling, that He was willing to give up everything most valuable to Him in order to reestablish His lost relationship with us.

Part of the reason God knows everything about you is, of course, because He is *omniscient* (all-knowing) and *omnipresent* (everywhere at once). How could He not know? If He is all-knowing, then He knows all. If His presence fills all, then He knows where you are—in fact, He is there with you. But God knows you from *His heart* more than from *His supernatural attributes*. He is "*intimately* acquainted" with you (Ps. 139:3, emphasis added).

GOD THINKS ABOUT US

God has lots of time on His hands. Since He is "from everlasting to everlasting," He is not short of time to do whatever He wants to do (Ps. 90:2). So how does God spend His time? With what does the God of everything occupy Himself? What does He think about?

Well, He thinks about the ones He loves. One of the ways we know that we are falling in love with someone is that we think about that person all the time—we can't get him or her out of our mind. Being in love is almost synonymous with always thinking about someone—where he is, what she's doing and things about his or her personality.

▲▲▲▲▲▲▲▲▲▲▲▲▲▲▲▲▲▲▲▲▲▲▲▲▲▲▲▲▲▲▲▲▲▲▲▲

If you tallied up all the thoughts God has about you, they would number as much as all the grains of sand on all the beaches and in all the deserts of the world.

▲▲▲▲▲▲▲▲▲▲▲▲▲▲▲▲▲▲▲▲▲▲▲▲▲▲▲▲▲▲▲▲▲▲▲▲

God thinks about us. In fact, if you tallied up all the thoughts He has about you, they would number as much as all the grains of sand on all the beaches and in all the deserts of the world. The psalmist exclaimed, "How precious also are Thy thoughts to me, O God! How vast is the sum of them! If I should count them, they would outnumber the sand" (Ps. 139:17–18). Wow! We are always on His mind. He thinks about us constantly. We never have to worry if He has forgotten about us.

Your life may take unexpected turns, or you may find yourself in lonely, desert places, but no matter what the conditions or how desperate life seems, God is intently thoughtful of you. Nothing about our lives escapes His notice. He is perpetually mindful of me and you.

Read Isaiah 49:14–16. Have you ever felt forgotten and abandoned by God?

_____
〰

How easy do you think it is for a nursing mother to forget her child?

_____
_____
〰

If you wrote someone's name on your hands, how often would you be reminded of them?

_____
〰

What does this make you realize about God, your Father?

_____
_____
〰

Did you know the Bible says that God feels good when He thinks about us? When He took a step back and surveyed what He had made in the beginning when He brought forth Adam and Eve, His comment about it all, and especially about us as the preeminent part of creation, was, "This is good—very, very good" (Gen. 1:31). Deliberations about us make Him happy. Sometimes He quietly celebrates over you; at other times His rejoicing as He thinks on you takes the form of shouted exclamations in the heavens—and even some dancing (Zeph. 3:17).

This knowledge of how God feels about us bumps into a misconception that can cause you lots of trouble in your walk with the Lord: Many people mistakenly believe that God is fundamentally disgusted with human beings—that He really doesn't like us because of how evil we are. It is true that God abhors the deadly sin in our life, but He hates it because of what it does to us.

> The LORD your God is in your midst, a victorious warrior. He will exult over you with joy, He will be quiet in His love, He will rejoice [to spin or twirl about] over you with shouts of joy.
> —Zephaniah 3:17

KNOWING GOD

Using your Bible, read Psalm 139:1–12. After each statement below, write down which verse corresponds to the truths in the statement:

God searches and knows me inside and out—so I do not have to wonder if He will still love me when He "finds out" what I am really like.

He knows every step I take, every thought I think—so He knows how I have ended up where I am, and what steps and thoughts will lead me to where He wants me to go.

He knows how and where I live—so I can rely on Him to point out elements in my lifestyle that do not correspond to His intentions for my life.

He surrounds me with His attention and touch—so even in the presence of my enemies, He is in control.

Wherever or however I end up, God is there waiting for me—so I never have to worry about being so far away from Him that I cannot find Him.

He can get hold of me anywhere, anytime—so I can rest in the knowledge that He can speak to me in a way I can truly understand.

Darkness and light are alike to Him—so no matter how dismal my circumstances may seem, or how lost I feel in the midst of them, God sees everything clearly.

God always loves us. Because He longs to be with us forever, because He delights so thoroughly in us, because He absolutely adores us—therefore He has made a way for our sins to be removed from our lives. He never confuses *us* with *our stuff.* His thoughts about our sins are exactly the opposite of His feelings about us—He wants to get rid of our sins so He can get next to us.

LET'S TALK ABOUT IT

▲ Describe how you viewed God before you read this chapter. Did you view Him differently than the Bible describes Him? If so, how?

_____

_____

▲ Why do you think people have a hard time believing that God loves them unconditionally? How would you explain God's love in your own words?

_____

_____

▲ Why did He create the world? What is God's purpose for us?

_____

_____

▲ Why does God prefer to be called "Daddy God"? What makes it hard for us to have a comfortable relationship with Him?

_____

_____

▲ God wants us to search Him out to have deeper, more meaningful relationship. Have you done this willingly, wholly, continually and intentionally? Have you let go of your old ways of thinking about and doing things? Why do you think God wants you to change your old ways?

_____

_____

YOUR TIME WITH GOD

Share your innermost thoughts and feelings with God. Tell God anything that is on your mind and release whatever has been bothering you to Him. God wants to accompany you in your life. Ask God for confirmation that He is there. Ask Him to use every situation in your life to disclose more of Himself to you. Ask God to hold your hand when you need courage, and ask Him to reassure you that you have strengths yet to discover and use.

Thank God for what He has already done and what He has already revealed of Himself to you. Perhaps you would like to include the following prayer in your conversation with God.

Father God, it's hard for me to say this, but I thank You for making me me. I look at myself and could point out several areas where I'm tempted to believe You made a mistake. But I'm choosing to believe instead that You framed me from the beginning with purpose and delight, and that even the things I don't like about myself are arranged by You for my welfare—and even for blessing other people. Show me how this can be true for me personally.

I want to draw near to You, Lord. Open my eyes to see Your heart toward me. Where I have been hurt or betrayed in the past . . . where I have guarded my heart against You . . . Lord, heal me. Help me to know You for who You are—my Daddy God. In Jesus' name, amen.

CHAPTER TWO

Being Loved Without End

NOTHING IN ALL THE WORLD IS MORE MEANING-FUL TO US THAN BEING LOVED. We love being loved—not just because of what those who love us do for us, but because of the special feeling we get by simply knowing that we are loved. Though humans are capable of getting by in life without being personally loved and delighted in by others, we all want to be loved. This is no accident, no evolutionary development of our emotions. We were made that way by a God whose whole purpose for creating us was to have a lasting relationship of mutual love and affection with us. From the very beginning of the cosmos and all the way through unfolding eternity, the single greatest hallmark of God's touch is love.

That's because God is more than merely a feeling or a force or an atmosphere of love—*He is love personified . . . love incarnate* (1 John 4:8, 16). As we saw in the last chapter, God is a knowable persona. He is an actual Being whose supernatural attributes and character are almost beyond human comprehension, but distinct and certain nonetheless. God is not *just* love, but of all the tangible or intangible elements in human experience, what is true of love comes the closest to depicting what is true of God. Love exemplifies God's essential character-istics. Love defines His nature, His motives and His dealings throughout all time.

At one point when Moses asked the Lord to reveal more of Himself, to more tangibly register His nature in a way that Moses could truly understand, the Lord agreed to "pass by" where Moses would be hidden in the cleft of a rock (Exod. 34:5–6). Moses wanted to know what sort of a God he would be following. The miracles he had witnessed in Egypt had convinced Moses of God's power, but Moses wanted to know His ways (Exod. 33:13). He wanted to know the full truth about the God of his fathers. What is God like? How does He choose to reveal Himself?

> Love exemplifies God's essential characteristics.

IN THIS CHAPTER YOU WILL LEARN THAT . . .

- ▲ God is love.
- ▲ We were conceived by God in love.
- ▲ God welcomes and honors us.
- ▲ God wants us with Him forever.
- ▲ We love God by accepting His love for us.
- ▲ God has adopted us into His family.
- ▲ God's love will keep surprising us.

The one who does not love does not know God, for God is love . . . And we have come to know and have believed the love which God has for us. God is love, and the one who abides in love abides in God, and God abides in him.

—1 John 4:8, 16

And the LORD descended in the cloud and stood there with him as he called upon the name of the LORD. Then the LORD passed by in front of him . . .

— Exodus 34:5–6

Now therefore, I pray Thee, if I have found favor in Thy sight, let me know Thy ways, that I may know Thee, so that I may find favor in Thy sight.

— Exodus 33:13

What is the nature of His glory?

The Lord's response to Moses is very revealing. God could have declared anything about Himself. Imagine if you were told to describe yourself in a handful of words. What would you say about yourself that you would want recorded for all time? Would you mention your accomplishments in school or at work? What boast could you truthfully make about yourself? Look at what the Lord told Moses:

> *Then the LORD passed by in front of him and proclaimed, "The LORD, the LORD God, compassionate and gracious, slow to anger, and abounding in lovingkindness and truth; who keeps lovingkindness for thousands, who forgives iniquity, transgression and sin."*
>
> —EXODUS 34:6–7

In Exodus 34:6–7 God gives us the most significant qualities about Himself. Read these verses and describe how each of His traits is a manifestation of love:

Compassionate _____

_____

Gracious _____

_____

Slow to anger _____

_____

Abounding in loving [merciful] kindness _____

_____

Abounding in truth [and trustworthiness] _____

_____

Maintaining loving [merciful] kindness _____

_____

Forgiving _____

_____

Love prompted God to conceive us. That love was not just a generic love for a species. He did not make all of us so that He could have lots of human beings milling about like so many pets. Quite the contrary is true. His love is such an intrinsic part of who

He is. It is so compellingly creative, so animating and life-giving in its makeup, that it generates His longing for relationship with one person after another. Every person in the world is born out of a unique yearning in God's heart.

GOD'S LOVE ARRANGES THINGS

God's love arranged quite a place for Adam and Eve! Everything they could ever want or need was in the Garden of Eden. What a lavish layout! They were given stewardship over all of creation and freedom to pursue their inclinations (with certain exceptions). The Garden of Eden is a picture of the sort of place God wants to make for us. It was not a tiny, spare or secondhand place. The accommodations were not Spartan quarters. Once we realize just how great Eden was, and grasp the fact of who made it (God) and why (for us to enjoy), we get a feel for what God has in store for our future.

The devil will continuously challenge what God says to us and what He arranges for us. Just as the evil one tempted Adam and Eve to doubt God's motive for setting certain things in place the way He did, so the devil will try to convince us that God is trying to withhold something good from us when He tells us how to live. (Read Genesis 2:7–9; 3:1–6.) The better we truly know God and His love, the better able we will be to resist the lies that come at us.

The first lie basically said, "God wants to keep you from what you really desire, what will completely satisfy you." That lie will come at you throughout your life with the Lord. It may take slightly different forms or relate to other matters than what you eat or see, but it will try to get you to turn away from the Lord's commands. So whenever we find ourselves thinking along those same lines, we ought to compare what the first couple enjoyed in Eden with what they ended up having after they bought into the lie. (Read Genesis 3:16–24.)

God does not wait until *after* we are born to love us. He loved us and knew us before we had physical existence. While we were still in our mother's womb, God was at work making us and framing the details of our being to match a desire that was already in His heart. (Read Psalm 139:13–16.) In other words, God started with who and what He wanted you to be, and then He followed that "blueprint" in the nine-month process of fashioning you. God's love is "from everlasting to everlasting" (Ps. 103:17), and that means His love for you predates your existence—before you had any chance to earn it or to deserve it.

Many times in your walk with the Lord, you will be drawn down a path of thought that questions whether or not God still loves you (especially after you have done some horrible thing). There are many other reasons why He will never stop loving you, and we will explore them throughout this book. But from the outset, let this simple truth give you a stay against the inevitable lies that will come your way: *You were loved before you were anything; "loved" was the first attribute of your being.* That is what the Bible means when it says, "He [God] first loved us" (1 John 4:19). Before our race existed, God's love motivated Him to create us; before you and I came into being by His hand, He already loved us.

God's love has history to it; it isn't a love for us that He decided upon recently. Like Him, it has been from everlasting. Because of that long-standing affection and lovingkindness toward us, God has done several wonderful things for us.

Read the following scriptures. What does God do as a result of His everlasting love for us?

Jeremiah 31:3 _____

_____

Deuteronomy 4:37; 7:8 _____

_____

Titus 3:4–5 _____

_____

LOVE (RE)DEFINED

God does not think the way we think—His ways are unlike our ways. Often, therefore, in our walk with Him we will have to adopt new definitions to words in order to understand what He is saying to us. What God means by love and what we mean by it are two very different things. Perhaps the best way to fill out our understanding of God's love is to look at the New Testament word *agape.* Two of our words that best translate *agape* are "welcome" and "honor." God's *agape* love welcomes us and wants us near to Him. He constantly invites us and draws us to Himself. Rather than being put out because of having to put up with us, He delights in the closest possible contact and connection with us. His love is totally welcoming.

Beyond that, His love bestows incredible honor and value on us. Although God has no peers, no equal in all of creation, He chooses to relate to us on terms of respect—much in the same way that a father interacts with a son in young adulthood. In other words, God is delighted not only in our nearness to Him, but also in who we are. He thinks highly of us, and He esteems us according to the place He has given us in His created order, as overseers of the earth. He Himself crowns us with "glory and honor" (Heb. 2:7).

Imagine that . . . God can't get enough of us. He cannot have us close enough to suit His tastes. And He values us, holding us in the highest regard. How differently God thinks about us than we think about ourselves! Most people imagine that God can barely stand the sight of them, or that they are far more trouble to Him than blessing. We tend to think ill of ourselves, and if we had the chance to somehow escape from our own presence, we would do it. Our natural thinking concludes that we must be barely tolerable in His sight. The truth is, we are "precious" and "honored" in His sight (Isa. 43:4).

> God is delighted not only in our nearness to Him, but also in who we are.

One of the best words to describe God's feeling about you is *delight*. He is not reluctant in His love, but unhesitatingly eager to shower us with delights.

Read Psalm 35:27. What does God enjoy with and for us?

_____

Read Proverbs 3:12. Why does God correct and instruct us?

_____

Read Isaiah 62:4. What nickname does the Lord give you?

_____

Read Micah 7:18. Why does God forgive you?

_____

Read Psalm 37:23. Why does God lead your path?

_____

God's love reaches out with an embrace that draws us to Him before we do anything, and it continues to draw us in spite of anything we may do. His love for you is never a response to what you do for Him; anybody can return love for love (Luke 6:32). No, long before we even wanted connection with God, His love activated our relationship with Him based on His giving and serving, not on ours (Rom. 5:8; 1 John 4:10).

> And if you love those who love you, what credit is that to you? For even sinners love those who love them.
>
> —Luke 6:32

> But God demonstrates His own love toward us, in that while we were yet sinners, Christ died for us.
>
> —Romans 5:8

> In this is love, not that we loved God, but that He loved us and sent His Son to be the propitiation for our sins.
>
> —1 John 4:10

FOR GOD SO (THUSLY) LOVED THE WORLD

God abounds in love (Exod. 34:6). It spills over out of His heart and floods toward each one of us personally and profoundly. Having set His affections on us, He has an insatiable desire for us. In the same way that we want to spend the rest of our lives on earth with the ones we love, God wants to be with us for all of His life—and that means forever. It can seem almost sacrilegious to put it this way, but God is addicted to you and me. His craving for us is intense and all-consuming. Everything about His life is focused on having us in much the same way that people become consumed by various pursuits or substances.

▲▲

Wondrously driven by His undying love for us
and propelled by His rich mercies,
God exchanged what was most precious to Him—
His only begotten Son—as a ransom to win
our release from the clutches of death.

▲▲

That is why He could not bear the prospect of eternity without us. We are not just a sideline interest of His, a way for God to idle away the eons. We are not just an occasional hobby He takes up in moments of dullness. We are, instead, the single, central focus of His heart—the whole reason He made the world. Wondrously driven by His undying love for us and propelled by His rich mercies, He exchanged what was most precious to Him—His only begotten Son—as a ransom to win our release from the clutches of death.

Read John 3:16. Using the analogy of addiction—that God was and is wondrously consumed with us, that He cannot get us out of His system or out of His heart—explain why the Lord "gave up" His Son. What did that mean?

_____

_____

That act of sacrifice manifested for all time the vast height, width and depth of God's love for you and me (Eph. 3:17–19; 1 John 4:9). God loved the world that much.

When God tells us to love Him with all our heart, mind, soul and strength (Deut. 6:5), He is not setting out some standard for an acceptable level of performance. He knows how love is supposed to work. He understands that the most fulfilling kind of love—the sort we want to have with our spouse, for instance—is total and

The Lord, the Lord God, compassionate and gracious, slow to anger, and abounding in lovingkindness and truth.
— Exodus 34:6

. . . so that Christ may dwell in your hearts through faith; and that you, being rooted and grounded in love, may be able to comprehend with all the saints what is the breadth and length and height and depth, and to know the love of Christ which surpasses knowledge, that you may be filled up to all the fulness of God.
— Ephesians 3:17–19

By this the love of God was manifested in us, that God has sent His only begotten Son into the world so that we might live through Him.
— 1 John 4:9

And you shall love the Lord your God with all your heart and with all your soul and with all your might.
— Deuteronomy 6:5

absolute. We dream about a relationship in which we love another person with the totality of our being. Anything short of that is unsatisfying. Loving God utterly is far more fulfilling than just loving Him a bit.

The main reason He tells us to love Him that way is because God Himself loves us with all of *His* heart, soul, mind and strength. He is totally in love with us.

He has made sure that nothing will ever again be able to separate us from Him and from all the love He has to give us. No distress, dismay or agony in our life will have the power to push us beyond the reach of His love. Whatever past we end up having, whatever future stretches before us, regardless of any and all spiritual forces arrayed against us—God will still, as always, love us.

Question: Have you ever worried that something has happened to separate you from God's love?

_____

Have you ever felt far away from Him—especially after you have done something that you know is wrong?

_____

Have you ever been so depressed or overwhelmed by the stuff of life that you forgot to even think about God?

_____

Read Romans 8:35–39. Our feelings often tell us it is impossible for God to still love us after all that has happened. The Bible tells us it is impossible for God to ever change His mind about us.

RECEIVING GOD'S LOVE

Notice how the Bible says that the love of God is in Jesus Christ (Rom. 8:38–39). Jesus is the tangible expression of God's love in the same way that He is the exact representation of all that is true of God Himself (Col. 1:15; Heb. 1:3). As we learned earlier in this chapter, love defines God's nature and His motives. It is an inseparable part of everything He is. God sent His Son (love) into the world. Whoever welcomes His Son receives His love. So if the question ever comes up in your heart, "Can God (still) love me and want relationship with me after what I have done?", ask yourself another question: "Do I (still) welcome Jesus in my heart?" Both questions have the same answer.

When God sent His Son, Jesus Christ, into the world, the

For I am convinced that neither death, nor life, nor angels, nor principalities, nor things present, nor things to come, nor powers, nor height, nor depth, nor any other created thing, shall be able to separate us from the love of God, which is in Christ Jesus our Lord.
—Romans 8:38–39

And He is the image of the invisible God, the first-born of all creation.
—Colossians 1:15

And He is the radiance of His glory and the exact representation of His nature, and upholds all things by the work of His power.
—Hebrews 1:3

> He came to His own, and those who were His own did not receive Him.
> —John 1:11

> And this is the judgment, that the light is come into the world, and men loved the darkness rather than the light; for their deeds were evil. For everyone who does evil hates the light, and does not come to the light, lest his deeds should be exposed.
> —John 3:19–20

invitation from Him was clear: "I love each of you, and I want to have relationship with you forever. Receive My love." The simple, sad truth is that most people did not, and do not, accept God's invitation. Embodying the love of God, Jesus came to the very people who had been created by the love of God, yet most of those people rejected Him (John 1:11). They chose not to identify themselves with Him because His presence cast light on wrong things they were doing and saying. They opted to remain in the darkness, away from God and His love for them (John 3:19–20).

As we are discovering, God's love is not a passive, internalized emotion. Though He thinks about us all the time, He does not *just* think about us. Our culture teaches us that love is mostly a feeling inside, one that occasionally manifests in doing something for the one we love. True love, *agape* love, is more than a feeling—it is a way of being toward others, a disposition, a set of behaviors, a manner of relating to people. It acts and initiates.

God's love *gives* and *extends* and actively *offers* itself to you and me. Our love must *receive* and *embrace* and *accept* His love actively in return. He initiates; we respond. He loves; we receive that love. This may seem like a small point, but it is one of the most significant truths you will ever learn.

It explains why we must intentionally receive Jesus Christ into our heart and welcome Him into our lives. God extends His love to every person in the world, but only those who receive His Son take in His love. It is exactly like gift giving at Christmas or on a birthday—someone can wrap a present and give it to you, but only when you take it and open it is it really yours.

Accepting Jesus into your heart is the only way to receive God's love. Until people receive Jesus, they have not received God's love.

> God's love *gives* and *extends* and actively offers itself to you and me. Our love must *receive* and *embrace* and *accept* His love actively in return.

This truth also defines how we express our love to God. The primary way in which we love God is to receive and accept His love for us. His love is always first. Our role is not to generate love for Him or to come up with ways to show our love—the greatness of His love has arranged for us to simply embrace His love. It is like being invited to a dinner party. Our host wants us to accept the invitation and come. Period.

Jesus tells a parable of a great wedding banquet that was to be hosted by a nobleman. (Read Matthew 22:1–14.) He invited everyone on his carefully prepared guest list, but most of them were too busy with other things to want to attend. So he got out the word that anyone and everyone was welcome to come and enjoy the celebration. People from every walk of life and every social stratum showed up on the big day. But one guest was dressed inappropriately for a wedding. He was kicked out.

Jesus made several significant points with this parable. None of the wedding guests had earned the right to be there. But everyone was welcome; no one was turned away. These same principles apply to the great marriage feast of Christ and His bride. We have all been invited. All we do is accept the free invitation—and acknowledge it as a special occasion by the clothes we wear.

Read Isaiah 61:10. What is the proper clothing, without which we cannot attend the feast in Heaven?

_____

Our natural inclinations will lead us to want to do things *for* God—to prove how much we love Him. In and of itself that is not wrong, but if we are not careful we can fall into a subtle trap that will make us feel unworthy of His love. It is perfectly acceptable, even desirable, to send a thank-you note in appreciation for the lovely dinner. But if, to somehow prove we are currently worthy to have been invited to dinner, we start to focus on all the things we know we should be—and are not—doing for God, we have missed the whole point.

We will feel condemnation every time we get confused about how our love expresses itself to God. All we can ever do *for* God is to receive and to accept His love for us. Whenever we try to do anything else for Him than just to respond with thankfulness for how He has first loved us, we set ourselves up for trouble. Pride will masquerade as love—suggesting that we can, and should, be on equal terms with God, doing for Him as He does for us.

UP FOR ADOPTION

Being on equal terms with God is as impossible as an adopted daughter's wanting to adopt her new parents. The emotions of gratitude and joy are understandable and completely fitting. As a response to her adoptive parents stepping into her life with love and provision, the little girl wants to return love in like fashion. But the parents have already accomplished the adoption. When we adopt someone as our own, we assume full responsibility to care for that person. Adoption is an act done by the provider and caregiver, not by the one who will receive that care.

God has adopted you. According to the kindness and affection

> God has only one *begotten* Son. But He adopts any and every person who wants to become a part of His eternal family.

He predestined us to adoption as sons through Jesus Christ to Himself, according to the kind intention of His will.
— Ephesians 1:5

So also we, while we were children, were held in bondage under the elemental things of the world. But when the fulness of the time came, God sent forth His Son, born of a woman, born under the Law, in order that He might redeem those who were under the Law, that we might receive the adoption as sons. And because you are sons, God has sent forth the Spirit of His Son into our hearts, crying, "Abba! Father!"
— Galatians 4:3–6

in His heart for all people, He made a way for us to have permanent relationship with Him through Jesus Christ (Eph. 1:5). God has only one *begotten* Son. But He adopts any and every person who wants to become a part of His eternal family. The adoption is not on the basis of how good we are or how well behaved we have been at the orphanage over the last several years. We are not adopted as a reward for how well we followed the rules of the orphanage.

God chose you and me simply because He delights in us. He wants us in His family. And the great news is that the rules of the orphanage no longer have any bearing on our standing once we begin living in our new home (Gal. 4:3–6). Children do things they should not do, but they do not lose their family identity. Regardless of all the wrong choices and mistakes children make, they are still sons and daughters.

Read John 1:12–13. What privilege do we receive from God when we receive Jesus into our lives?

_____

Whose will and whose strength accomplish it?

_____

Now read 1 John 3:1. Why does God want to call us His children?

_____

Once again, we see how impassioned God is about having an eternal connection with us. By adopting us He has settled for all time the nature of that relationship. From now on we are addressed as children in God's household. This ties back in with receiving Jesus Christ, the Son of God, and the love of God. God extends His loving gift of adoption; we respond to His offer by welcoming Jesus into our life. Jesus, the only *begotten* Son of God, has invited us into His life as brothers and sisters. We become part of His family when we receive Him into our life.

LOVE REMOVES FEAR

By this, love is perfected with us, that we may have confidence in the day of judgment; because as He is, so also are we in this world. There is no fear in love; but perfect love casts out fear, because fear involves punishment, and the one who fears is not perfected in love.

—1 JOHN 4:17–18

One of the most difficult truths to grasp in the kingdom of God is how all-encompassing God's love truly is for us—and how totally forgiving. Deep down in our anxious hearts we worry about the possibility of being punished for all the stuff we have done wrong. After all, our minds tell us, we cannot get away with anything since the Lord knows all and sees all. We dread the Day of Judgment when every "careless word" we have ever thought or said will be brought out into the open (Matt. 12:36). We imagine every deed or thought will be played on a giant video screen for the gathered multitudes to see. *Good thing He loves me,* we think, *because otherwise I'd really get a harsh sentence.*

God has indeed fixed a day in which He will judge the world in righteousness through Jesus. (Read Acts 17:31.) Jesus is the one appointed by God to judge the living and the dead, and the basis for His judgment will be the words He has spoken—and how people have responded to them. (Read Acts 10:42 and John 12:48.) The coming Day of Judgment, when every person whose name is not written in the Book of Life will be judged according to their deeds, is a looming reality when God will deal out punishment upon all unrighteousness. (Read Revelation 20:11–15.)

But for those who have put their trust in Christ and His righteousness instead of their own, the Day of Judgment will be a day of incredible joy. Our names will be in the Book of Life, and all our unrighteous deeds and words will be "hidden in Christ." His words and what He did on the cross will be the only focus when our name is called in judgment. (Read Colossians 3:3–4.)

What's more, when we are brought to stand before the throne of God in the presence of every created being, Jesus will interrupt the court proceedings just before a list of our sins and the judgments against us would have been read. He will call for all charges against us to be dropped—on three accounts:

1. He Himself has already paid the penalty for our sins, and we cannot be tried a second time for previously paid-in-full crimes. (Read Romans 8:3; Hebrews 9:26; 10:12–18.)

2. Our names were permanently inscribed in the Book of Life, so we have bypassed any court trial. We have immunity from judgment and cannot be prosecuted. (Read John 3:18; 5:24.)

3. He is happy and proud to call us His own family. Because we confessed Him before people on earth, He gladly confesses us before the Father. He vouches for us. (Read Matthew 10:32; Mark 8:38; Hebrews 2:11; Revelation 3:5.)

God wants to eliminate the fear of punishment from our lives. His love doesn't just reduce our sentence—it removes it. He doesn't change a felony to a misdemeanor—He completely wipes away the offense from our record. Think of it this way: On the Day of Judgment the video of your whole life will have been edited with love and forgiveness. The resulting version will be shorter than the original—and rated cleaner than "G" for all audiences.

He wants you to have confidence in His love—but not a swaggering bravado that says, "My Dad is God, so I can do anything I want with impunity." As you sincerely try to live your life in the Lord (and fail to live it perfectly), He wants you to rely on His love to cover all your shortcomings. The longer you walk with God and mature in your understanding of Him, the more you will stand in awe of His love and the less you will worry about getting in trouble.

TRADEMARKS OF GOD'S LOVE

True love is like a multifaceted gemstone, cut and polished to radiate God's splendor in every imaginable situation and from countless different angles. God's love is a constant variable like a warm tropical climate. It is not generated by anything in us; it simply and always is the way that it is. A tourist landing in Hawaii doesn't expect to affect the weather; the tourist just plans to enjoy it. God's love is a prevailing condition like that.

Because He loves us, and because He is always the same (James 1:17), God is always constant in how He acts toward us and in how He thinks about us. Love always expresses itself in actions. So how does God's love cause Him to behave toward us? What responses should we expect from a loving God, as opposed to an unloving God? What is His disposition toward us? What manner will He take in dealing with you throughout your life?

First Corinthians 13:4–7, one of the most well-known passages in the Bible, talks about the true nature of *agape* love. By expanding the single words used to define love in these verses, we can arrive at a more complete picture of just how magnificent the Lord's love is for each of us. God's love for you is always:

1. *Patient (long-spirited, not short-tempered)*—God patiently continues to care for and about us throughout all our years. He forbears (refrains) from enforcing the rightful consequences we deserve for our behavior. When we are sure that we have "really done it now" and that we are "going to get it," God will keep surprising us with His mercy. Even when we run out of patience with ourselves, He has lots and lots of patience left.

2. *Kind (usefully helpful, not removed from our real lives)*—God always thinks about what would most benefit us in each situation, and He gears His activities toward being of service to us in very practical ways. He works to put us at an advantage in life. He keeps performing "little kindnesses" for us, doing favors and making things work out that wouldn't work out otherwise. Since He cares about the daily needs of our life, He clothes and feeds us in kindness. (Read Matthew 6:25–34.)

Every good thing bestowed and every perfect gift is from above, coming down from the Father of lights, with whom there is no variation, or shifting shadow.

— James 1:17

Love is patient, love is kind, and is not jealous; love does not brag and is not arrogant, does not act unbecomingly; it does not seek its own, is not provoked, does not take into account a wrong suffered, does not rejoice in unrighteousness, but rejoices with the truth; bears all things, believes all things, hopes all things, endures all things.

— 1 Corinthians 13:4–7

3. *Not jealous (contentedly generous, not anxious about getting any-thing for Himself)*—Because God has everything and is totally complete in who and what He is, He has no thoughts about what He might be losing or missing by continuously giving us what we lack. He is not stingy, miserly or jealous of the good He does for us. Envy does not cloud His vision as it does ours, and He never draws back from giving to us because "it is about time" we gave to Him.

4. *Not boastful (promoting us, not Himself)*—As the Almighty, the Lord of lords, God has no need to boast or to secure His own position. Over and over again He acts as our Advocate, to advantage and aid us, and to elevate our standing in life. His notion of true greatness, of having the "top spot in the cosmos," is to serve and do for others (Matt. 23:11–12). He doesn't just boast of His greatness, but He uses it for us and allows us to discover how great He is through what He does.

5. *Not arrogant (gently thoughtful, not overbearing)*—He uses His preeminent place and power in the cosmos, His magnificent and stately majesty, not to remain distant from us or haughty, but to give us dignity, self-esteem and value through His attention. He is not arrogant or aloof. Instead, He bends down, stooping the way an adult does to speak kindly with a child, in order to relate to us on our level. He comes into our world even though we live worlds apart.

6. *Not unbecoming (seemly in behavior, not odd)*—God always does what fits best and works most perfectly for all the unique situations in our lives. How He expresses His love for us will never cause us embarrassment. He is supernatural, not weird. He offers us soundness of mind and heart, not strangeness.

7. *Not selfish (generous, not self-seeking)*—The Lord does not love us for what He can get out of the relationship—He loves us for what He knows He can give to us. He does not seek what works best for Him—He opts for what works best for us. He is like a math major in college offering to help a fourth grader with an arithmetic assignment; other than the simple pleasure of doing something for the sake of another, there is no possible benefit.

8. *Not provoked (steadily patient, not easily exasperated)*—Although God's wrath comes out against sin, which ruins the lives of His children, He is never exasperated with us. He never gets pushed to the brink or over the edge by what we do. Sooner or later we expect Him to say, "That's it; I have had it up to here with you." If we had earthly fathers who flew into rages, we imagine that God is going to become

> But the greatest among you shall be your servant. And whoever exalts himself shall be humbled; and whoever humbles himself shall be exalted.
> —Matthew 23:11–12

> Lo, for my own welfare I had great bitterness; it is Thou who hast kept my soul from the pit of nothingness, for Thou hast cast all my sins behind Thy back.
> —Isaiah 38:17

> Above all, keep fervent in your love for one another, because love covers a multitude of sins.
> —1 Peter 4:8

annoyed and outraged, and that He will come down on us with lightning flashing. But He won't. Not ever.

9. *Forgiving (forgetful, not mindful of wrongs)*—God does not dwell on the things we have done to disappoint or to hurt Him; rather, He consciously chooses to set them aside so that His heart is only filled with pleasant memories of us. In fact, He casts our sins behind His back where He cannot see them (Isa. 38:17). Since we are so conscious of all the times we have brought our sins to Him, it seems only reasonable to expect Him to bring them back up to us. But He doesn't. Not ever.

10. *Righteous (focused on good, not bad)*—God has no delight when anything hurtful or sad happens in our lives, nor does He compute with satisfaction that those terrible events are our just desserts. He is thrilled by every opportunity to make things right, good and true for us. We humans find it hard not to notice the bad things others do. Though we do not want to get what we ought to get, we can see how other people should. God, on the other hand, causes the sun to shine on everyone—regardless of what they deserve.

11. *Truthful (mercifully covering, not uncovering)*—God knows and sees everything in our lives, including all our inner thoughts and past behavior, but rather than bringing up all those embarrassing realities time after time, He puts a roof over them and covers them in silence. If anyone could blow the whistle and uncover us, God can. However, the truth of His love covers a multitude of violations and wrongs in our lives (1 Pet. 4:8). He does not hide things to keep them covered; He covers things to release us from their shaming power.

12. *Vulnerable (entrusting, not withholding Himself)*—No one has been rejected more often or more completely than God has been. Even in the face of how we turn away from Him or refuse to open up our hearts to listen to Him, He puts up no defenses against us and knows we will likely reject Him again. We put Him on hold; we ignore Him; we tell Him we do not want to talk to Him today. Still He offers Himself to us and is always there for us without reproach or indignation.

13. *Hopeful (excited about the future)*—God is always looking forward to a great future with us. In anticipation of times to come, He confides things to us about what He has in mind. His long-range thinking never loses sight of happy days ahead for us with Him. He has plans for us and our future. Those plans are meant to give us something hopeful to hold onto when our current situation is painful. He says, "I'm going to show you things you never dreamed of" (Jer. 33:3).

14. *Enduring (solidly persisting, not frail under pressure)*—God's love is a rock-solid foundation that is so strong, so fortified, that it outlasts virtually everything else in life. It can bear up under incredible loads of junk—the stuff that normally breaks relationships. No one on earth would put up with the kind of garbage we have thrown God's way—lies, betrayal, inconsistency and more. Underneath all our days and all our foolish ways are His everlasting arms, locking us in a loving embrace (Deut. 33:27).

15. *Unfailing (determinedly focused, not erratic)*—God has set Himself unswervingly on the course of loving us no matter what we do. His intention to love us through everything will never drop off or fail. His love, like His existence, has no end—it is everlasting.

> God's love is a rock-solid foundation that is so strong, so fortified, that it outlasts virtually everything else in life.

> The eternal God is a dwelling place, and underneath are the everlasting arms.
> —Deuteronomy 33:27

LET'S TALK ABOUT IT

▲ Describe how you defined love before you read this chapter. What does God mean by love? Put in your own words how love is more than just a feeling—it is a determined way of acting toward others. In what ways does the Lord relate to us in love?

_____

_____

▲ In what ways does God *honor* us? Does it surprise you to realize that He wants to be with you more than you want to be with Him? How does that change the way you feel about Him?

_____

_____

▲ Why does God want us to love Him with our heart, mind, soul and strength? What is the best way we can love God? Have you accepted the Lord's invitation to the big banquet that He is hosting in heaven?

_____

_____

▲ How did God make sure nothing ever again would separate us from Him and from all the love He has to give us?

_____

_____

▲ Why do you think it is difficult for people to receive God's unconditional love? What makes us try to earn His favor and love? Can you identify some area in your life where you are insecure in His love—something you have done that makes you wonder how He can still love you?

_____

_____

▲ Read back through the attributes of true love found in 1 Corinthians 13. Select three of love's qualities and meditate on how God's love causes Him to relate to you. What responses will you now expect (different from what you imagined before) from a loving God?

_____

_____

▲ Have you run out of patience with yourself? Do you ever feel that you have really done it now and are going to get it? In what ways has God surprised you with His mercy and love?

_____

_____

YOUR TIME WITH GOD

Ask God to help you in very practical ways. Ask Him to make things work out that wouldn't work out otherwise. God wants to be your advocate. He cares about the daily needs of your life and wants to perform little kindnesses for you.

Reflect on the wrong in your life. Remember that God's love covers a multitude of violations and wrongs. God covers things to release us from their shaming power. Thank Him.

Thank God that in every moment of your life you are being blessed by His love. The Lord's love consoles, soothes and uplifts you. When you are in need of comfort, know that God is always right there with you. In God's presence discouragement is transformed into courage and hope is transformed into reality.

As part of your prayer time with God, you may want to include the following prayer:

Eternal Father, I'm amazed that it is possible that You could truly love me this way—You are so full of delight, so welcoming and embracing. Neither my heart nor my mind can grasp it. I just presumed that You would be less intimate, less eager to be close to me. I think that is why I have stayed remote and impersonal with You—except in those moments of great need.

There is nothing remote or impersonal about You, is there? I open myself to Your overwhelming love, Lord, and ask that You help me get over my wrong kind of fear of You. I thank You that I don't ever have to work at earning Your approval—it was You who wanted me before I could even begin to want You at all.

Now I come to You, wanting to trust You more for all the things Your love provides: advantage, shelter, encouragement, hope, mercy and fulfillment.

I receive the gift of love You offer me in the person of Jesus, Your Son. I am humbled and so very grateful to be welcomed by Him into Your presence, and to share with Him all the privileges of being called Your beloved child. In Jesus' name, amen.

CHAPTER THREE

Being Forgiven

IN THIS CHAPTER YOU WILL LEARN . . .

- ▲ What sin is.
- ▲ What sin does to cut off relationship.
- ▲ What forgiveness is.
- ▲ Why we need forgiveness.
- ▲ What forgiveness does to remove and lift the stain of sin.
- ▲ Why we no longer need to make sacrifices.
- ▲ Why every wrong we will ever commit is already forgiven.

WHEN WE TRULY REALIZE THAT EVERYTHING GOD HAS DONE THROUGH THE AGES HAS BEEN FOR THE SOLE PURPOSE OF (RE)ESTABLISHING THE CLOSEST AND MOST FULFILLING RELATIONSHIP POSSIBLE WITH US, WE LOOK AT THINGS VERY DIFFERENTLY THAN WE DID BEFORE. God really isn't the aloof Judge in the sky we expect Him to be, writing people off one after another as we each fail to live up to His expectations of us. He is, instead, a God of love who agonizes over the wrong, with resultant death, we introduce into our own (and others') lives. When we choose ways of believing or living that cut Him out of the equation, the loss He feels is more rending than the multiplied loss of every parent on earth suffering the death of a child.

He created every one of us very purposefully and particularly, desiring above all else to share His whole life with us forever. At all costs He intends to maintain the closeness and intimacy of our relationship with Him—even when He has to pay the price Himself.

So what's the problem? God is God . . . can't He do whatever He wants to do? If He wants something to be a particular way, *presto*, He can make it that way, right? Why does God's relationship with human beings need to be maintained and repaired? Couldn't God just fix it once and for all time—and make it foolproof? That way everyone could live happily ever after.

> In order to understand the magnitude of what God has done for you, you must first grasp a reality that people do not like to hear much about—sin.

This brings us to the most central issue in all of creation. In a way, it is the whole story—the theme, the plot of God's dealings with each of us. In order to understand the magnitude of what God has done for you, you must first grasp a reality that people do not like to hear much about—sin. The reason most people do not want to talk about sin is simple. However anyone defines their personal boundaries between right and wrong, between acceptable and unacceptable behavior, everyone knows that they have blown it. No one has been able to live up to his or her own standard for conduct.

We instinctively recoil at the recollection of our wrong doings. We do not like being reminded of the bad things we have done— either because we feel badly about them and wish they had not happened, or because we plan to do them again and do not want to have to hurdle our conscience to do so. We do not want our mental, emotional or physical excursions into darkness exposed.

Literally, *to sin* means "to miss the mark—to come up short, to be off target, to end up missing where you are supposed to be and, ultimately, to miss out on what you would have received if you had hit the target." A sin is both the wrong we do or think *and* the consequences for that wrong.

Consequences are not the same as punishments that may or may not be administered. A child may or may not be grounded or punished for breaking the vase his mother told him not to touch. Either way, though, the consequence of his wrongdoing is the same—the vase is now broken.

According to the following verses, what is the automatic result or outcome when we sin?
Romans 6:16, 21

_____

Galatians 6:8

_____

Everyone wants sin buried in the past, with no aftereffects in the future. We all want to be done with what we've done and not to have to face it. The problem is, sin doesn't just go away on its own—it has a lingering outcome. Perhaps if sin somehow had no consequences—if breaking the vase didn't break it—sin could be forgotten or passed over as though it did not exist.

SIN SEPARATES US

But sin does have consequences. In fact, if you think about ways in which others have wronged you, what you are left with is not so much what they did, but what the what did to you—the outcome it had in your life. Once someone sins against us grievously, a curious thing happens—that person's wrongdoing becomes more prominent on the landscape of our relationship than he or she is. We lose sight of the individual because the sin looms enormously in our way. What we "cannot get over" or "put behind us" blocks our relationship.

> For the wages of sin is death, but the free gift of God is eternal life in Christ Jesus our Lord.
> —Romans 6:23

> Therefore, just as through one man sin entered into the world, and death through sin, and so death spread to all men, because all sinned . . .
> —Romans 5:12

Sin always ends in death—not always a physical end of one's life, but a cutting off of relationship with the person against whom we sinned and an end to the future life we would have enjoyed if we had not sinned (Rom. 6:23). *Death*, as the Bible defines it, is a loss of relationship and a loss of future.

You may want to think of it this way: One of the spiritual laws governing how life works is that sin results in death. You cannot have relationship with both a person and that person's sin against you. Their actions or their words become the focus of your attention. If you hang on to their sin, you have to let go of the relationship. As Adam and Eve chose to disregard God's instructions, sin entered the world, and death came along with sin. Then death spread to all people from that point on because they (and we) kept making the same sorts of terrible decisions that Adam and Eve made (Rom. 5:12).

Question: Can you think of something that someone did or said to you several years ago that the individual has probably forgotten—but it still pains you deeply?

_____

That person's words or deeds probably left no lasting impression. Nor did the behavior affect the rest of the world. It landed primarily on you, and you are having a hard time getting out from underneath the personal consequences of the sin. It is almost impossible to separate what the person did from what it did to you. Your vase was broken once they broke the vase.

Question: Why is it hard to continue in relationships with people who have betrayed or violated us?

_____

_____

Can you see what God's dilemma was?

_____

> Against Thee, Thee only, I have sinned, and done what is evil in Thy sight, so that Thou art justified when Thou dost speak, and blameless when Thou dost judge.
> —Psalm 51:4

Sins committed against other people also have a consequence on the one who committed the sins—even though they may not be aware of that consequence. As surely as sin affects others with its deathly consequences, so it brings long-lasting consequences into the life of the sinner. Every wrong we have done—though it was done to other people or to ourselves—has ultimately been an offense against God. Each wrong cuts across and disregards boundaries God has set for His creation (Ps. 51:4).

That is why, in relationship to God, you were "dead in your trespasses and sins" (Eph. 2:1). In other words, you were cut off from connection with the Lord, "excluded from the life of God" (Eph. 4:18). You had forfeited future (eternal) life with Him. (Read Ephesians 2:12.)

▲▲

In order to restore what people had done away with, God had to do away with the cause of all the devastation; He had to get rid of our sin.

▲▲

Though not physically dead, we have lived a life spiritually removed from the Lord's presence. Adam and Eve had to give up their place in the perfect garden. They found themselves hiding from God—rather than relating to Him intimately and conversationally as they had before their sin (Gen. 3:8). So too have we lived life away from God's presence and plans.

Sin and death ruined everything God had ever wanted for us to enjoy with Him. In order to restore what people had done away with, God had to do away with the cause of all the devastation; He had to get rid of our sin.

FORGIVENESS: THE ONLY SOLUTION

Sin is a permanent mark on our record. It is like a blotch of indelible ink spilt onto a white cotton shirt. God's original intent was for no one to sin, just as our hope is that no one will ever do anything to hurt and offend us. It is a great plan as long as no one messes up, but when everyone has dark stains on their shirts and blouses, another plan is needed. God saw that there was no one on earth who was perfect; everyone turned aside from His ways. Therefore He Himself acted to rescue us from our hopeless condition (Isa. 63:5).

The subject of sin is central to the good news God wants to share with the world. The issue of sin—who has committed it and how it can be removed—is one of the surest ways to distinguish false religions. Some religions teach that people can become so spiritual or pure that they no longer sin. Other ideologies are convinced of the basic goodness in people—a goodness that is hindered only by external factors in the environment, upbringing or lack of education.

And they heard the sound of the Lord God walking in the garden in the cool of the day, and the man and his wife hid themselves from the presence of the Lord God among the trees of the garden.

—Genesis 3:8

And I looked, and there was no one to help, and I was astonished and there was no one to uphold; so My own arm brought salvation to Me; and My wrath upheld Me.

—Isaiah 63:5

Read the following verses and see what they have to say about that.

2 Chronicles 6:36

_____

_____

~~~~~

Romans 3:10–12, 23

_____

_____

~~~~~

James 3:2

_____

_____

~~~~~

> Therefore the Law has become our tutor to lead us to Christ, that we may be justified by faith.
> — Galatians 3:24

One of the first things the Lord did was to "shut up all [men] in disobedience [under sin]" (Rom. 11:32). He heightened everyone's awareness of wrong by furnishing the world with a readable instruction manual for how things were to work (and not to work) called *the Law*. The whole point for giving it was to convince all of us that we need forgiveness for our sins (Gal. 3:24). We have absolutely no hope of maintaining our life in God by means of our own flawlessness. As the saying goes, "Nobody is perfect . . . "

Our culture uses that line as an excuse: "Compared to most other people, I do pretty well. You make mistakes, too." But God is faultless. He made the worlds to work in perfection and beauty, not in shortcoming and blemish. His kind intention is for things to be right, not wrong. He cannot reconcile evil with His goodness; there is no place for distortion in the midst of perfection. That would be like a master woodworker trying to fit wrongly cut boards into a exquisitely designed cabinet. Wrong and right cannot fit together. If even one wrong is allowed to be part of an equation, the error throws off the whole answer.

For the sake of what He has always wanted with us, God could not have just said, "Oh well, good try. Never mind about your wrongs; we'll find some way to work them into our future together." Our sin could not be accommodated—it had to be dislodged. Our wrongs could not be entertained—they had to be eliminated. There was no possibility for God to "look the other way." The very nature of sin and trespass and evil is to ruin what is right. Wrong acts to destroy; it always introduces death. God could not allow it to perpetuate itself forever. To do so would be like a doctor who knowingly lifted the quarantine of patients infected with a highly contagious and deadly virus like Ebola.

There was only one solution: forgiveness.

WHAT IS FORGIVENESS?

Next to love, forgiveness is the most basic and most powerful dynamic of the good news Jesus has delivered to the world. Through forgiveness God restores what is lost, He repairs what is broken and He reestablishes His life with us. Forgiveness is the foolproof plan God has implemented so that our relationship with Him remains in constant repair instead of in need of constant repair. It is why and how we will live happily with the Lord ever after. Forgiveness is the miraculous working of God to save us from the consequences of our sin. It takes us from the wrong place we have ended up in as a result of our sin to the right place to which God has invited us.

> ▲ Forgiveness is
> ▲ the miraculous
> ▲ working of God
> ▲ to save us from
> ▲ the consequences
> ▲ of our sin.

Read Romans 1:16 and 1 Corinthians 1:18. The word for *power* is *dunamis*—from which we get the word *dynamite*. It means "force, miraculous power, ability, mighty work." In our culture we tend not to think of forgiveness as a powerful force but as a fairly feeble response from someone who has been victimized. In what ways can you see forgiveness as being a very strong power?

Rom. 1:16 – It is the power of God at work
1 Cor. 1:18 – We who are being saved recognize this msg. as
the very power of God.

GRACE

forgiveness provides
FREEDOM

What our natural language communicates about forgiveness is a far cry from what it truly entails. We mostly use it after making small social gaffes ("Forgive me; I didn't realize that seat was taken"), or we ask others for it only infrequently for specific offenses ("Forgive me; I should never have said that"). Consequently, we fail to realize the magnitude and might of forgiveness.

What does the Bible reveal about forgiveness, and how does it work out in our walk with the Lord? To begin with, forgiveness is one of the most imposing features of the Lord: "There is forgiveness with Thee, that Thou mayest be feared" (Ps. 130:4). Forgiveness is the last word, the final statement that can be uttered about someone's ultimate destiny. Forgiveness has the authority to grant a pardon. If you committed a capital crime and were caught, tried and sentenced, you would face several people, each of whom had an authority over your life. These would include the detective who arrested you, the prosecutor who brought evidence against you, the jury who convicted you, the judge who sentenced you and the warden who jailed you. But none of them could match the authority held by the governor with the power to grant you clemency.

Jesus told us not to fear the one who can affect only this life, but to fear the One who has authority to affect our eternity. (Read

For judgment will be merciless to one who has shown no mercy; mercy triumphs over judgment.

—James 2:13

Luke 12:4–5.) Mercy and forgiveness can always outdo judgment because they come into play *after* the verdict and sentence have been handed down (James 2:13). Forgiveness has the undeniable right to have the last word, and once it is spoken, nothing more can be said—except "Thank you."

FORGIVENESS LIFTS, CLEANS AND SENDS AWAY

Two images help us picture what forgiveness is and what it does. First, forgiveness lifts a load from us; it carries away what we were carrying. All of us can relate to struggling under the weight of bad things we have done. They "weigh" on our conscience. Like a heavy debt, our wrongs burden us and overwhelm our heart. Yet most of us dismiss the weight of things we do after a few hours or days. But sin is a heavy encumbrance, and in the spiritual realm all the wrongs committed by a person accumulate into a massive load over the entire course of that person's life—a heavy debt that is impossible to carry. Forgiveness lifts the amassed weight off our lives.

Forgiveness also wipes away the stain of sin. Forgiveness is not preventative, like an unfolded napkin across your lap. Napkins are good things—they guard against many spills that would otherwise spoil your clothes. Forgiveness takes the next step—it takes care of what your napkin misses. It washes your clothes and makes them as clean as new. Forgiveness removes the cranberry stain from your white cotton shirt, making it "as white as snow" (Isa. 1:18). Have you ever noticed how the smallest stain draws all the attention? A splotch on a dress or a pair of pants stands out more than all the rest of the fabric because it is so out of sync with the original pattern. So it is with sin.

Read Psalm 51:1–9. Find all the words David uses to ask God to forgive his sin.

_____

_____

Does David see his sin?

_____

Against whom has he sinned?

_____

What does David say to God in verse 7?

_____

_____

Does that give you hope for your own sins?

_____

We have spilled countless numbers of items across the fabric of our being. We have wiped dirty, greasy hands with our heart linen. We have engaged in rough and careless play that has besmirched and soiled our soul. Forgiveness cleans away all stain and any trace of what once dirtied us.

The common theme in both these pictures is that forgiveness removes our wrongdoings by separating our sins from us. It severs the link between us and what we have done—our crimes are no longer connected with us. They are put away from and behind us. That's the very thing we want—to have our sin done away with, left out of the equation, no longer with the power to affect our future. The only real power we have on our own is to *pretend* that our sins never happened. God offers us actual slate-cleaning, stain-removing forgiveness for the undeniably real sins in our life.

FORGIVENESS, NOT WHAT WE DESERVE

That sounds great! It's just what every person wants. So, why would anyone struggle with forgiveness? As strange as it may sound, people in general—even believers—have a hard time accepting God's forgiveness. Over the course of your life with the Lord, you will discover that forgiveness is one of the most difficult spiritual truths to keep embracing. That's because, as usual, we do not think as God thinks—His way of doing things is almost always the opposite of ours.

If you have ever purchased a new car, you know that the stack of payment coupons far outlasts the thrill and the smell of that new vehicle. Month after month you pay off the debt by sending in a payment coupon with your check. Forgiveness is like having someone else pay off the loan. The stack of coupons is of no account, but it is sometimes hard to get used to them being meaningless. Force of habit can make us feel as if we should still be sending them in.

Forgiveness is a free gift from God to all who accept Jesus as their Savior (Rom. 6:23). (That is the meaning of *Savior*—"the One who rescues us from the power of our sins.") We do not do

For the wages of sin is death, but the free gift of God is eternal life in Christ Jesus our Lord.

—Romans 6:23

anything to earn forgiveness. A pardon that commutes a sentence is not the same as "time off" for good behavior. There is absolutely nothing we can do to gain forgiveness on our own, to somehow work for it. Forgiveness is not a wage we earn; we cannot increase our take-home pay of forgiveness by putting in extra hours or effort. The only wage we have been able to earn from our sin is death.

OLD AND NEW TESTAMENT WORDS FOR FORGIVENESS		
Language	**Word**	**Meaning**
Hebrew, OT	*Nasa'* (pronounced *naw-saw'*)	Lift off or up, carry or cast away, pardon, take away
Greek, NT	*Aphi'emi* (pronounced *af-ee'-ay-me*)	Send forth or away, lay aside, let go of, forsake

Because humans like to accomplish things on their own, it bothers us when we are told we cannot do anything to affect our life situation. Our pride finds it difficult to accept that forgiveness is completely unconnected to our behavior. There is no link between the gift of forgiveness and what we do or do not do. If we pause to think about it, it is ridiculous—we want to be forgiven, which is to have every connection between us and our deeds removed, but we are tempted by a desire to have forgiveness earned by what we do.

This is another of the many traps waiting to ensnare you as you live life as a believer. The lies will come, whispering their (true) accusations but bringing us to a horribly misleading conclusion: *You don't deserve to be forgiven after what you have done. God will never forgive you now.* We can never deserve to be forgiven. That is the whole point. A guilty, convicted felon on death row cannot do anything while awaiting execution to earn forgiveness. His only hope lies in a pardon from the chief executive of the government. Our only hope lies in the Ruler of the universe!

NO MORE SACRIFICES

Another of the themes God introduced into the world after sin entered it was sacrifice. As we learned in the last chapter, sacrifice has always been a way to maintain God's close relationship with

His people. Sacrifice is directly tied in with forgiveness. Sin always acts like a wedge—its presence drives people apart from one another. Sin, as the precise opposite of what God wants, separated our race from Him. It brought in death, so God had to find a way to remove sin from our lives. Otherwise there was no possibility of keeping us together with Him.

Consequently, He implemented a way for people to transfer their sin away from themselves and onto an animal. The sin-carrying animal was sacrificed—put to death—as a guilt offering. (Read Leviticus 1:4; 4:13–21; 5:15–16.) The penalty for sin is always death. In the Old Testament system of sacrifice, when the penalty was paid by a sacrificial animal, there was no longer any death fine to be paid by the guilty person. This process was called *atonement*— "covering over and wiping away sin with the blood of another."

▲▲

The atonement God offers to us through the sacrifice of His Son gives us forgiveness and freedom forever.

▲▲

Have you ever heard of a *scapegoat?* We generally use the word for someone who takes the rap for and bears the punishment deserved by another. Actually, though, that is not its original meaning. In fact, that is the opposite of what it means in the Bible passage from which it was taken. The word *scapegoat* comes from one of the specific details God gave about atonement.

Read Leviticus 16:7–10. Describe what happens to the goat chosen for sacrifice.

_____

_____

What happens to the scapegoat?

_____

_____

Which of the two goats are you?

_____

Which one is Jesus?

_____

Otherwise, He would have needed to suffer often since the foundation of the world; but now once at the consummation of the ages He has been manifested to put away sin by the sacrifice of Himself... And every priest stands daily ministering and offering time after time the same sacrifices, which can never take away sins; but He, having offered one sacrifice for sins for all time, sat down at the right hand of God, waiting from that time onward until His enemies be made a footstool for His feet. For by one offering He has perfected for all time those who are sanctified.
—Hebrews 9:26; 10:11–14

And their sins and their lawless deeds I will remember no more.
—Hebrews 10:17

The Law, which alerted people to their countless shortcomings, and its sacrifices, which *temporarily* cleansed people's stains, could never make anyone perfect (sinless) forever. (Read Hebrews 10:1–4.) Jesus came into the world expressly to offer Himself as the sacrifice that would "put away" our sins once and for all (Heb. 9:26; 10:11–14). Because of Jesus' atonement for our sins, God never again remembers our wrongdoings or takes them into account in His dealings with us (Heb. 10:17). The atonement God offers to us through the sacrifice of His Son gives us forgiveness and freedom forever.

WHY BLOOD FOR ATONEMENT?

Our modern sensibilities recoil at the thought of blood sacrifices. They seem too raw, too violent, too primitive for a loving God's approval—much less His requirement. Yet the consequence of sin is always death. The debt cannot be paid except through the loss of life. In His mercy, God allowed the sins of our race to be transposed to sacrificial animals in order for the beasts to pay the penalty in people's place. This process is called *atonement* (think of it as "made *at-one-ment*" with God)—covering over our sin with the blood of another.

Why would God choose such an unsanitary and seemingly gruesome way to take care of our sin problem? Why is the shedding of blood so central to God's plan for our restoration? When God formed Adam out of the dust of the ground and "breathed into his nostrils the breath of life," what carried that breath to the cells in his body? (Read Genesis 2:7.) It was Adam's blood. In that perfect original world, Adam was *inspired* by God—given physical breath *and* inner motivation. He was animated in both body *and* spirit through what God breathed into Him.

Adam's blood was an agent of life designed by God to connect Himself with His child in much the same way that a mother passes life to the infant in her womb by means of the umbilical cord. That is why the Lord declares, "The life . . . is in the blood" (Lev. 17:11). Adam's whole being, body, soul and spirit worked in perfect harmony with the Lord.

When sin entered the world, everything was cut off from its original relationship with God, and it all became subject to death and decay—even the very blood that had once carried the breath of God to our race. From that point on, the blood carried a "gene" of death. Our "image" no longer matched that of our Father Creator. The breath of His life was expelled from our blood, and in its place came the curse of death.

God was left with only one option to restore us to Himself. He had to provide a substitution for us—something that would satisfy the death penalty under which we would otherwise remain imprisoned. That sacrifice had to involve shed blood, because that's where the life resides. God had to furnish a blood sacrifice that would perfectly cover the stain of our sin. He foretold His solution on the very day Adam and Eve fell from communion with Him—the seed of woman (not tainted by the life-blood of man) would bruise the head of the serpent. (Read Genesis 3:15.)

Jesus, born of a virgin without the "sin gene" of man in His blood, was God's solution to fix the problem of sin once and for all. His blood was both completely human and absolutely sinless. He was the fullness of God in human form, the perfect likeness and image of both. As such, He could represent our race as no beast ever could, and as His blood was poured out, the final atonement took place for all time. In modern terms, our race received a complete blood transfusion to rid our bodies of a deadly disease. His blood carried the "breath of life" from His Father, and it perfectly matched the blood of humanity—except it carried no fault, no sin.

Long, long ago God had told Abel and Cain there was a way to overcome sin—the sacrifice of a lamb. (Read Genesis 4:4.) Every lamb that was sacrificed from Abel onward foreshadowed Jesus, who was, as John the Baptist introduced Him, "the Lamb of God who takes away the sins of the world" (John 1:29). That title is the one most often used of Jesus in the Book of Revelation because it best summarizes what He has done to redeem the world from the curse of sin and death. "Worthy is the Lamb who was slain" will be the resounding chorus of our gratitude in heaven (Rev. 5:12–13). And here on earth, we overcome that curse, as well as the serpent of old, by "the blood of the Lamb" (Rev. 12:10–11).

Once we have received forgiveness for something, there is nothing more to be done about it (Heb. 10:18). Forgiveness means the deed is no longer connected with us; we have nothing to do with it or it with us. Forgiveness is absolute and complete. When we have been forgiven, there is nothing left for which we can be forgiven again. Trying, then, to offer a sacrifice to God to prove our sincerity or to live up to His free gift misses the truth of forgiveness.

God forgets about our sin, but we do not (and neither does the devil). As part of the Law, sacrifices were meant to remind people of the inescapable sin in their lives—in order to point them to the need for forgiveness from God in Jesus. The reminder serves no purpose after the fact. It would be like tying a string around your finger to remind you not to forget to buy the carton of milk you purchased at the market two days ago! I have been forgiven; you have been forgiven—for all things for all time.

> Now where there is forgiveness of these things, there is no longer any offering for sin.
> —Hebrews 10:18

PERPETUAL AND TIMELESS PROVISION

We sinned regularly before we accepted Jesus' atonement for our sins, and we will continue sinning with grievous regularity for the rest of our lives. However, the amazing message of the gospel is that when we receive God's forgiveness through the cross-borne sacrifice of His Son, we instantly have forgiveness for all of our sins regardless of when they transpire in our life—past, present or future.

Among the many verses in the Bible that tell us what the Lord does for us when He forgives us, there are two scriptures that sum up what is true about God's forgiveness in relation to our sins. As a beginning place for memorizing and meditating on Bible verses, read Hebrews 8:12 and 1 John 1:9, and commit them to memory.

Question: What does God say He will remember about our sins?

_____

If we confess our sins, how much of our sin will He cleanse away?

_____

God's forgiveness covers us perpetually. Some people have mistakenly taken the promise from the Lord in 1 John 1:9 and turned it into a limiting requirement, concluding that unless we confess, we will not be forgiven. In other words, forgiveness is yours for the asking, but it's up to you to ask for that forgiveness, and until you do God doesn't forgive you. Even if we tried to ask God to forgive us for each sin we could think of, we would surely forget about or be unaware of many others! All of us would live in a constant state of unforgiveness with the Lord because of our poor memory or blindness.

To the contrary, this promise tells us that when we do sin, we have security in the fact that His forgiveness *always* covers our sin and washes it away. Consequently, when we confess a sin, it is not so much that we are asking Him to forgive us (in the hope that He will decide to do so), but rather to thank Him that His provision through the cross enables us to be fully released from sin's evil effects.

God's forgiveness is like a great pool of cool water on a very hot day. By receiving Jesus' forgiveness, we jumped into this pool where we get to revel in its refreshing waters every moment of every day. We dwell continually in these waters, which offer the forgiveness that we need even before we commit a sin. When we become aware of a particular sin in our life, we can simply cup our hands together, fill them with His forgiving waters and pour it down our heads, faces and bodies. It's simply a reminder of what God has done for us, and this reminder cleanses our guilty conscience and draws us near to God to enjoy relationship with Him.

Because of the price Jesus has already paid on the cross, the just and right thing for God to (always) do is to forgive and cleanse us from our sin. The atonement has been made. It would be unjust and unrighteous for God to accept payment for the sins twice; that would be like chasing down and killing the scapegoat after it was set free. God's judgment and righteousness are based on forgiveness as His first choice for every situation. God is never unwilling to forgive. The problem is only with people who either do not seek His forgiveness or do not accept it.

BEING BAPTIZED IN WATER

For those who have sought—and found—the forgiveness of God for their sins, one of the most important first steps a believer can take is being baptized in water. It not only makes a powerful public statement about your conversion and your decision to live no longer for your own desires, but being baptized in water is one of the most profound acts of obedience you can do. (Read 2 Corinthians 5:15 and Galatians 2:20.)

Being *baptized* literally means to be immersed or submerged into something. By being placed in it, you take on its qualities as though they were your own, and you end up where it takes you. Floating down a river is the perfect picture of being baptized—while you do not actually become water instead of flesh, you take on the river's speed, direction and view, and unless you swim against its current, you will follow its course and go where it flows. You become one with the river, not in any mystical sense, but simply by virtue of its activity and your willingness to "go along with it."

Jesus Himself, though He was sinless, chose to be baptized in water as a way of fully identifying with our human need to be washed clean from our sin. If He identified with us by being baptized in water, it must be very important for us to be baptized as well.

It is not correct to say that a person cannot go to heaven unless he or she has been baptized—rather baptism *represents* what happens to us when we accept Jesus' death as payment for our sins. But water baptism is supposed to be so interwoven with, and follow so closely on the heels of, a person's decision to die to himself or herself and live to God, that in the Bible the act of being baptized presumes the intentional choice to become a Christian—and vice versa. While the sacrament of baptism will always be a bit of a (wonder-full) mystery, it is safe to say that every believer ought to follow the Lord in obedience into the waters of baptism.

- ▲ It is not so much
- ▲ that we are asking
- ▲ Him to forgive us
- ▲ (in the hope that
- ▲ He will decide to
- ▲ do so), but rather
- ▲ to thank Him that
- ▲ His provision
- ▲ through the cross
- ▲ enables us to be
- ▲ fully released from
- ▲ sin's evil effects.

Read Romans 6:4. Though baptism is symbolic, what does this verse suggest the act of baptism gives us power to do?

_____

_____

Read 1 Peter 3:21. Though the act of being baptized does not save anyone who has not received the forgiveness of God extended in Jesus Christ, for those who do believe in Him, baptism acts like a huge eraser, wiping away what?

_____

_____

Believers in Jesus are baptized in water as a symbolic expression of being buried in the grave. The old nature, with its carnal desires and its separation from God, is pronounced dead—and buried. We are baptized into, and fully participate in, Jesus' death on the cross, which paid the penalty for our sins once for all time. (Read Colossians 2:12–13 and Romans 6:9.) When kids float along in a river, the real force propelling them and carrying them is the river; that's the whole point—letting the river do the work. Likewise, Jesus' death is the real power that transports us to a sinless condition. The river of His life and His death, not our swimming, has enabled us to enter the presence of God free from our sin.

We are going to explore more of God's provisions for our earthly walk with Him in the coming chapters—including the importance of repentance and confession. There will be help for forgiving other people in the same way that God has forgiven us. But the most important truth for you to take away from this chapter is this: Whenever we ask for it, we receive forgiveness as a free gift. Amazing!

FORGIVING OURSELVES

Sometimes it is harder to forgive ourselves than it is to receive forgiveness from others — or God. We keep getting knocked over with regret about what we did — especially when it radically altered our life or the lives of others. How can we experience relief from the terrors of self-reproach? How can we forgive ourselves for the terrible past? Here are some starting places:

Make a clear, verbal confession to the Lord by saying aloud: "Lord, I fully acknowledge that I did 'X'; it was my doing, and I am the one responsible for doing it. I have no excuses. It was wrong, and I was absolutely wrong for doing it. All the consequences that have resulted from it—the ones I cannot see, as well as the ones I can see—are my responsibility, too. They would not have happened if I had not done 'X.' Forgive me, in Jesus' name." Then thank the Lord for forgiving you.

If it is possible without renewing unnecessary painful contact between you and anyone who has been affected by what you did, confess your sin to the people you hurt. Make no excuses. Be simple and straightforward, openly declaring that you did "X." Acknowledge how "X" has severely affected their life and brought death to them. Make a statement, and ask a question: "I have sinned against you, and violated you by doing 'X.' I deserve every bad thing you think about me for what I have done, and though I cannot expect you to forgive me now—or even in the future—I humbly ask you to forgive me. I do not ask for your forgiveness to put pressure on you to forgive, but to remind you that I have done you a terrible wrong. You do not need to answer this question—just hear it: 'Will you forgive me?'"

Accept the consequences your sin has brought about. God is able to intervene now, today, in the midst of where things have ended up. Tell Him you will put your trust in what He is able to do from now on—rather than living under the power of what you have done. Pray like this: "Deliver me, O Lord, from what I have brought on myself. Rescue me and those I have sinned against. I can and will live with whatever You allow or do. Thank You, Lord, for Your mercy."

Remember that God offers us a future based on what He has done, not on what we have done. Not being able to forgive yourself is one of the psycho-spiritual lies the enemy puts in your mind and heart. It is like he buries smelly old tin cans in the vegetable garden you have tried to tend so carefully. The cans do not belong there, but there they are. The *I-cannot-for-give-myself-for-what-I-did* feelings, impressions and sensations are real. But they are not true. Consciously take the cans—those thoughts of shame, regret, self-hatred—and pull them from the soil as often as you have to. Ask for God's grace to take the feelings from you.

The accuser, the liar, wants us to believe the opposite of the truth. The devil calls God a liar, and tells us to listen to voices other than the Lord's. "I cannot forgive myself" is not the truth of God. It feels so real, so big and so loud. But it is a lie. It makes you feel helpless, hopeless and forever weakened. You keep getting stuck because of it. It is like a compulsion—an addiction to regret, shame or self-loathing. Do you see how evil it is? Even though it seems rightly motivated—acknowledging you have done wrong—it is a twisted and incorrect conclusion.

Finally, confess that wrong conclusion—the sense that you cannot forgive yourself—to the Lord. Acknowledge that it is a sinful thought, and then receive His cleansing forgiveness for it. You may still have the memories and be aware of the magnitude of your past wrongs, but when you face those memories, whisper aloud, "Thank You; thank You; thank You, Lord Jesus, for forgiving me!"

LET'S TALK ABOUT IT

▲ How has your thinking about sin changed as a result of reading this chapter? Did you realize that sin is both the act (thought, behavior, etc.) *and* its built-in consequence? How would you define sin (in your own words) to someone who had never heard of it?

_____

_____

▲ What are most people afraid of when the subject of sin is brought up? Why does God talk about it? What is His purpose for making it such a central theme in His dealings with us? Why did He "shut up all [men] in disobedience [under sin]"?

_____

_____

▲ How does sin cut off relationship between us and others—especially the Lord?

_____

_____

▲ What is forgiveness? Can you think of an analogy for what forgiveness is and what it does to sin?

_____

_____

▲ Why is every wrong we will ever commit *already* forgiven?

_____

_____

▲ In what ways have you missed the mark, come up short or ended up missing where you are supposed to be? Even when you knew you were doing wrong, and went ahead and did it anyway, the Lord forgives you. Receive that forgiveness.

_____

_____

▲ Is there something in the past causing you regret even though you have already gone to the person or persons involved and said, "Forgive me"? Forgive yourself. Allow yourself to be in

God's presence and feel the burden of regret being lifted from you. The desire to be forgiven is your acknowledgment that you wish you had done better in the past and your commitment to doing better now and in the future. But most of all it is an acknowledgment that you cannot live as you should without His power and grace.

_____

_____

▲ How has God restored what is lost and repaired what is broken in your life?

_____

_____

YOUR TIME WITH GOD

Thank Him for full and complete forgiveness that washes away every bit of residue from bad choices and willful points of rebellion in your life.

Here are two simple prayers—the first one is for you if you have not yet welcomed Jesus into your life to fully forgive your sins. The second prayer is for you if you have previously accepted God's forgiveness through Jesus, but have grown a bit distant from Him. You may want to pray both prayers because they express in words what our heart most wants to say to the Lord.

To receive forgiveness for your sins and to become a Christian . . .

God, I acknowledge that I have done many wrong things in my life. I have sinned against You by sinning against others. My mind and my heart have engaged in so many different forms of wrong and wickedness. I have used myself in countless inappropriate ways. I am guilty of many sins. I cannot blame anyone else for what I have done.

I ask for Your forgiveness. I believe that You gave Your Son, Jesus Christ, to be a sacrifice for my sins. He paid the penalty for my wrongs when You had Him die on the cross. Thank You both for Your great love and mercy for me. I want to accept what You have done for me. I welcome the new life You offer me—fully forgiven for my sins.

Jesus, I invite You into my heart. I believe that You have been raised from the dead—just as You will raise me from death so I can live forever with You in heaven. I want You to lead me and guide me so that I can know You better. I want to live my life for You instead of for myself. Be the Lord of my whole self. I give my days to You.

Thank You for hearing my prayer. Thank You for Your Holy Spirit now dwelling in my heart. Amen.

To renew your commitment to the Lord and to feel renewed in His forgiving grace . . .

Lord Jesus my Savior, I know I have blown it. There are things I wish I had never done and things I didn't do that I wish I had. Not only have I stained my own clothes, I have stained other peoples' clothes as well—especially those I love the most.

I am still tempted to cover over my wrongs and to work hard to get myself right before coming to You. Show me, Lord, where and how I'm trying to earn my place with You rather than accepting the free and forgiving place You have already made for me. I want to start trusting Your forgiveness more and my efforts less.

Jesus, Your blood on the cross covers every stain of sin I've ever made (and will ever make). You were willing to give Your life so that I could be pardoned from the sentence that my failings have earned for me . . . the sentence of death. I confess how badly I need the forgiveness that only You have the power and authority to grant me. So I come to You now to receive the cleansing of Your blood, by which You separate me from what I've done and through which You restore me to Yourself.

Father, free me from the sins that so easily entangle me, and lead me in Your way of obedience. In Jesus' name, amen.

CHAPTER FOUR

Experiencing Grace

PEOPLE WITH AN IMPOSING PHYSICAL STATURE, LIKE OFFENSIVE LINEMEN ON A SUPER BOWL TEAM, ARE MINDFUL OF THEIR BODILY PROPORTIONS AND WHAT THEIR SIZE DOES TO INTIMIDATE OTHERS. Without having to say or do much, they are forces to be reckoned with simply because everyone knows they could compel the lesser bodies around them to do their will fairly easily. The sheer strength they possess by virtue of their size has a way of giving their opinions, preferences and wants a bit more weight than might otherwise be the case if they were as small as the rest of us. Maybe it is a holdover from the days when "might made right"—when the guy with the biggest sword or fist was left standing—but our eagerness to comply with comparatively huge and powerful people stems from a basic resignation to reality—they can do whatever they want anyway. We couldn't stop them even if we wanted to.

Unless their actions violate our conscience, we are happy to team up with them—being on their side is far better than facing them across the field. In fact, when we line up behind them, they become our champions, and all the attributes of their gross frame, which previously made us nervous, now become points of celebrative discussion with teammates or taunting boasts flung at the opposition. We love "big" when it is on our side. That is why, when we are around people whom we judge to be more notable than ourselves—in girth and strength, intelligence, position, experience—we eagerly search their voices or mannerisms for clues about how they feel toward us. Do they act friendly? Are they gentle and patient with us? Are they selfish or kindly disposed toward us?

It brings such relief to learn that the huge guy whose paw nearly swallowed your entire arm as you shook hands is "really gentle." You smile inwardly when someone tells you that the brainy coworker asked to be assigned to your project. Few things feel better than knowing your boss's boss has plans for your bright future in the company. When you are facing a serious stomach operation, you are comforted by the fact that your surgeon, who happens to be head of the department, has been performing such procedures as routine for dozens of years—since she was in residency.

IN THIS CHAPTER YOU WILL LEARN . . .

▲ What you instinctively know about grace.

▲ God wants to be your champion.

▲ What grace is and the condition in which it leaves you.

▲ Why God loves to be gracious.

▲ What grace means for your eternity and for your daily life.

This very normal mentality—of wanting the biggest and the best, the smartest and the strongest, the most powerful and helpful on your side—is not an evolutionary expression of the survival of the fittest. While it may be true in the animal kingdom that the strongest and most able tend to outlive their weaker counterparts, no animal or protoplasm ever has the hope and longing for a champion. Animals that live in a pack or herd do follow the largest or strongest of the group, and that leader brooks no resistance until an even stronger or larger rival makes a challenge. The longing for someone bigger to be on our side, to come to our rescue even though we do not have much to offer in return, is a uniquely human capacity—one placed in our hearts by God as a clue to what He wants to do for us. It is our earliest and finest inkling about one of God's surest and finest features—grace.

Question: Why do children boast in the size or strength of their dads—"My dad is bigger than yours"?

_____

_____

Why do we want to be under the care of the "foremost expert" on the medical condition we have?

_____

_____

Read 1 Chronicles 16:25 and Psalm 97:9. What do they say about our God?

_____

_____

Read Exodus 15:11 and Psalm 35:10. In what ways does the mightiness of God manifest itself on our behalf?

_____

_____

> God's love compels Him to intervene on our behalf.

GOD AS CHAMPION

God's love compels Him to intervene on our behalf. As we have seen, He is not an aloof God, content to let the world He created spin through eternity on its own skewed course. He is ever-present to put things back on course—to come to the aid of people for whom He made everything in the first place (Ps. 46:1). One of the most consistent pictures you will find of the Lord in the Bible is that of a champion—someone who uses his great strength and

> God is our refuge and strength, a very present help in trouble.
> —Psalm 46:1

battle prowess to defend and fight for others. Jeremiah calls God a "dread [awe-inspiring, terror-striking] champion" who makes spiritual enemies go weak in their legs (Jer. 20:11).

As you come to know the Lord better and better, you will encounter Him as an intervening champion over and over because it is one of His most telltale activities—to come as "a Savior and a Champion" (Isa. 19:20). In countless ways He will "rise up" for your help, as King David experienced Him, taking hold of shield, spear and battle-axe to meet those who were pursuing David (Ps. 35:2–3). He will deliver you from traps, save you from deadly infections—both physical and spiritual—and faithfully shield you from attacks that come your way (Ps. 91:3–4).

God is the perfect champion; His stature is more than imposing to the opposition, and He can do anything He wants to do without anyone stopping Him (Isa. 45:21–22). What could be better than being on the same side with God—not in anything so small and inconsequential as a football game, a legal dispute or a lottery—but in the whole of your life?

Question: Imagine, if God is for you and actively working as your defending champion, who could possibly be against you—and have it mean anything?

_____

Who is bigger than God?

_____

Read Deuteronomy 4:35–39. What does it mean when God tells us, "There is no other"?

_____
_____

How does God involve Himself on our behalf?

_____
_____

Read Romans 8:31–34. How has God demonstrated that He is for us?

_____
_____

How do we know that He wants to give and do good things for us?

_____
_____

Take hold of buckler and shield, and rise up for my help. Draw also the spear and the battle-axe to meet those who pursue me; say to my soul, "I am your salvation."
—Psalm 35:2–3

For it is He who delivers you from the snare of the trapper, and from the deadly pestilence. He will cover you with His pinions, and under His wings you may seek refuge; His faithfulness is a shield and bulwark.
—Psalm 91:3–4

Declare and set forth your case; indeed, let them consult together. Who has announced this from of old? Who has long since declared it? Is it not I, the LORD? And there is no other God besides Me, a righteous God and a Savior; there is none except Me. Turn to Me, and be saved, all the ends of the earth; for I am God, and there is no other.
—Isaiah 45:21–22

He Himself has said, "I will never desert you, nor will I ever forsake you.
— Hebrews 13:5

The one who comes to Me I will certainly not cast out.
— John 6:37

I will not leave you as orphans; I will come to you.
— John 14:18

Through Jesus we conquer overwhelmingly every circumstance of this life. He has promised never to leave our side (Heb. 13:5), never to push us away (John 6:37) and never to leave us alone or defenseless (John 14:18). The Lord God Almighty, Maker of the heavens and the earth, bends down the way that a towering adult stoops to speak affectionately to a child and draws us close to His side. His loving, protective *don't-even-think-about-messing-with-My-little-one* posture sends an unmistakable signal throughout every realm of the cosmos: "I am this one's Champion."

For the most part, as we will see, God's intervention on our behalf is mostly to introduce good and bounty into our life. He is, after all, a giver. That is the nature of His loving character. He gives life, hope and meaning. He creates out of nothing and fills our cup to overflowing. Like a happy parent taking his four-year-old son to the beach to play for the day (and dragging along the sand toys, the ball, the extra towels, the change of clothes, the umbrella, the folding chair he'll never get to sit in, the Frisbee, three different UV levels of sunscreen and a *dream-on-you're-not-really-going-to-try-to-read-that* magazine), God is happily absorbed in being with us for the whole day. The kid has no concept of what Dad has had to do to pull the day off.

It is not, of course, an accurate metaphor for the Lord's dealings in our life—because He doesn't have to work at making the day work. But for a moment, just to get a sense of a most important understanding about how God feels in relation to us, bear with the image. The dad is basically happy to share the beach; he has little interest in anything else that may be happening in the water or on the sand. He just wants to enjoy the day with his son.

Now, if an older kid, say eleven or twelve, comes up to the four-year-old son and begins to grab at him, push him down and choke him, the dad will be there with only one thing in mind. The son, at that age, may or may not be fully conscious of what was happening to him, and even if he had known he was being bullied, he could not have done anything about it. Isn't that one of the main taunts of a bully—"What are you going to do about it, huh?"

It would be great if there were no beach thugs in life, if the water had no rip currents, if sand never got in anyone's eyes—but there are, and it does.

Whenever anyone or anything messes with God's kids, He takes a keen interest. Throughout the days of our lives, a lingering question comes up in our hearts. We want to know—to put it in the language of a four-year-old—if our God is bigger than all the others. Can He rescue us from the bullies and the tides? The answer? Most definitely yes.

Read Isaiah 49:24–26. Can you think of a physical circumstance in your life that seemingly holds you hostage? How would you describe it to the Lord?

_____

_____

Is there an emotional tyrant in your life—inner fears or feelings—that holds you captive and keeps you from being free? If you could get away from one thing in your mind or heart, what would it be?

_____

GRACE DEFINED

Though we might not realize it in these terms, our longing for a champion is a longing for *grace*. God adopts our cause and fights on our behalf as a champion because He is full of grace (Exod. 22:27). In fact, when He was giving Moses the Ten Commandments, He named Himself as, "The LORD God, compassionate and gracious" (Exod. 34:6). In order to understand who the Lord is and what He is like—as opposed to what other gods are like—we must come to understand His graciousness.

So what is grace, and why is it so important in our spiritual growth? Most people think of *grace* as a religious word, an expression of something good, but they are not really sure what. To begin with, think of grace as a condition, a situation *you end up being in* as a result of what someone did for you. The something they did for you is something you could never do for yourself. For a homeless nine-year-old street urchin from New Delhi, grace would be like getting to go to Disney World—on his own, there is no way he could transport himself across the oceans to get there, and no hope of affording the entry fee once he arrived. Grace is the better standing a student ends up in after his professor "throws out" an exam the student had failed miserably—that which would have lowered his overall test average is no longer a factor.

Over and over in the Bible we see this theme in action because it typifies what God does all the time on our behalf. If we do not understand how grace works, it can seem as though God enjoys making a big point out of the fact that we didn't do such and such—He did. For instance, in Psalm 44:1–2, the writer acknowledges that God was

And it shall come about that when he cries out to Me, I will hear him, for I am gracious.
—Exodus 22:27

Think of grace as a condition, a situation *you end up being in* as a result of what someone did for you.

the real reason behind all the victories his ancestors enjoyed in previous generations, and he concludes his summary by saying:

> *For by their own sword they did not possess the land; and their own arm did not save them; but Thy right hand, and Thine arm, and the light of Thy presence, for Thou didst favor them.*
> —Psalm 44:3

Question: Is this a put-down? Is this God wanting to make sure He gets all the credit, and none of it goes to people? Why do you think God stresses His solo role so much?

_____

_____

Now read Psalm 44:4–8 and answer the same questions.

_____

_____

Grace is not only a great kindness done to or for someone, but it is also the condition in which they are left—that which is true about them or their now-changed situation as a result of what someone else did. It is both a "favorable action" and "the well-being, delight or benefit produced by the action." For instance, as an act of grace a complete stranger gives you his unused tickets at a theme park, and you end up being able to do lots more than your own budget would have allowed. A champion fights on your behalf against an opponent who is too strong for you, and that act of grace saves you from certain defeat. You were fought for, *and* you are now victorious.

Question: Being a gracious hostess means doing for the guests what they cannot do for themselves. Think of some specific examples of what a gracious host or hostess does at a dinner party. In what ways can you imagine God being gracious?

_____

_____

List three sorts of gracious acts He does in your life.

_____

_____

_____

God "longs to be gracious to you" (Isa. 30:18). Feats of grace are God's favorite activity. If you have ever been around a young mother of a newborn infant, you have caught a glimpse of how God totally enjoys being gracious. At the least sign of the baby's discomfort or need, Mama sweeps into action to feed, cover, pick up or gently shush the little one. Though she might enjoy having others help her with the routine of caring for her baby once in awhile, she will not willingly let go of that special role. She would feel robbed if she were denied the opportunity to take care of her child. Taking care of one who cannot take care of himself is the essence of grace.

GOD'S WORKOUT ROUTINE

One way to look at why God is so strong in grace . . . why grace is one of His most distinguishing features . . . is to examine what activities gratify and satisfy Him most. (Read Jeremiah 9:23–24.) He takes great delight in doing three sorts of repetitive exercises. Over and over again He looks for opportunities to "work out" in the world. Not only does He not grow weary of these practice sessions in our lives, He is actually invigorated by them. When it comes to talking or thinking about God, always remember to remember what He likes doing the most, exercising:

Lovingkindness	*Judgment*	*Righteousness*
Being kind toward us	Pointing out root causes of trouble	Making things right for us
Extending mercy to us	Straightening out tangles	Fixing situations we broke
Treating us as favorites	Separating us from our sin	Scrubbing everything clean
Restoring our original beauty	Giving good and accurate directions	Bringing well-being into our lives

As humans, we like to boast or complain (the flip side of boasting) about how smart (dumb) we are, how capable (or inadequate) we are, and/or how much (little) resource we have. Wise people boast about the grace of God and how He more than makes up the difference for what we need in life.

FAVOR IN THEIR EYES

Grace, then, changes the condition in which you end up by God's doing for you what you could not have done for yourself. What's more, grace is always a voluntary choice made by someone stronger, more powerful or more endowed with resources and authority to do good to the less powerful or capable. Grace is never obligatory or necessitated. In other words, you "find favor" with someone and receive some sort of special treatment for no other reason than their decision to pick you. Nothing can explain why they have chosen to benefit you as opposed to someone else. Grace is granted and given, but it is never earned or deserved. You find favor in their eyes; they do not first spot something admirable or advantageous in you, then grant you favor as a result of the potential they can see in you. "Noah found favor in the eyes of the Lord" (Gen. 6:8).

> Grace, then, changes the condition in which you end up by God's doing for you what you could not have done for yourself.

In fact, grace almost always comes to us as a surprise. We are puzzled at what we see in their eyes because we can find no reason in ourselves as to why they would be looking favorably upon us: *I can't believe it, but I think it's true—for some reason he really likes me.* The favor is in them; the grace originates with them, and we are merely the recipients of that grace. When an adult catches a stray foul ball at the stadium, then offers it to a kid three rows up—one of several boys all around him—that is grace in action. Nothing in the boy drew the gift of the ball to himself; something in the heart of the man prompted him to give the ball to the boy.

This is why God says, "I will be gracious to whom I will be gracious" (Exod. 33:19). The emphasis is not on grace as a whimsical act, randomly and unpredictably carried out by a capricious God who just does what He wants to do ("So tough!"). Rather, He wants us to know that His choice of us occurred long before we did anything worthy of favorable treatment (Rom. 9:11–12). It is His grace in action; it is not a result of our actions.

Grace does not evaluate people and their behavior to determine whether or not they deserve grace. God does not choose His people because of the special qualities He sees in them; He chooses them because He loves them (Deut. 7:6–8). Parents *choose to have* a baby (whom they *will* love simply because it is theirs); they do not *choose to love* a baby whom they already have.

> Grace does not evaluate people and their behavior to determine whether or not they deserve grace.

> For though the twins [Esau and Jacob] were not yet born, and had not done anything good or bad, in order that God's purpose according to His choice might stand, not because of works, but because of Him who calls, it was said to her, "The older will serve the younger."
> —Romans 9:11–12

> The LORD your God has chosen you to be a people for His own possession out of all the peoples who are on the face of the earth. The LORD did not set His love on you nor choose you because you were more in number than any of the peoples, for you were the fewest of all peoples, but because the LORD loved you.
> —Deuteronomy 7:6–8

The Bible makes quite a big deal out of the fact that we are a "chosen people," hand-picked by God before the worlds were even founded. Jesus told His disciples, "You did not choose Me, but I chose you" (John 15:16). Remember that grace is both the choice of us and the condition we are put in as a result of that choice.

Read the following verses and write down what ends up being true of us as a result of what God (and God alone) does for us.
Ephesians 1:4

_____

_____

Colossians 3:12

_____

_____

1 Peter 2:9–10
" . . . a royal _____, a holy _____, a people for _____ . . . now you have received _____."

His choice of us makes us special, not the other way around.

UNACCOUNTABLE ACTS OF GOODNESS

We find grace (favor) in the eyes of the Lord—in His heart-choice of each of us—not in the deeds of our lives. Though it has struck us as unfair when someone (else) has been the "favorite" of a coach, teacher or boss, our indignation comes from the fact that he or she "can do no wrong" in the leader's eyes. We can see plenty of places where our teammate or coworker is messing up. And, likely, the coach's blindness cannot see our excellent effort and performance. God is not blind, nor does He take one person's side to the disadvantage of another person, but because of His grace, we "can do no wrong" in His eyes. We are "favorites" of His, and there is no telling why.

As with His love for us, His choice of us is something we can either accept or reject. But we cannot do anything to influence His choice by what we do—either good or bad. It is a bit bewildering to us humans to receive something for which we did not work. Again, our pride wants to be able to point to some contribution we made to how things have ended up. But if you earn something by working, it is called a *wage*—some reward or payment due to you—not grace (Rom. 4:4). This is why some people struggle with

> Now to the one who works, his wage is not reckoned as a favor, but as what is due.
> — Romans 4:4

God's grace—and why you too will be challenged throughout your walk with the Lord; we have a hard time thinking in terms of other than what we deserve.

Not getting what we deserve is the essential promise of the good news in Jesus. God keeps no account of your wrongs or failings—regardless of whether they are willful or accidental—but neither does He tally up your good deeds and righteous acts, then reward you like a frequent-flier program. Grace frees you of a debt you have no hope of paying off on your own. But you cannot earn points with God. He redeems you from your old life into your new life, but you cannot redeem spiritual coupons or script for additional life upgrades.

Not getting what we deserve is the essential promise of the good news in Jesus.

Oh, yes, there is a thing called *obedience,* and we will look at it closely later. But here is a fundamental point of confusion for many Christians: They imagine that obedience gains them more favor with God. That is not true. Not now . . . not ever. "Favor with God" is grace—two expressions for exactly the same thing. Grace is never earned or lost, increased or diminished as a result of what we do. God's acts of grace, and where they transport us, are always unaccountable.

Read Isaiah 43:25 and 2 Corinthians 5:19. What act of grace does God do with regard to us and our sin?

_____

What condition does that put us in?

_____

Read Galatians 2:16. Can anyone be justified (made perfectly acceptable to God) by their good deeds?

_____

Read Ephesians 2:4–9. How does God demonstrate the wealth of His kindness, mercy and grace to all of creation for all time?

_____

_____

LOVE AND GRACE

Love moved God to create us; love moved God to rescue us and forgive us; love moved God to save us. But love alone could not have done the job. Love was the motive, but grace was the means. Because of our sin, we were in a fix—cut off from God and His intended course for our life. Because of Adam's original sin, and our continual disobedience, death reigned on earth (Rom. 5:17). We were caught up in the "course of this world" like tiny twigs swept along by a flooding river (Eph. 2:1–3). We were in a hopeless condition. On our own, we could do nothing about it, nothing to change it.

The mounting interest from our sin-debt was so great that even if we miraculously managed not to sin again for the rest of our lives, we could still never hope to pay for the wrong we had done. The sum total of our so-called "righteous deeds" amounted to the value of an old, dusty-smelling suit coat at a thrift shop (Isa. 64:6). We had no righteousness in our account derived on our own from keeping the Law (Phil. 3:9), and the certificates of debt, the spiritual IOUs decreed against us, were absolutely unanswerable with our own resources.

That is when grace entered the picture. When we were "dead in our transgressions," God "made us alive" by "canceling our debt" and "nailing it to the cross." (Read Colossians 2:13–14.) God's act of grace was sending Jesus as the Atonement to die in our stead. As a result of that act, we are now debt free. We have been delivered from "the domain of darkness" and transferred to the kingdom of God; the consequence of that gracious act has been to bring us back to life in a perpetual state of *having-been-forgiven-ness*. (Read Colossians 1:13–14.)

Why would God want to do something so extreme? Why would He willingly forgive such massive debts and zero out the balance sheet on the entire accounts of our lives? What does it accomplish in His eternal purposes?

First, God will do anything to have us in His life forever. He paid the highest possible price in order to secure our rescue—the life of His only Son (remember John 3:16). No matter what, He always wants us close, so God's grace has "seated us with Him" and with Jesus "in the heavenly places" as a timeless declaration of the place we will occupy for all eternity. (Read Ephesians 2:4–6.)

Second, God wanted to send an eternal message that would reverberate throughout the ages. He wanted to convince everyone beyond a shadow of a doubt that He has a mind-boggling wealth of grace. Eliminating all the sin-debt of all the people of all time

For if by the transgression of the one, death reigned through the one.
—Romans 5:17

For all of us have become like one who is unclean, and all our righteous deeds are like a filthy garment.
—Isaiah 64:6

. . . and may be found in Him, not having a righteousness of my own derived from the Law . . .
—Philippians 3:9

would not even put a dent in God's assets of grace. He always has enough to spare, plenty of grace left over.

The enemy of your heart will try to convince you that God must ration His stores of grace; He can only afford to give you a limited amount of grace at set intervals (like an allowance). The devil wants to convince you that if you need grace too many times a week or a day, God will eventually have to tell you, "No more for now. You live without My grace for awhile, then maybe you will be more careful and not waste it so badly. Do you think I have an unlimited supply for people like you?"

> God graces us with total forgiveness forever so that we will look to Him and not to ourselves for the needs of our everyday lives.

One of the best ways to resist the lies of the devil is to quote scripture that directly counters his false claims. From your Bible, read 2 Corinthians 9:8 and 1 Timothy 1:13–16 aloud.

Question: What can you now quote in order to answer the lie that says God must ration grace to keep from running out of it?

_____

_____

Third, God graces us with total forgiveness forever so that we will look to Him and not to ourselves for the needs of our everyday lives. On the one hand, grace has taken care of our eternity—forever converting the condition we were in as sinners to the condition we find ourselves in as saints. But God doesn't want to wait until after our earthly life to grace us. He loves to be gracious to us right now.

GRACE AS A DAILY PORTION

Your faith in Jesus, and the grace work He accomplished by dying for you on the cross, secures your eternity. The Atonement was made, finished for all time. Nothing is bigger to us or more impossible for us to accomplish on our own than eternal forgiveness.

If God gladly does that—having both the desire and the riches to do it for us—think of how much more He wants to do for us. Having freely given up the life of His Son, it makes no sense that He would tell us the rest is up to us (Rom. 8:32). No, He wants to keep giving to us and doing for us by His grace (1 Cor. 2:12). He wants to fill our daily lives with His gracious acts, His unaccountable gifts of kindness to change our life situations. By grace,

> He who did not spare His own Son, but delivered Him up for us all, how will He not also with Him freely give us all things?
> — Romans 8:32

> Now we have received, not the spirit of the world, but the Spirit who is from God, that we might know the things freely given to us by God.
> — 1 Corinthians 2:12

He wants to heal our sickness, supply our need, restore our family and remove our pain.

He doesn't say, "Look, I did My part—taking care of your eternal condition. Now you have to pull your own weight. Eternal life was on Me; daily life is your responsibility." God wants His grace to be our daily portion.

That is why Jesus teaches us to pray for God to give us our daily needs, forgive us our sins, lead us where we should go and deliver us from evil. (Read Matthew 6:9–13.) It is why most of the New Testament letters begin with the salutation, "Grace to you." Life is full of situations beyond our resources—money crunches, emotional devastations, family breakups, physical afflictions and diseases. We find ourselves in circumstances we wish we could change, but we have no power over them even though we scramble to do something about them.

Grace is absolutely counter to this life's teaching that you are alone and must rely on your own resources—"Work hard. Invest wisely. Give it your best shot. Do all you can do, and be all you can be." Grace, on the other hand, teaches us to . . .

- ▲ Boast of our weaknesses instead of our strengths (2 Cor. 12:9).
- ▲ Acknowledge that we are not self-made people (1 Cor. 15:10).
- ▲ See ourselves as His workmanship, not our own (Eph. 2:10).
- ▲ Strengthen our hearts not by our own religious rigors, but by His grace (Heb. 13:9).
- ▲ Make Him our champion, instead of trying to fight the battles on our own.

Such times—when the neighbor is so grumpy with your kids; when there isn't enough money for the mortgage payment; when the doctors diagnose you with Hepatitis C; or when your heart is broken, seemingly beyond repair—are times for grace. Grace is like an extra tank of gas. When you find yourself on empty, switch tanks. That's what it is for. Grace is like a lamp. When it is too dark for us to be able to see, we can quit squinting and turn on the light.

God invites us to live in His grace; it is a daily—indeed hundreds of times daily—experience. Just as His lovingkindnesses are "new every morning," so His grace is ever fresh for the needs of our lives (Lam. 3:22–23). As you walk with the Lord, your life will not magically become problem free. The very nature of life on this planet means that you will regularly encounter difficulty,

---

And He said to me, "My grace is sufficient for you, for power is perfected in weakness." Most gladly, therefore, I will rather boast about my weaknesses.
—2 Corinthians 12:9

But by the grace of God I am what I am.
—1 Corinthians 15:10

For we are His workmanship, created in Christ Jesus for good works.
—Ephesians 2:10

Do not be carried away by varied and strange teachings; for it is good for the heart to be strengthened by grace, not by foods, through which those who were thus occupied were not benefited.
—Hebrews 13:9

pressure, need and helplessness. We are too poor, too weak to take care of the things life throws at us.

But God's power is perfectly suited for those situations. His "power is perfected in our weakness" (2 Cor. 12:9). His grace is the perfect answer to our daily needs. The whole reason that Jesus willingly changed His condition by leaving heaven to come to earth, by setting aside His riches for a humble birth and death, was to enrich our daily and eternal lives beyond anything we could do on our own. (Read 2 Corinthians 8:9 and Philippians 2:5–8.)

God is great; we don't have to be . . .

LET'S TALK ABOUT IT

▲ What is a champion, and when and why does a champion fight for someone?

_____

_____

▲ God wants to come to your aid. Ask Him to come to your aid and shield you from your attackers. The Lord is loving, protective and gentle toward you, but He acts as a dread champion intervening on your behalf. How do you feel when you see someone being taken advantage of by a bigger or stronger person?

_____

_____

▲ What is grace? (Define it in your own words.) What two things does grace change? How does that relate to doing someone a favor or feeling favorable toward another?

_____

_____

▲ Why is grace important in our spiritual growth? Can we do anything to earn God's grace? How have you tried to earn His favor or grace?

_____

_____

▲ What acts of grace or gifts of kindness done to change your life situations have you received today, this week, this month and this year? What were they growing up as a child and later as a young adult?

_____

_____

▲ Give three reasons why God willingly forgave massive debts and zeroed-out the balance sheet on the entire account of our life. What does it accomplish in His eternal purpose?

_____

_____

▲ Are there circumstances in your life that seem too big to handle? Call out for the grace of the Lord, and entrust yourself to your Father in Heaven, just as Jesus did while dying on the cross. Do not try to direct the grace of God according to what you can think needs doing; rather, ask Him to do what He knows is the best for you.

_____

_____

YOUR TIME WITH GOD

Are you in circumstances you wish you could change even though you have no power over them? Is your heart broken, seemingly beyond repair? Is life too difficult, and you feel helpless? These are times for grace. Grace takes you where you want to be but cannot get to on your own. Watch for God's grace in your life and thank Him for making up the difference for what you need in life. As you thank Him you may want to include the following prayer:

Thank You, God, for loving me. Thank You, Jesus, for so willingly coming to my rescue. Your love inspires and comforts me through the ups and downs of my life and in the peaceful times in between. I see Your love acting in grace, flowing in and through every one of my days. I believe that You love me, care for me and guide me in every moment.

Thank You, Lord, that You are always there for me. The abundance of Your grace is far beyond anything I could ever realize or imagine. The power of Your love blesses me in the most amazing ways. You love me unconditionally, and I want to do all that I can to honor Your gift of love and to honor You, the giver and sustainer of my life.

Lord, thank You that there is nothing that will ever happen and no situation I will ever face that is beyond Your touch. Thank You that You love to extend grace to me. Give me a heart that is always willing to receive from You. Help me to put away my defenses and all the ways I think I can do things on my own.

Thank You that You do not measure my goodness, but You love to come into my life's circumstances and meet me exactly where I am. Lord, I want to live today in the abundant grace You offer.

CHAPTER FIVE

Worshiping God

WHEN WE LOVE SOMEONE, WE LONG FOR AN ENGAGING RELATIONSHIP WITH THEM. Though true love can love from a distance and even sustain itself in the face of outright rejection, its primary urge is to connect us with the person we love. Being in love means we want to be around them and with them, doing things and experiencing things together. Love is all about joining together with, sharing with and communicating with someone else at the deepest level of our being. Love is like a language—it transforms feelings into expressions that can be understood by others. Love must express itself.

Nothing is more important to God than relationship with us. From the very beginning, He desired living interaction with us, and He has paid an incredible price to securely reestablish lasting connection between us and Him. He wants to relate to us in such intimate and profound ways that we experience Him for who He truly is and find ourselves drawn into deeper and deeper communion with Him. Over and over again He communicates how much He loves us. Knowing how fulfilling it is for love to be able to express itself, He wants us to have a way to declare our love for Him, so He enables us to engage in one of the most satisfying and meaningful activities in all of creation—worship of the Most High God.

Many people mistakenly imagine that worship is something God requires—either because He likes to hear Himself praised (as an ego-starved, insecure deity), or because He lives in a perpetually bad mood and we have to appease His wrath with verbal sacrifices (like throwing people into a volcano to pacify a rain god). The heart of God for worship has nothing to do with what He receives from our praise—as though He needs something from us or takes some kind of self-satisfying pleasure in having us reaffirm His preeminent place in the cosmos.

Worship, like every aspect of truth God has provided for our

IN THIS CHAPTER YOU WILL LEARN THAT . . .

▲ Worship is the language of love between us and the Lord.

▲ Worship is for our sake, not the Lord's.

▲ We can worship anytime, anywhere.

▲ Worship is an external activity.

▲ Worship transforms us.

▲ Worship is a powerful spiritual force.

▲ Pride keeps people from worshiping God.

> Nothing is more important to God than relationship with us.

walk with Him, has one great purpose—to bring us into closer relationship with Him. Worship is the language of love and understanding we get to use with the Lord. Just as His love welcomes and honors us, so our worship verbalizes our delight in Him.

When we worship the Lord, we are focusing our attention and affection on Him. We are thanking Him for all He has done for us. We are acknowledging His hand at work in our lives, and we are telling Him how glad we are to know what we know about Him. Like best friends rehearsing all the joys of their lifelong relationship or a daughter reflecting on those special moments when her mother first let her play with her jewelry box, worshiping God acts as a rejuvenating reminder that we are not alone—nor have we been. We are known, loved and helped throughout our lives. We worship the Lord for what He has done and for who He has been to us. Going over all that has been true of His dealings with us in days and years past creates incredible anticipation for our future.

Question: Praise is a powerful declaration of truth about what God has done in the past, as well as what He has been like. Why do you think that rehearsing His past dealings increases our faith for the Lord's future work on our behalf?

_____

_____

Read Psalm 56:4 and Psalm 71:14. Describe the connection between praise and hope you find in these verses.

_____

_____

Read Jeremiah 17:14. According to this verse, why is the Lord Himself our praise? What do you think that means?

_____

_____

Read Exodus 15:2. Whose God is the Lord?

_____

What do you think it means to have God be your strength and salvation?

_____

_____

The expression "I will praise Him" is difficult to translate fully because it communicates an entire picture not contained in any single word in our language. Think of preparing a beautiful guest room that is both cozy and exquisite—the kind of place someone would hardly want to leave even to go eat. The room is so comfortable and inviting that your guest feels completely at home. Can you see how praise welcomes the Lord? Why would you like the Lord to be a permanent guest in your home?

_____

_____

"THANKS, DAD, FOR EVERYTHING"

In the midst of forces and events much too large for us to grapple with on our own, we are presented with an intimidating message of aloneness. Dwarfed in the face of the size of the cosmos, the uncertainty of the future, the needs of food and friendship—we are like that solitary high school freshman who has just moved from out of state and is standing in front of his new school on the first day of classes, knowing no one. Anything awaits us. That is when we want to know with certainty that we are not alone. Worship is a way of thanking the Lord for being with us closer than any friend could ever be (Prov. 18:24).

At the very heart of worship and praise is *thanksgiving*—gratitude to the Lord for all that He has done and for all that He is. With worship we acknowledge the Lord's hand in our life, and we tell Him how glad we are for it. It is simple and spontaneous, like the thanks expressed to a father by a youngster who has just caught his first fish: "Thanks for taking me fishing, Dad." So much is wrapped up in those words, and they become the highlight of the trip, cherished for years by the father.

▲▲

At the very heart of worship and praise is
thanksgiving—gratitude to the Lord
for all that He has done
and for all that He is.

▲▲

Worship is not the acknowledgment of a stranger—it is the gratefulness of a child for whom the father has arranged and done so many other things. Though the child knows nothing, really, of the preparations for the trip, much less for daily life back home, the father accounts the simple thanks as more than enough reward

> There is a friend who sticks closer than a brother.
> —Proverbs 18:24

for everything. Almost nothing else can make a father feel so successful with his life. That is how God receives our worship—as saying, "Thanks, Dad. I love You." Though our worship cannot possibly encompass all that the Lord is or all that He has done for us, He receives it as His most cherished honoring. The angels cry out in majestic worship all the time, but the Lord loves the sound of our simple worship more than all the angelic anthems that could ever be sung.

SPIRIT AND TRUTH

What exactly is worship? How do you worship God? Probably the best place to begin is with Jesus' explanation to a woman who had similar questions. (Read John 4.) As we will see, Jesus was explaining aspects of worship that make it much more than a mere ritual and far more powerful than just a physical exercise. The more we realize what is truly happening while we worship, the more we will want to do what we were created by the Lord to do—bring praise and honor to Him.

The cultural upbringing of the woman to whom Jesus was speaking had taught her that worship had to be done in a special place and according to a religious formula. Her religion said that true worshipers of God should go to a holy mountain to meet Him. Jesus told her that the physical setting for our worship is not very important because we worship God "in spirit and truth" (John 4:23).

Worship is a spiritual activity that transcends our physical surroundings. That means we do not have to make a pilgrimage to a holy river or shrine; there is no need to travel to sacred mountains, to face a particular direction or to ascend some lofty peak to "get in touch" with God. God lives in the spiritual dimension of reality. He is not attached to any earthly location, and there are no "dead zones," like with cell phones, where He cannot pick up our prayer signal. We do not have to wait until we can get to the right place before we can worship the Lord. He is Lord over all, and His glory is over all the earth (Num. 14:21; 1 Chron. 29:11).

One of the differences between the *religions* of false gods and *relationship* with the true God has to do with access—when, where and how we can come into contact with the one we worship. Are certain days of the year more auspicious than others? Are there elaborate rituals of cleansing or concentrating that must be followed in order to approach God? Must we have accouterments such as incense or beads in order to find our way to Him? Are there levels of enlightenment or attainment we must pass through on our spiritual quest toward God?

All the earth will be filled with the glory of the LORD.
— Numbers 14:21

Thine, O LORD, is the greatness and the power and the glory and the victory and the majesty, indeed everything that is in the heavens and the earth; Thine is the dominion, O LORD, and Thou dost exalt Thyself as head over all.
— 1 Chronicles 29:11

Read the following verses. What do they tell you about when, where and how to worship the Lord?

Psalm 34:1

_____

Psalm 103:21–22

_____

Hebrews 13:15

_____

Romans 14:11

_____

Read Hebrews 10:19–22. Tell what these verses say about worshiping the Lord.

_____

_____

Right where we are, in the midst of the most hectic schedule or while chasing down the last Cheerio from our toddler's breakfast, on the busiest street corner or alone in our room—anywhere, any time we can worship the Lord. "Thank You, Lord. Praise You, Jesus. I love what You're doing in me these days. You are great. I surrender afresh to You because You have been so faithful to me." What a privilege to have instant admittance to God! We do not need to meditate or sit in particular positions in order to get in touch with and worship God. We do not have to wait for the right time or place to worship.

▲▲▲

> Right where we are, in the midst of the most hectic schedule or while chasing down the last Cheerio from our toddler's breakfast, on the busiest street corner or alone in our room—anywhere, any time we can worship the Lord.

▲▲▲

Wherever we worship, we touch the realm of spirit. Not only does worship take place at a nonphysical dimension, but as Jesus explained to the woman at the well, worship also involves a dimension of "truth" that comes only through spiritual revelation. He did not mean some sort of mystical, peculiar and arcane "secrets of the universe." He just meant that the natural mind cannot grasp the truths of God. By means of our native intelligence

For since in the wisdom of God the world through its wisdom did not come to know God, God was well-pleased through the foolishness of the message preached to save those who believe.

— 1 Corinthians 1:21

At that very time He rejoiced greatly in the Holy Spirit, and said, "I praise Thee, O Father, Lord of heaven and earth, that Thou didst hide these things from the wise and intelligent and didst reveal them to babes. Yes, Father, for thus it was well-pleasing in Thy sight."

— Luke 10:21

And Jesus answered and said to him, "Blessed are you, Simon Barjona, because flesh and blood did not reveal this to you, but My Father who is in heaven."

— Matthew 16:17

Therefore I make known to you, that no one speaking by the Spirit of God says, "Jesus is accursed"; and no one can say, "Jesus is Lord," except by the Holy Spirit.

— 1 Corinthians 12:3

you and I cannot know God for who and what He is (1 Cor. 1:21). Did you know that at one point Jesus actually thanked His Father for hiding the simple truths of the kingdom of God from people who insist on figuring them out on their own (Luke 10:21)? Interesting, isn't it, that the truth of God is not easier for smart people to get than it is for the rest of us.

The Spirit of God, whom Jesus calls the "Spirit of truth" (John 14:17), imparts understandings to our spirit and discloses insights about God to us. (Read John 16:13; 1 Corinthians 2:10, 12–13.) The Holy Spirit is the only One who alerts us to Jesus' true identity (Matt. 16:17). God has leveled the playing field so that His ways are available to every one who comes humbly to Him. In fact, no one can worship Jesus as Lord, except by revelation from His Spirit (1 Cor. 12:3).

Remember the concept of grace? If we could grasp spiritual truth by means of our natural intelligence, we would not need grace. The Lord hides His wisdom and His ways in simple truths that the world scorns as foolish nonsense. (Read 1 Corinthians 1:18–25.) Because His ways are so much higher than our ways, and His thoughts transcend our very limited mental ability, He has intentionally made the truths of His kingdom on earth very, very simple. In a sense, He has hidden them *beneath* where worldly intelligent people would think to look.

Aside from the fact that He is God, so whatever He chooses to do is the way it is going to be, God has chosen to use seemingly foolish things to accomplish His purposes for two basic reasons: First, He wants us to believe Him and His words, rather than to think we can figure everything out on our own. Second, He wants us to be able to boast in Him, not ourselves. The temptation to rely upon and boast about our accomplishments is rather foolish in His kingdom. But "boasting in the Lord" (i.e., worship) is incredibly wise, and it sets many powerful forces into motion. In a way, worship is the highest form of name-dropping in the cosmos. In the midst of complicated, difficult circumstances, we will always make much more progress by "throwing His name around" than we will by trying to convince everyone how great we are.

Read 1 Corinthians 1:18–25. What does the world think about the wisdom of God? What does God think about the wisdom of the world? Why would the Lord choose to use a "foolish" way to save the world when He could have done something much more impressive in the world's eyes?

_____

_____

Now read verses 26–31 and complete the following statements.

God chooses:

Foolish (hidden, not obvious, unimpressive, silent) things to befuddle and confound the _____.

Base (ordinary, not noble-born, without connections in high places) things to shame the _____.

Despised (thought nothing of, least valued) things to bring to nothingness the _____.

WORSHIP AND REVELATION

Aside from receiving the love of God in Jesus, worship is the smartest thing you can ever do—it is like instant (spiritual) intelligence. Worship is profoundly wise because it declares what is true of God; consequently, it is the closest we can ever come to uttering pure truth. During times of worship, we thank the Lord (like the little boy whose father took him fishing) for "a great trip." As we offer our simple thanks, our heart and mind will begin understanding much more that He has done for us. It is like coming to the realization that the very pleasant man we sat next to on the plane, who gave us his card to call if we ever needed anything, was the owner of the airline! Our Father in heaven wants to disclose Himself to His children. One of the main ways in which He opens Himself to us and reveals more of His character is through worship.

If you want to think of it this way, worship heightens your sensitivity to spiritual truth because it is in itself such a spiritual activity. Worship sets your eyes upon the Lord so that you become more attuned with His slightest gesture (Ps. 123:2). It is no coincidence that you will often receive points of revelation in church during the worship. If we will let ourselves worship freely—without laboring so awkwardly with it and worrying about what others think of us—we will surprise ourselves with how much our spirit "understands and knows" God (Jer. 9:24).

> Behold, as the eyes of servants look to the hand of their master, as the eyes of a maid to the hand of her mistress; so our eyes look to the LORD our God, until He shall be gracious to us.
> —Psalm 123:2

REJOICING ALWAYS

Rejoice always; pray without ceasing; in everything give thanks; for this is God's will for you in Christ Jesus.
—1 THESSALONIANS 5:16–18

"Rejoice always." Why would God tell us to keep celebrating even when life is not going well? That can almost sound like the spiritualized version of "keep a stiff upper lip." Is that what God wants to tell us—not to cry, to tough it out or at least to remember it could be worse? Are we supposed to pretend that we are happy about a lost job? A chronic illness? An empty apartment? Is God testing us to see whether or not we can remain cheerful when terrible things happen to us or to those we love?

Nothing could be further from the truth. The truth always begins with, "For God so loved the world that He gave . . . " He is not a God who wants His children to pay or to prove anything. He wants to do for us what we cannot do for ourselves. He is a God of grace and affection. Whenever we read our Bible, we must always interpret its words in light of what we know to be true of the Lord. This statement, *"Rejoice always,"* is a good case in point.

Our heavenly Father isn't telling us to thank Him *for* everything — the flat tire, the lost job, the broken friendship. Rather, *in the midst of* everything He is reminding us to let our attention be focused on the One who is above and beyond the brokenness that surrounds us. He did not fashion the world as it has become — with all of its loss, barrenness, futility and pain; He fashioned Eden — with everything that was pleasing and good. (Read Genesis 2:9.) He wants our portion to be every good thing and abundant life.

But since we live on a broken, derelict planet, we will inevitably encounter situations where ruin, bleakness and degradation spill into our life. So, what is there to celebrate at such times? We celebrate the Lord and His goodness — that He does not forsake us in our time of need; that He does not despise our afflicted state. (Read Job 36:15; Psalm 22:24; Isaiah 63:9.) He can redeem even the worst of situations, making us fruitful in our affliction and turning them to ultimate spiritual profit in our lives. (Read Genesis 41:52; 50:20; Romans 8:28–29.) Look at how wise Solomon put it:

> Remember also your Creator in the days of your youth, before the evil days come and the years draw near when you will say, "I have no delight in them" . . . Remember Him before the silver cord is broken and the golden bowl is crushed, the pitcher by the well is shattered and the wheel at the cistern is crushed; then the dust will return to the earth as it was, and the spirit will return to God who gave it. "Vanity of vanities," says the Preacher, "all is vanity!"
>
> —ECCLESIASTES 12:1, 6–8

God is not interested in having us do exercises or activities just to prove we are willing to do what He wants us to do. Worship is not a proving ground for devotion or an obstacle course for elite forces' ("good Christians'") training. The Lord doesn't say, "I don't care how hard life gets, just keep praising Me because that's all you're good for." No. He is telling us that He is our resource and our recourse when life gets hard — He has ample supply for any need, and He can change the course of things in our life.

If we, through worship and praise, will keep focused on who God is and what He has done in our lives thus far, it will produce an incredible peace and joy deep in our hearts. When the hard times come, we can thank Him for being with us and seeing us through. No matter what, His promise of miraculous intervention is still true. "Thank You. Thank You, Lord. Amen."

If you have ever wondered why you feel awkard or foolish while worshiping, why you get embarrassed, the explanation is simple. The world around us is so off tune from the Lord's original score that the voice of anyone who worships Him stands out in the chorus crowd. That is part of the catch, isn't it? Most of us do not like to be different from those around us, which is one of the main reasons we do not worship as frequently or as freely as we could. When our spirit wants us to lift our voice and our hands in praise, our self-consciousness often tries to veto the idea. We can easily think more about being in the presence of others than in the presence of the Lord.

> Worship is one of the best ways to overcome doubts because it proclaims, "Yes, I believe."

Furthermore, the natural world, especially our own mind, considers the truth of God to be foolish and inconsequential—a waste of time and beneath our bother. Since worship expresses thanks for God's ways, our old self thinks it is doubly dumb. Our self-sense challenges us with two questions: *What good do you think those little truths are going to do?* and *Do you really want everyone to know you are trusting in invisible remedies?* As you walk with the Lord, you will confront those lies over and over. Worship is one of the best ways to overcome doubts because it proclaims, "Yes! I believe."

Read Isaiah 43:21; Psalm 147:1; 150:6; Matthew 21:16 and Romans 14:11. Do you suppose worship is meant by God to be an awkward activity for us? In other words, is worship foreign to how the Lord created us, or has something of our original constitution been stolen from us?

_____

_____

A WHOLE-BEING EXPRESSION

Since worship is the language God has given us to enable us to express our devotion to Him, and since we are to love Him with all of our being—body, soul and spirit—it is only fitting that worship should be a presentation of our heart, soul, mind and strength [body]. Worship starts in our heart and spills over to our lips because we speak out of what fills our heart (Luke 6:45). The more our heart is filled with adoration and delight in God, the more we will want to declare it. Contrary to what many people imagine,

> The good man out of the good treasure of his heart brings forth what is good; and the evil man out of the evil treasure brings forth what is evil; for his mouth speaks from that which fills his heart.
>
> —Luke 6:45

worship and praise are mostly external activities and postures, not internalized thoughts and emotions.

You could almost say that worship is our body language. In worshiping, we adopt a posture of humility, acknowledging God's greatness and our desire to serve Him. In fact, worship (*shach'-a,* pronounced *shaw-kahw*) literally means "to bow, to kneel, to crouch prostrate before the Lord." That is why we bow our head when we pray and why we often kneel. But the emphasis in worship is on approaching the Lord, not just remaining frozen in fear before Him. Just as a puppy might lovingly lick his master's hands, eagerly pressing to get close to his face, so we "kiss" the Lord with our worship. Worship is tender and intensely personal between us and the Lord.

WHY DO WE LIFT OUR HANDS IN WORSHIP?

▲ To signal our surrender to God and to His purposes for us
▲ To acknowledge that our hands are empty of needed resources
▲ To "give Him a hand," thanking Him for His work
▲ To ask to be lifted and carried by our "Daddy God"
▲ To focus everyone's attention on Him, pointing toward Him
▲ To embrace the greatness of all He has in store for us

Praise boasts. In song or in announcement, praise celebrates God and His doings; it centers all the attention on Him and gives Him credit for what He has done. Praise [*tehillah,* "a hymn"] sings a song that makes it clear how you feel about God. You make your inner feelings clear to the outside world. Praise is like polishing silver to shine it up and to show it off—it lifts God up and holds Him out in front of everything for everyone to see.

Thanksgiving [*towdah,* pronounced *to-daw*] literally means "to extend your hands, to lift your hands." The posture of lifted hands that so profoundly communicates our surrender, as well as our inability to accomplish what needs doing by means of our own (empty) hands, declares to all the world that we lift God up. We want Him to stand out and above, so we lift Him up. King David, the greatest worship leader of all time, understood this. That is why, in thanks for God's love and kindness, he says, "My lips will praise Thee . . . I will bless Thee . . . I will lift up my hands in Thy name" (Ps. 63:3–4). Jeremiah, a mighty prophet of old, also understood the connection between physical activities and postures and spiritual realities; he says, "Let us lift up our heart with our hands unto God in the heavens" (Lam. 3:41, KJV).

Question: Read each of the following verses, and look for a detail about physical expressions of worship:

1 Chronicles 29:20

_____

Psalm 34:1

_____

Psalm 40:3

_____

Psalm 47:1

_____

Psalm 95:6

_____

Psalm 134:2

_____

Psalm 141:2

_____

Isaiah 12:5

_____

Praise and worship bless God. Throughout the Bible we are encouraged to bless the Lord. In the Old Testament, blessing [_barak_, pronounced _baw-rak_] God actually meant to kneel as a physical statement of adoration and respect. It was a salute to God—pressing the knees to the ground instead of pressing the hand to the forehead as we do in a military salute to a superior. And in the New Testament, blessing [_eulogia_, pronounced _yoo-log-ee'-ah_] primarily had to do with speaking well of someone—it is the word from which we get _eulogy_. On earth we eulogize someone after they have died. Since God is alive forever, we bless Him day after day throughout our lives.

THE FRUIT OF OUR LIPS

Because our culture has tried to convince us that our faith is a "private matter" between us and God, we have a subtle resistance to speaking aloud to Him or about Him. This affects the way in which we witness—we want our lives to "speak" to people. That is good. Our life choices and behavior should communicate to other people that we have a relationship with God—one they could have as well. But if we do not actually tell them about the good news of Jesus' sacrifice, they are not going to have the opportunity to believe.

The "private" nature of faith in our society also affects our worship. Society is fairly accepting of *reverence* as an act of worship; being quiet, observing moments of silence, is OK even for nonbelievers, because such observances do not have an impact on them. They can easily ignore the moment of silence; it does not say anything to them that they are forced to consider. If, on the other hand, we who exalt the Lord do so aloud, our praises become very disturbing to them. They overhear something they do not want to hear—they are confronted with our belief in a God whom they do not follow.

The point is not to rattle people with public praise. But it is interesting to see the difference in impact between silent and spoken worship. What we speak has more definition than just what we think within ourselves. It puts more on the line. Believing and speaking always go hand in hand in the Bible.

It is not surprising, then, that the Word of God talks about praise and worship as the "fruit of our lips" (Hos. 14:2). Through Him, then, "let us continually offer up a sacrifice of praise to God, that is, the fruit of lips that give thanks to His name" (Heb. 13:15).

In fact, the Lord says that the people He will form for Himself—like you and me—will "declare [His] praise" with our mouth (Isa. 43:21). Verbal worship is the one of the primary ways for us to give glory to the Lord. (Read Isaiah 42:12.) That is why David prays, "O Lord, open my lips, that my mouth may declare Thy praise" (Ps. 51:15).

It is not as though we have done something wrong by praising the Lord only in our heart. He can "hear" us when we do. And many times inner worship is more appropriate to a situation than outward praise might be. We can pray silently as well as aloud, and we can worship with our lips or without them. But especially in church with other believers, we want to sing aloud new songs and old songs. (Read Psalm 149:1.) We want to celebrate Him with our words. (Read Psalm 35:18.)

I have proclaimed glad tidings of righteousness in the great congregation; behold, I will not restrain my lips, O Lord, Thou knowest. I have not hidden Thy righteousness within my heart; I have spoken of Thy faithfulness and Thy salvation; I have not concealed Thy lovingkindness and Thy truth from the great congregation.

—Psalm 40:9–10

PRESENTING OURSELVES FOR TRANSFORMATION

Beyond these particular activities of worship (and others, like clapping, shouting and playing instruments), we also can express our praise to the Lord by how we present our whole lives to Him. As newly adopted children of God, we are living testaments "to the praise of His glory," meaning that our recovery and restoration communicate to all of creation just what God is like, what is really true of Him. (Read Ephesians 1:5–6, 12.) We are ambassadors of His kingdom, and the more we come to live His way of life, instead of our own former way, the more attention we draw toward Him. Our lifestyle reflects on Him.

Paul defines the ultimate "spiritual service of worship" not as a song meeting at church, but as an offering you make to the Lord of yourself (Rom. 12:1)! The most profound worship statement I can make is to lay myself on the altar as a sacrifice and say, "Here is my life, Lord. Use me as You want to use me. I surrender all to You." In our culture, a sacrifice is generally seen as something I give up, a choice I make to do without or to deny myself something I really want. So it is understandable that many people get confused about what God wants to do with them when they sacrifice themselves. They think, *Well, my life won't be as full or as fun as it would have been, but I want God to know that I choose to live for Him.*

God's purpose for sacrifice has never been to have us end up with less. As we are learning, everything God has arranged for us on earth is to bring us closer to Him in love. Primarily, sacrifice is a means of eliminating the blotches on our record—taking care of the wrongs that separate us from God. The atonement transfers sin and its penalty from us to another.

In addition to being a means of removing sin from someone's life, sacrifice is also a means of bringing transformation. A sacrifice made on earth is meant to ascend into heaven. Somehow it transfers a message from one dimension of reality to the other. A lamb cannot be offered up to God in the heavens in its physical, bodily form because it is flesh and blood. A person can try throwing a lamb into the sky in an effort to send it to heaven, but it will always tumble back to earth. How then does one get the lamb into the sky to stay? Transform it into a sweet-smelling savor; turn the tangible carcass into intangible smoke by burning it as a sacrifice.

And that is a hint about one of the greatest benefits (to us) of worship—worship changes us. You will discover that the lifelong process of walking with the Lord brings about huge changes in our thinking and living. The world wants to keep us conformed to its

▲ Worship changes us.

patterns, but God works to transform our lives so they resemble His. Our thoughts and actions need lots of realignment to fit His patterns. When we bring ourselves to the Lord and offer our whole life to Him, He is overjoyed and delighted to help us change because He knows we do want to live His way. Worship and praise miraculously aid in that transformation. (Read 2 Corinthians 3:18.)

Read Deuteronomy 5:7–8. Have you ever wondered why God warns us not to worship any image of other gods?

_____

Read Psalm 115:1–8. What happens to people as they worship an idol or a false god?

_____

_____

Read Luke 16:13. Why do you think that worshiping (serving) one god makes us unsuitable for worshiping another?

_____

_____

　　Our worship of the true and living God will increasingly shape us into His image. Sacrifices of praise and worship will change the way we think and feel. This can be a daily offering to Him, not just a once-in-a-lifetime experience. When you received Jesus into your life and surrendered to His lordship, you received a once-for-all-your-life forgiveness and adoption, but your "forever connection" with the Lord means you can have daily guidance from and interaction with Him. There is no better way to receive both from Him than in times of worship.

TWO TRAPS TO AVOID

The first trap is believing that you are not good enough to worship the Lord. Throughout your life, you will have days and seasons when the accumulation of your own wrongdoing or discouragement will make you feel unworthy or unacceptable to the Lord. That is not true, of course, because Jesus' sacrifice has made us perpetually acceptable—even pleasing—in God's sight. But in your own soul, you will feel that you are not "doing well." At such times the temptation will be to draw back from worship, to withhold yourself from Him out of a sense of shame or guilt. We feel better about praising God when we feel better about ourselves.

　　It is natural to think that way, but it is not correct. Worship is always about how God has done, not how we have done. We have blown it, but He never has. All His works are done perfectly (Deut. 32:4). He is worthy of our praise even when, and especially when, we do not feel worthy of praising Him. At such times, the best thing we can do is focus on how different His works are from our own. Hallelujah!

Among the many hindrances to full and free worship, pride is probably the worst. That is because pride and worship are antithetical to one another. Worship thanks God for how He has arranged things and for what He has done; pride is sure it could do better and that it knows more.

The devil, whose name used to be Lucifer, was the chief worship leader in heaven before pride entered his heart. (Read Isaiah 14:11–14; Ezekiel 28:1–18.) He wanted things his way, not God's way. Ultimately he declared that God was wrong. Pride always leads us to that conclusion.

Read Deuteronomy 32:4; Daniel 4:37 and Psalm 145:7.
Why is praise is the antithesis to pride?

_____

_____

Worship automatically puts everyone in the right place—God above, the Great and Mighty One, and us on earth where we can receive all that He wants to do for us.

Read Psalm 25:9 and James 4:6. What does the Lord want to do for us—especially as we worship?

_____

_____

A second trap is worrying that your worship is not good (or frequent) enough to please the Lord. Devotion to God and thankful praise for who He is and what He has done can inadvertently be turned into a legalistic mandate—something we better do or suffer the consequences. We can put lots of pressure on ourselves to worship God ("It really is something I ought to do!"), and so can well-meaning worship leaders.

Especially in churches where the wisdom and beauty of worship get expressed freely and regularly, the prodding toward higher or more worship can become very fleshy. The result is a charismatic legalism. Worship and devotion to God are heart attitudes that will manifest in behavior, but when the behavior is focused upon more than the attitude—when devotion gets turned into devotions—danger is not far off.

The Rock! His work is perfect, for all His ways are just; a God of faithfulness and without injustice, righteous and upright is He.

— Deuteronomy 32:4

Legalism looks holy on the surface, but it always transfers the burden from the Lord to us. It concentrates on our works rather than on His. Worship is supposed to celebrate everything Jesus has done for us, and we cannot really do that by exerting pressure on ourselves or others to work harder! The benefits of worship are unmistakable, and the more frequently and freely we worship, the greater blessing we will experience. But that is not because we earn the blessing the way a dog might earn a biscuit for retrieving a newspaper. God doesn't say, "There's a good little worshiper." Worship is like having air conditioning in a Texas summer heat wave—turn it on as often as you want.

AN ACTIVE FORCE

There are many physical forces, powers and processes that propel things in the world and make things happen—magnetism, gravity, electricity, wind, fission, to name a few. Our natural world is "governed" by various laws—actions have reactions; friction slows movement; matter and energy may change form, but they do not cease to exist; and everything tends toward chaos. Living your life in the Lord will expose you to spiritual forces, powers and processes that affect everything in life. Worship is among the most powerful of these spiritual dynamics, and the enemy of your soul does not want you to understand it, much less make use of it.

Not only does worship signal our allegiance to the Lord, but it also accomplishes great things in and around us. As we have seen, it postures us to better receive His instructions and intentions. That is partly due to the change it effects in us, but it is also because it actively invites the rulership of God to establish itself in our life situations. Did you know that God is "enthroned upon the praises" of His people (Ps. 22:3)? In a spiritual sense He inhabits our praise, so worship compellingly invites Him to invade our circumstances with His kingdom power.

Read 2 Chronicles 20:1–23. What was the situation for the people of God? Why did they cry out to the Lord (v. 12)?

_____

_____

What did God tell the king to do (v. 17, 20)?

_____

_____

What did the king do (v. 21)?

_____

_____

What happened as they praised the Lord (v. 22)?

_____

_____

By praising God, we reassert that He is "far above all [other] rule and authority" that may be trying to direct how our life turns out (Eph. 1:20–22). The next time you are facing an attack from circumstances or spiritual forces, what will you do?

_____

_____

Worship is a powerful agent of deliverance and rescue. When Paul and Silas were in prison, their songs of praise before the Lord—even in the midst of their confining circumstances—brought about a miraculous earthquake that opened the jail cells. (Read Acts 16:25–30.) The more familiar you become with the Bible, the more you will see how the people of God choose to exalt and magnify the Lord when they are surrounded by enemies or in the midst of danger. (Read Psalm 57:4–11.) Why? Because worship acts as a special call for deliverance. Worship acknowledges God's place as the Most High, as the Faithful One, and worship signals to everyone that we are helpless on our own to do anything about what faces us.

> Worship is a powerful agent of deliverance and rescue.

When we are in the midst of a hard time, our natural inclination is to do anything but praise God. (Little lies whisper that He is at least somewhat responsible for us being where we are.) Worship is tailor-made for times of trouble. That is a lesson you will have to keep learning throughout your life. Worship magnifies our sense of God's presence and work.

Worship also ushers us into His courtroom—not physically or in some sort of weird, out-of-body transport, but in the realm of spirit. Worship is the primary activity in heaven, and it is one of only a few things we can do on earth as it is done in heaven. Hence, the Bible tells us we can enter His gates and courts with our praise and thanksgiving (Ps. 100:4). Just as we pray for His will to be done on earth as it is in heaven, so our praise can be done on earth as it is in heaven, too. (Read Matthew 6:9–10.) Truly, worship draws us closer to the Lord and brings us nearer to Him.

> Enter His gates with thanksgiving, and His courts with praise. Give thanks to Him; bless His name.
>
> —Psalm 100:4

WHAT DOES JESUS SAY ABOUT PRAISE AND WORSHIP?

Read Matthew 4:9–10. While resisting temptation in the wilderness, Jesus quoted a very important truth to Satan: "You shall worship the Lord your God, and serve Him only." Worship, service and bonded allegiance are the same concept. We worship the Lord by looking only to Him for our ultimate outcome and our daily instructions. Worship is a signal of allegiance we make to our God. Difficulties and sadness in this life will try "to bring us to our knees," to make us acknowledge defeat. However, when we voluntarily bend our knees to the Lord in worship and surrender to His lordship, we can defeat the very circumstances that sought to overwhelm us.

Read Matthew 21:16. When the religious leaders grew indignant at the praise being given to Jesus by the multitudes, He told them that even little children instinctively know enough to worship. God designed us for the special relationship He wanted us to have with Him, so He created in us an inborn desire to worship Him. As they grow older, most people become too sophisticated or knowledgeable to worship the Lord, or they bow down to false gods. When people refuse to celebrate the Lord, they completely miss one of the most basic purposes for mankind. Hence, Jesus explains that God uses children and their innocence to repair and adjust worship among people.

Read Luke 19:40. In fact, the whole of creation is so bent upon worshiping its Creator that if people do not exercise their privilege as the only ones on earth who can loose their tongues in praise, even inanimate objects like rocks will find a way to cry out in adoration. The ability of humans with speech and language — all the intricate and creative ways we could verbally thank the Lord — far exceeds that of any other creature. How sad it must be to the Lord to have people choose to be as inarticulate as sheep, as silent as stones.

Read Mark 7:7. Even though some religious activities and practices may seem spiritual, the essence of worship is obedience (paying close attention, listening attentively) to what God has said, not just imposing man-made rules or doctrines on ourselves (or others). He wants us to have ears to hear what God is telling us, not just a general openness to all sorts of spiritual input.

LET'S TALK ABOUT IT

▲ If you are like most of us, your thinking about worship was quite different than how the Bible talks about it. How have your thoughts changed about worship from reading this chapter?

_____

_____

▲ Did you ever wonder why God wanted to be worshiped? In what ways is worship really for our sake? How would you encourage a friend to engage in worship to the Lord?

_____

_____

▲ Since God is the One whom we worship, it only makes sense that we should worship Him the way He wants to be worshiped. How do we worship God? What does it look like? Why do you think that people want to make their own choices about how to worship Him?

_____

_____

▲ Can you explain why the Lord warns us not to worship false gods? How does worship transform us?

_____

_____

▲ In this chapter we learned about some things that keep us from worshiping God. In your own life, what makes it difficult to praise the Lord?

_____

_____

▲ Why do you think people struggle with worshiping the Lord with their whole being? What would you say to a friend who asked you the reason you lift your hands in praise and speak words of worship to the Lord?

_____

_____

YOUR TIME WITH GOD

Thank God for all that He has done for you. Acknowledge His hand at work in your life. Tell God how glad you are to know what you know about Him.

Are you in any danger or trouble? Are you in the midst of hard times, or do you feel surrounded by enemies? Worship God. Acknowledge His place as the Most High, as the Faithful One. Thank God for how He has arranged things and for what He has done. Surrender everything to God. Lift your hands and begin to praise Him, simply, with your lips.

Father, I love You. Thank You for what You have done in my life. Thank You, Lord, for Your mercy and forgiveness. Thank You that You have a plan for my life.

And praise You, Jesus, that You are always with me, and that You died for me. Thank You for Your faithfulness to me.

Praise Your name, Lord. I love You. I worship You as the Almighty One, the Maker of heaven and earth, who spoke the worlds into existence, who made me as Your child. I serve You and surrender afresh to Your purposes for my life. Thank You that You go before me and lead me in the way I should go.

How I bless You for all You have done for me. Receive my worship and praise as an offering, as incense before You. Hallelujah! Hallelujah! Hallelujah!

CHAPTER SIX

Reading the Bible

THERE IS A HUGE DIFFERENCE BETWEEN *RELIGION* TOWARD GOD AND *RELATIONSHIP* WITH GOD. *Religion* essentially outlines ways in which people like you and me must live in order to be acceptable (to come) to God. Religion puts the emphasis on what we need to do for Him. Relationship with God, on the other hand, is completely based upon what God does for us. With religion, the great question mark is whether or not God will find what we do adequate enough to measure up to His standards. Will God accept what we do for Him? Will He willingly receive us into His presence? What the Bible teaches about God, and the relationship He wants with us, is exactly opposite to that—the issue is not whether He will accept what we do for Him, but whether we will accept what He has done for us.

Religion is one of the worst enemies to your relationship with the Lord. A religious mentality, lurking in the fleshly corners of every soul, attempts to interpret or characterize our walk with the Lord as a series of steps we must take for Him, things that we need to do to prove something to Him or to show Him how hard we are trying.

God wants to do good to us all the days of our lives and to pursue us with mercy (Ps. 23:6). Religion tells us we have to do good to God and pursue Him by following rules and regulations all the days of our lives. God wants to lift our burdens and sustain us (Ps. 55:22); religion wants to add other loads and put the burden of sustaining our connection with God upon us (Matt. 23:4).

▲▲

Religion is one of the worst enemies to your relationship with the Lord.

▲▲

The Lord desires to be the One who "daily bears our burden" (Ps. 68:19), the One who breaks "the yoke of [our] burden" (Isa. 9:4). That is why Jesus invites us to come to Him when we are loaded down with all the stuff life puts on us—because all the things He gives us to carry are handy and pleasingly helpful for hauling the rest of the junk to the dump. Everything God does for us and offers to us comes with these words attached: "Here, you will find that this

IN THIS CHAPTER YOU WILL LEARN . . .

▲ The difference between religion and relationship with God.

▲ Why God wrote the Bible for our sake.

▲ The power God's Word has to renew and to restore us.

▲ Why the Bible is unlike any other book on earth.

▲ That the promises in God's Word can change our lives.

▲ How the Bible reveals the truth about God and about ourselves.

Surely goodness and lovingkindness will follow me all the days of my life, and I will dwell in the house of the LORD forever.

—Psalm 23:6

Cast your burden upon the LORD, and He will sustain you; He will never allow the righteous to be shaken.

—Psalm 55:22

And they tie up heavy loads, and lay them on men's shoulders; but they themselves are unwilling to move them with so much as a finger.

— Matthew 23:4

really helps you . . . " Religion twists God's words around to sound like this: "If you want Me to help, you better do this . . . "

As you learn to walk with the Lord on your journey and to distinguish His voice from all the others vying for your attention, try to remember to listen to the *tone* of what you hear. If it is kind and merciful, offering to bless you and assist you, it is far more likely to be the Lord than if it sounds condemning, threatening, withholding or conditional in its love. Your own sincerity and zeal can fool you into engaging in activities in order to somehow do something *for God* when He has actually meant those activities to do something *for you*. His posture of grace toward us always means that He wants to do things for us, rather than for us to do things for Him. Whenever He tells us to do something, we can be assured that it is meant to benefit and advantage us, instead of satisfying and further enriching Him.

Read the following two sentences, catching the tone in which they are written:

▲ "If you do not do what I tell you to do, you are not going to be blessed."

▲ "If only you had followed my instructions, you would have been so blessed."

Can you hear the difference? The first sentence sounds angry, threatening and authoritarian. The second is merciful, concerned and advisory. Though the Lord is the ultimate authority in life, He speaks to His children differently than He does to His enemies. He wants to teach us how spiritual life really works, so He instructs, counsels and guides us. He does not bully, threaten or condemn.

Read the following scriptures with the sound of the second sentence in your ears, and then put them into your own words. Deuteronomy 5:29

_____

_____

Psalm 81:13–16

_____

_____

Isaiah 48:17–18

_____

_____

Matthew 11:28–30

_____

_____

One of the easiest places to get confused about what our role is vis-à-vis the Lord's provisions for us is in reading the Bible. God wants you to read the Bible, not in order to prove something to Him or to earn something from Him, but because He wants to do you good.

Everyone who has walked with the Lord will tell you that reading your Bible is one of the most important and helpful things you can do to grow spiritually strong and stable. We are going to look at some of the reasons why that is true, and explore many of the incredible benefits that come to us from reading the Word of God. But throughout your journey with the Lord, remember that His intent for His Word is to serve you, not for you to serve it. Reading the Bible is not a religious obligation—it is a marvelous, life-giving opportunity available to you whenever you want it.

> Reading the Bible is not a religious obligation—it is a marvelous, life-giving opportunity available to you whenever you want it.

MAN WAS NOT MADE FOR THE SABBATH

In one of Jesus' frequent conflicts with religious leaders of His day, He was accused of violating the Sabbath because He had allowed His disciples to pick some grain to eat while they were walking along in the fields. (Read Mark 2:23–28.) The legalists said, "Hey, God has a rule: no work on the Sabbath. Period." Jesus replied by telling them they had missed the heart of God—His intentions for us. God did not create mankind so there would be someone to obey His rules. He made the Sabbath as a blessing for people—giving them regular rest and a regular reminder that God is the only One who can completely make things the way they are supposed to be.

God did not make people so that there would be someone to read His Word. He wrote the Bible, just as He made the Sabbath, as a blessing for the sake of people. It was to give us regular refreshment and a regular reminder that God is the only One whose words can gain us real life, the kind of life He so earnestly desires us to experience (Matt. 4:4). The Bible, like the Sabbath, is only meant to do us good. If we think of reading the Bible primarily as a requirement mandated by God for anyone who wants to do what

> But He [Jesus] answered and said, "It is written, 'Man shall not live on bread alone, but on every word that proceeds out of the mouth of God.'"
> —Matthew 4:4

. . . seeing that His divine power has granted to us everything pertaining to life and godliness, through the true knowledge of Him who called us by His own glory and excellence. For by these He has granted to us His precious and magnificent promises, in order that by them you might become partakers of the divine nature, having escaped the corruption that is in the world by lust.
— 2 Peter 1:3–4

By faith we understand that the worlds were prepared by the word of God, so that what is seen was not made out of things which are visible.
— Hebrews 11:3

they are supposed to do, we will lose much of our incentive for reading it. If reading His Word is merely a discipline of obedient devotion, a compulsory exercise of our *religion*, then we will miss all the advantage God wants to bring to us through it.

▲▲

God's Word is filled with a creative power so life-giving that it framed the cosmos. That power still reverberates in His written words to us.

▲▲

So, why would the Lord want us to spend time regularly reading His Word? Where is the advantage to us? What spiritual benefit do we derive from taking His Word into our heart? What can be found in the Bible that cannot be found anywhere else? To start, let us focus on what the Bible is—and is not. It is not just paper and ink, words divided into books, chapters and verses. Those are just the means by which the Bible can be read. As simplistic as it may sound, the Bible is the Word of the Lord—what He has said about everything pertaining to real life and to godliness (2 Pet. 1:3–4). When you read a chapter or several verses, you are actually reading what the Lord has recorded for all time concerning that subject.

Think for a moment about the power of God's Word. In the beginning of time as we know it, He spoke, and out of nothing, all of creation came into being. (Read Genesis 1; Romans 4:17.) God's Word is filled with a creative power so life-giving that it framed the cosmos (Heb. 11:3). That power still reverberates in His written words to us.

SCIENCE OR SCRIPTURE?

Science has several theories about the origin of the cosmos and life on earth. The odds against life—against existence (period)—are so enormous that any plausible explanation for why we are here must factor astronomical sums of natural substances (like time or energy) into the equation. Life is simply too big of an improbability to have happened without some huge element outside of our present experience and what we can see in the world as we know it now.

Scientific investigation concludes that something "just happened." Amidst the vastness, out of the primal energies and elements of the infant cosmos, life (somehow) began and evolved to its present form. What could have been powerful enough to scatter the galaxies or to bring forth life of any kind—much less humanity—on the earth? For believers in the Lord, the origin of our species is far more than a matter of idle curiosity. It sits at the center of what is true of Him—that He created the worlds as an arena for His creation of and loving relationship with us, and that He did so intentionally, personally and miraculously.

What does the Bible say about how we got here?

Read Genesis 1:1, 27. The Hebrew word for *create* is *bara* [pronounced *baw-raw'*]. Along with meaning "to create," it suggests a deliberate choice — in the way you might select the choicest tree to cut down for lumber to build a house. Science says things exist because of chance and accident, but the Bible says what?

Read Hebrews 11:3. The Greek word for *prepared* or *formed* [*katartizo*] means "to complete thoroughly, to make completely perfect." Science tells us that the cosmos and everything in it is evolving toward a higher order even though the evidence points to the fact that it is actually falling apart. What was the power behind the perfect and complete cosmos when it was made by God?

Read Romans 4:17. What two things can God do by His Word?

After six days, God rested—"He completed His work" of speaking things into existence (Gen. 2:1–2). He wasn't tired or worn out. Rather, He was finished, and everything was perfectly the way He wanted it to be. Just like a student who knows all the answers on a test and finishes before the time is up, so God finished the cosmos with plenty of time to spare. His rest was a silent commentary about how pleased He was with what He had made. God arranged the cosmos exquisitely—exactly as He wanted it. Like a designer with an unlimited budget and endless amounts of time and energy, God decorated the universe and put His signature touch on even its smallest details.

Read 1 Chronicles 16:14; Psalm 119:60, 89 and 1 Peter 1:25.
Since God's Word never changes, what can it do in our lives? In what way can the Word of God act as a reference point for our lives today?

Now read John 1:1–3; Colossians 1:15–17 and Luke 6:46–49. Why does Jesus claim that His words are a sure foundation for our lives?

_____

_____

God no longer needed to speak creative words; instead, He could have conversation with the people whom He had created. He loves to talk with us and speak to us. That has always been the point. But the counter-directive voice of mankind's rebellion reconfigured the worlds, splashing garish colors everywhere and knocking the furnishings out of place. Sin messed everything up. What God had made, we unmade; what He had fixed and arranged, we broke and scattered in disarray. When sin came and broke the worlds, it cut off much of the dialogue between God and us.

And so, in love God began to speak again—not creative, *call-into-being-out-of-nothing* words, but curative, *get-everything-fixed-back-up* words. His Word still has the same power it had to create the worlds and give birth to us. But now that Word wealth expends itself to renew and to restore us. Of all His creation, God has always placed the highest value on people; therefore, His primary focus for restoration is on us. Like a man returning to find that intruders have broken in and ransacked his home, God's first thought is for what He cherishes most—His family. The shambles can be taken care of later; the broken drawers can be fixed tomorrow. Right now, He wants to make sure everyone is OK, and He wants to relieve them of the trauma they have suffered.

> This is the essence of what God's Word does in our lives— it reframes and reconstitutes our being.

So it is with our heavenly Father. In the midst of a wayward, off-based world, God's Word soothes and repairs the damage we have suffered. It situates us to fit in with all the arrangements He has made for the new life we will be enjoying with Him forever. Because His Word is exactly the same as it has always been (Isa. 40:8), it is perfect for perfectly restoring us to our original condition (Ps. 19:7). That is the essence of what God's Word does in our lives—it reframes and reconstitutes our being.

So, how does the Bible work? How does it do its restoration in our lives?

> The grass withers, the flower fades, but the word of our God stands forever.
>
> — Isaiah 40:8

> The law of the LORD is perfect, restoring the soul.
>
> — Psalm 19:7

THE ESSENTIAL TRUTH
ABOUT THE TRUTH

The Bible is unlike any other book in the world. What is true of it is not true of any other volume on the planet. To begin with, it is the Word of *God*, not man (2 Tim. 3:16). Though penned by people throughout the ages, it is inspired [literally *God-breathed*] by God who "watches over" it to assure that it does what it is supposed to do (Jer. 1:12). Men "moved by the Holy Spirit spoke from God"—they did not write the Scriptures as "an act of human will" (2 Pet. 1:21). This point—the ultimate authorship of the Bible—receives great assault in our culture and in your own mind. Why? Because as long as the Bible is just a good book, a collection of nice stories, an anthology of historical fiction, a moral code or a treasury of quotable quotes, it does not have any real authority in someone's life. They can take it or leave it; read it or not read it; follow it or dismiss it.

It is not as though God gets offended when people disregard His words. He is grieved, not peeved. He loves us so profoundly, and He wants us to experience an abundant life (John 10:10), as free as possible from the ravages of wrongness all around us. That is the whole point for the Bible having authority in someone's life. As people really come to view the Scriptures as a message from God Himself, they are able to get to know Him for who He really is. He wants us to know Him and His heart and His ways. He wants us to see what He is like by reading the record of what He has done for and what He has said to people through the ages (Rom. 15:4).

Once you believe that the Bible is written by the Lord, you will read it differently and more attentively, the way that you would read a long letter from someone who loves you. The Scriptures reveal how He thinks about things, stuff He did before we got to know Him and ways He handles problems like ours. Reading the Bible is the best way for us to get to know the Lord, to grow familiar with His voice and to become acquainted with His manner of doing things. In that way we get a feel for His style and can highlight patterns and themes we will encounter over and over in our own spiritual lives.

Read 1 Corinthians 10:1–11, especially verse 11. The examples from history contained in the Bible have been personally chosen by the Lord (like an artist's sample portfolio) to do what in our lives? How can others' examples *instruct* (call attention to) us?

> All Scripture is inspired by God and profitable for teaching, for reproof, for correction, for training in righteousness.
> —2 Timothy 3:16

> The thief comes only to steal, and kill, and destroy; I came that they might have life, and might have it abundantly.
> —John 10:10

> For whatever was written in earlier times was written for our instruction, that through perseverance and the encouragement of the Scriptures we might have hope.
> —Romans 15:4

GOD'S PROMISES

When we "give" someone our word, we are pledging to stand behind what we have said. "I give you my word" means "I promise; this is true." The Bible contains all the promises that God has made to you. It is full of declarations about how He will provide for your needs, how He will contend with your spiritual adversaries, how He will carry you, answer you, change you and love you throughout your life. Most people know almost nothing about what God wants to do for them. That does not make Him mad; it makes Him sad that the people whom He loves have so little idea of what He has in mind for them as His children.

He wants you to know about His promises for several reasons. First, they are born out of His heart of love for you. Love promises a future; love loves to enumerate what it is going to do for the sake of another. Parents awaiting the birth of a child understand this. So do brides and grooms, young boys with their first puppy, and closest friends moving away to another city. True love calls forth promises from the deep places in our heart—pledges, commitments and vows of what we will (always) do and feel for the one we love.

Read Isaiah 26:9. What do we learn about when we experience one of God's words in life?

_____

_____

Read Joshua 21:45 and 2 Corinthians 1:20. What do we know about the promises of the Lord?

_____

_____

Read Romans 10:17 and Hebrews 11:33. How do we receive the promises from Him when we read the Bible?

_____

_____

> For bodily discipline is only of little profit, but godliness is profitable for all things, since it holds promise for the present life and also for the life to come.
> —1 Timothy 4:8

Though sincerely meant and well intentioned, human promises have nowhere near the power of God's promises. People often break their promises, or they collapse under the weight of uncontrollable circumstances. Human promises offer little to change how someone's life turns out. God always keeps His Word, and He is in control over all of life's circumstances. His promises carry through from this life into eternity (1 Tim. 4:8).

As you read the Bible, you will be amazed at just how much God has sworn to give to you and to do for you. If you do not know about His promises—say, to never desert you no matter how bad things get—you will go through unnecessary and agonizing uncertainty, hoping that He will do something that He already promised He would do. The more of His promises you know, the more you can stand with certainty and without fear. His promises are the mainstay of your inheritance—all He has bequeathed to take care of you and to bring you incredible fulfillment.

▲▲

God gives us His Word as a kind and careful mentor who watches over us.

▲▲

We are "commended" to God's Word (Acts 20:32); that is, we are encouraged to place ourselves in its safekeeping and under its benevolent care. The Bible is not a taskmaster driving us to do God's will. Neither does God appoint overseers to make sure that we read as much as we are supposed to read. Instead, God gives us His Word as a kind and careful mentor who watches over us. Not only do His words alert us to our full inheritance, but they also "build us up." As we read the Bible, our inner person, our spiritual life, is developed and matured like a fast-growing adolescent (Eph. 4:14). God's words increase our strength and confidence. His Word adds a weightiness to our character so that we become firmly established in His ways.

CHANGE AGENTS

As we have been seeing, God wants us to read His promises in the Bible because of the supernatural capability they have to change us. Just as worship has a transforming power in our lives, so too does reading the Bible. The Bible is the truth (John 17:17). All of its parts put together add up to the whole truth about God's will and way for us here on earth (Ps. 119:160). Not only do the promises of God neutralize corrosive influences in our life, but also His words proactively enable us to become more like Him in how we think and behave (2 Pet. 1:4). Scripture teaches us what is true about life and how it works. It realigns our thinking and adjusts the course we are on. Like a practiced mother cleaning up her teenage boy's room, the Bible can, if we allow it to, sweep into our heart and mind to put things back where they belong.

In other words, even though our lives have been tragically infected and corrupted by the ways of a world gone bad, a world pursuing its own fulfillment no matter what the cost, the

As a result, we are no longer to be children, tossed here and there by waves, and carried about by every wind of doctrine, by the trickery of men, by craftiness in deceitful scheming.
— Ephesians 4:14

Sanctify them in the truth; Thy word is truth.
— John 17:17

The sum of Thy word is truth, and every one of Thy righteous ordinances is everlasting.
— Psalm 119:160

For by these He has granted to us His precious and magnificent promises, in order that by them you might become partakers of the divine nature, having escaped the corruption that is in the world by lust.
— 2 Peter 1:4

... that the man of God may be adequate, equipped for every good work.
— 2 Timothy 3:17

promises of God act as a counterbalance and an antidote. The Word of God has an incredibly restorative power to fix the inner damage that has been done in our lives as a result of the wrong ways we have of thinking. Reading the Bible will change how we think and feel about life, making us complete people, instead of the fragmented beings we have been (2 Tim. 3:17).

> The Word of God has an incredibly restorative power to fix the inner damage that has been done in our lives as a result of the wrong ways we have of thinking.

Read John 8:32. Jesus tells us that the more of the truth we really know, the more liberated we will be from false and deadly mentalities. Why do you think the truth sets people free? What sort of truth do you think Jesus is talking about?

_____

_____

ATTRIBUTES OF THE BIBLE AND THE ADVANTAGES TO US IN READING IT (FROM PSALM 19:7–11)

The Bible is . . .	Reading it will . . .
Perfect—exactly right and correct in every detail pertaining to life. It is wholly complete, and it lacks nothing that we need for life.	Restore your mind, heart and conscience to how God intended them to work. His Word will bring your thoughts and emotions to different conclusions than they have had, and it recovers areas of your inner life that have been broken, bound or bruised by wrong ways of thinking or feeling throughout your life.
Sure—absolutely reliable and trustworthy as a basis for living life and making decisions. It is a firm foundation upon which to stand, no matter what the circumstance.	Make you unbelievably wise, with keen insights on what to do, think or say in any situation you may face. Rather than having to rely on your own limited experience and expertise, you will find that Bible stories and verses come to your mind, offering you counsel and direction for making the right decisions.

The Bible is . . .	Reading it will . . .
Right—precisely as it should be, like a clear, sunshiny morning or an exquisitely set dinner table. It doesn't get any better than the genuineness of God's Word.	Bring a deep-seated joy to your heart in the same way that you might drink in the beauty of an evening sunset. Constant exposure to the Bible counteracts the pollutants of life and introduces a fundamental sense of well-being and prosperity to your life.
Pure—completely free of any worldly contaminants or other elements of distortion. It has no mixed motives or mixed messages that need to be filtered out.	Reveal all sorts of counterfeits, subterfuges and falsehoods to you that you would otherwise not discern in life. The Bible is like a powerful flashlight shining on the path in front of you; it lets you see hidden pits and traps and points out the best path to take.
True and righteous—thoroughly and expertly revealing the way God intended life to work and to be. The righteousness and truth of God come to us only through revelation, and the Bible is God's disclosure to us.	Make you aware of what lasts unto eternity and what is merely passing away. The Word of God abides forever, and when the dust finally settles in this life, only those things lined up with eternal truth will remain standing.
Sweet and desirable—intensely craved by your spirit as the most delightful food imaginable. Nothing tastes better to your soul than the Bible, and nothing can offer such perfect nourishment for growth and health.	Develop your spiritual immune system, guarding you from external disease agents and internal ailments that might otherwise exploit your vulnerabilities. Scripture provides you with a great line of defense against all sorts of infections.

ALIVE AND ACTIVELY PENETRATING

This leads us to another way in which the Bible is unlike any other book you will ever read. It is not an inert textbook to be memorized and studied like a science volume. It is not just a static collection of facts like an encyclopedia, or a set of principles and axioms like in a geometry book. It isn't even just a list of rules and moral guidelines to follow. It does spell out the truth, and it does offer reliable principles and guidelines for life. The more of it you memorize, the better.

But beyond all this, it has a life of its own, an animated quality that enables it to "perform" and do its intended work in us almost on its own (1 Thess. 2:13). It is like a chemical compound that reacts to other elements; much like hydrogen peroxide fizzes and bubbles in response to infectious agents, so the Word of God has a spiritual reaction to things in us. The Bible works like a solvent, getting down and under even the deepest issues in our psyche, bringing with it God's restorative and healing power.

Let's do a little Bible study on Hebrews 4:12–13: "For the word of God is living and *active* [powerfully effective, efficient] and *sharper* [able to cut right through to the real issue] than any two-edged sword, and *piercing* [reaching through] as far as the division of soul and spirit, of both joints and marrow, and able to *judge* [discriminate between and among] the thoughts and intentions of the heart. And there is no creature hidden from His [God's] sight, but all things are open and laid bare to the eyes of Him with whom we have to do" (emphasis added).

Question: In your own words, what two traits are true of God's Word?

_____

_____

What three things can God's Word do?

_____

_____

What should we be expecting to happen in our own heart and mind as we read the Bible?

_____

_____

> The more we read the Bible, the better able we are to "read between the lines" of life.

As we read our Bible and let it wash into our heart and mind, it fixes and rebuilds aspects of our God-given personality—without requiring us to know ahead of time what the problems are or where the woundings may be in us. Like a time-release cold capsule or super-potent multiple vitamin, the Bible really starts to work after we have ingested it. It nourishes our inner person and strengthens us against spiritual attack. The truth of God's Word penetrates even deeper than our consciousness, to sift through all of our feelings and thoughts. It "judges" them with truth, meaning it alerts us to false ways and unreliable mental footings. It points out wrong motives in us and convicts us of hidden faults.

Additionally, the Bible supplies us with heightened discernment and a keener sense of what is going on—inside and out. The more we read the Bible, the better able we are to "read between the lines" of life. Scripture is like "a lamp" shining in the dark, "a light" along our way, chasing back the shadows so we can see clearly (Ps. 119:105). To God, day and night are alike (Ps. 139:12); He sees perfectly well in both. Nothing is hidden from His sight, and His Word has that same capacity to navigate in the hidden recesses of our being, going where it needs to go and doing what it needs to do. (Read Hebrews 4:13.) Simply put, the Bible counsels us with the most reliable therapy available on the planet.

The wisdom contained in God's Word transfers itself to the seat of our thoughts and emotions so that from reading it, we know much better what to do, say and think in various situations. Since God knows how everything is supposed to work, His counsel gives us a huge advantage for living and becoming everything God intends for us to be in life and ministry. A steady diet of Bible verses will create an inner sense of peace and joy (Ps. 119:165)—a kind of optimism that enables us to believe God has everything under control.

God's Word is especially suited to rejuvenate us from the past and to outfit us for the future. Reading the Bible will build us up and provide us with all the resources and tools God has intended for us to use and enjoy. Since God has the final word in everything, His written Word (given to us long before the final end) is the surest and longest-lasting foundation upon which to base our life decisions. His truth outlines a path that we can reliably follow with all our heart. Because of all the rewards that come to us through the Bible, it is the most satisfying and most valuable resource in all the world. Life just works so much better when we read the Bible.

> Darkness and light are alike to Thee.
> —Psalm 139:12

> Those who love Thy law have great peace.
> —Psalm 119:165

HOW TO GET THE MOST OUT OF YOUR BIBLE READING

1. Begin by believing what you are reading is true, rather than reading and then deciding if it is true or not.

2. Pray a simple prayer: *"Lord, teach me from Your Word. Plant these verses in my heart to bear fruit later in my life."*

3. Read as regularly as possible—a little each day is better than a lot once in a while.

4. Read the Bible as you would read a treasure map—looking for things in your life that resemble what you find in the verses.

5. Expect revelation. Listen to what comes to your heart about issues in your life or concerning matters about which you have wondered.

6. Mark or underline every verse that sticks out to you—especially verses that build you up. Keep your eye out for promises or commands that reveal the heart of God.

7. Look for contrasts between what the Bible says and how you think, feel or act. When you spot those differences, ask the Lord to change you.

8. Read on four basic levels: a) *literal*—what God says or does in the lives of actual people; b) *thematic*—principles and understandings about the ways in which God works; c) *prophetic*—promises about what God is going to do in the flow of human history; and d) *personal*—points of instruction and encouragement for your own life.

9. When you come to passages that you do not understand, put a question mark in the margin and keep reading. Do not get stuck. It just means that the Lord isn't speaking to you from those verses at this time.

10. Look for qualities or attributes in the lives of key Bible characters that resemble you. Then ask if they are good or not-so-good things—depending on how God dealt with them in the Bible story.

11. Meditate on what you read by thinking about it throughout the day. You will be amazed at how many things God will show you about your life as you reflect on His Word.

PERFECT MIRROR

The Bible also acts as a magnifying mirror, giving us an up-close glimpse of two images. First and foremost, it reflects the glory of the Lord in the same way that a giant mirror enables astronomers to see objects in the heavens through a telescope. Stars that are faint to the natural eye because of their physical distance from the earth are brought close by huge mirror lenses. In similar fashion, God's Word, which is "very near you" (Deut. 30:14), offers us a firsthand look at God, who inhabits another realm in the heavens and who, therefore, is experientially distant from us. As you look into the Bible, it will present you with the truth about God—what He is like in personality, character and activity.

The Bible mirror has no warps or distortions. It is perfectly smooth and shaped to give back an exact picture of God. The contorted view many people have about God comes from their own impressions, not from the pages of the Bible. Sometimes well-meaning people take a few Bible verses out of context and attempt to interpret God's ways in light of a small portion of the whole mirror. If the mirror lens is not smooth, the warp of the lens creates a distortion in the magnified reflection. The whole Bible must be seen in light of the whole Bible; individual stories or verses can be misleading if taken only on their own.

TAKE THESE STEPS

During times of Bible reading, when you feel convicted or alerted to some area of your mind or heart that does not line up with God's way, try doing two things:

1. Meditate on the verse(s) throughout the next several days—repeat it in your mind, think about it, look for connections to events in your life or to other thought patterns. Ask Jesus to teach you from His Word and to open your eyes to what He is saying to you.

2. Look up similar verses and look for more patterns and connections—use the cross references in your Bible or a concordance to discover the whole counsel of God as it relates to the specific issues He is bringing to your attention.

Reading the Bible is also like holding up a mirror to ourselves. It will return an accurate portrait of our likeness, and it will help us with things we cannot see with our natural eyes. (Read James 1:21–25.) Without a mirror, no one can see the back of his own head to know how the strands of hair are standing up and out. Faults and needs in our soul can remain undetected and unanswered when left only to our natural perceptions. The Word of God has a miraculous way of bringing hidden things to light in our heart. Not only can we behold wonderful truths about the Lord in the mirror of His Word, but we can also see some not-so-wonderful realities about our life. The amazing promise from the Lord is that He never draws our attention to broken or sinful areas of our life just to inform us about them. He intentionally sends forth His Word to heal and deliver us. (Read Psalm 107:20; Matthew 8:8, 16.)

As you go about your days, you will be reminded of verses and phrases from the Bible that alert you to what God is saying. In fact, recalled Scripture that comes to your mind is one of the primary ways in which the Lord will guide you. Discovering God's will for your life, being led by the Spirit, hearing God's voice, ministering to other people, resisting temptation—and virtually every other aspect of your journey with the Lord—develop largely as a result of spending time reading the Bible.

Always remember, however, that we do not earn spiritual growth, like a merit badge, as a result of doing something for God (such as putting in the required amount of Bible study). God never meant for reading His Word to become a legalistic obligation for us to fulfill. Rather, the Bible is one of the most useful, all-purpose tools for your growth in understanding the Lord and His way of doing things. The Bible will introduce as much blessing into your life as you allow it to.

SOME WAYS THE BIBLE WORKS FOR US

The Bible is the best all-purpose tool for growing in our relationship with the Lord and for navigating life in general. Here are just a few of its uses taken from Psalm 119 (the longest and most detailed description of how the Word of God works in a believer's life). Open your Bible and take time to read Psalm 119. See if you can find the verses from which these promises come. Take the time to underline any verses you especially like.

The Bible . . .

Provides us with answers and direction as we seek the Lord.

Revives us when we are down or broken, giving hope and comfort when all looks lost.

Strengthens us in the midst of draining circumstances.

Enlarges our capacity for receiving the things of God.

Gives us answers for the condemnation we sometimes feel.

Keeps us walking in freedom, unentangled with distractions and difficulties.

Teaches us discernment, knowledge, wisdom and understanding.

Provides light so we can see where we are walking and where the path will take us.

Offers us great peace and stability even in the midst of rough waters.

Counteracts our tendency to wander away and get ourselves lost or in trouble.

Makes us wiser than even the smartest person in the world.

Heightens our awareness and dislike of every evil way.

LET'S TALK ABOUT IT

▲ Before you read this chapter, what was your thinking about the Bible? How has that changed as a result of what you have read?

_____

_____

▲ Why did God write the Bible? What is God's primary purpose for giving us His Word?

_____

_____

▲ Why do you think that most people struggle with reading the Bible regularly, and why do they feel guilty for not reading more? Why does God want you to read the Bible? What advice would you give to a friend who asked you if they should read the Bible?

_____

_____

▲ Most people are looking for a philosophy for living—some sort of guidelines for decisions and actions. Why is the Bible the best philosophy for living? How would you explain the connection between the creative power of God's Word and the restorative power it has?

_____

_____

▲ In light of what you have learned in this chapter, what is the importance of Jesus being called the Word of God?

_____

_____

▲ Jesus says that even though our lives have been tragically affected by the ways of a world gone bad, the promises of God act as a counterbalance and an antidote. How do God's words enable you to become more like Him in how you think and behave?

_____

_____

▲ Do you sometimes have fears or negative thoughts? Look for promises from the Lord in the Bible that relate directly to those painful emotions and thoughts. The more of His promises you know, the more you can withstand the lies that come against you. What do God's promises reveal about God's heart toward you?

_____

_____

YOUR TIME WITH GOD

Look into joining a Bible study with other Christians from your church or at work.

Read the Bible one book or several chapters at a time. Get a feel for the overall story—who the characters are, what the time and place were like. Get to know the whole story. The more you get from the details of each episode, the more you will get a grasp of the whole context. Take some time to think about it, meditate on it, look at it from every angle—really study it. Go deep and ask God if there is anything else you can personally learn. Perhaps the words of the following prayer can help you express your thoughts:

Dear God, thank You that You have given me the Bible to support me in every area of my life. Help me to have a heart that loves the Bible and wants to learn more. Thank You for the many promises You give to me through Your Word—the instruction provided and the principles that are life-giving to me. Father, I ask that You speak to me through Your Word and that I grow more each day.

Thank You, heavenly Father, for giving me Your words in the Bible. They are perfect, sure, true and righteous. Reading Your words restores my mind, heart and conscience to how You intended them to work. Your words introduce well-being and prosperity to my life.

Open the eyes of my heart to see what You are saying to me personally as I read the wonderful letter You have written to the world. I want to line my life up with Yours. Thank You . . . in Jesus' name.

CHAPTER SEVEN

Asking for God's Intervention

TO THE SECRETARIES AND JUNIOR ASSOCIATES OF A LARGE CORPORATION, THE CEO CAN BE A FEAR-SOME PRESENCE AND NOT SOMEONE TO INTERRUPT LIGHTLY. They would never think of walking into the BIG BOSS's office and fiddling with the items on his desk—some things are just not done, no matter how casual the working environment claims to be. Rarely would the rank-and-file workers approach the top executive to request a raise or to ask for some situation to be looked into. That simply isn't done. There are managers to handle such matters.

But on a school holiday, the granddaughter of that powerful person can walk into the office, climb up on grandpa's lap and make paper-clip necklaces. She can suspend international negotiations or multimillion-dollar business plans to ask for another color pen to draw with, or to announce that the stapler is empty. Though some employees might grow indignant at the interruption and secretly marvel at the way the little girl is so oblivious to the fact that this is a workplace, not a living room, no employee would miss the main point—adored family members can get in to see the boss anytime they want.

Learning how to welcome God's activity and purposes into your life is much like learning how to be a child in the lap of God. You will be amazed at how many resources He has offered to put at your disposal, and how easy it is to ask for them in times of need. But before explaining some of the simple *ins and outs* of prayer, it will help us if we dispel some of the faulty impressions most people have about conversation with God. Spiritual truth is so opposite from how we would naturally think about things, and if we are not careful, our natural and religious thinking can race ahead to choke the life out of what the Lord wants us to know.

A good example of this is the story of the

IN THIS CHAPTER YOU WILL LEARN . . .

▲ That God delights in having us come to Him anytime, anywhere.

▲ Why we do not have to be "good enough" to pray.

▲ How prayer is for times when we don't "have a prayer."

▲ How the invisible realm is affected by our prayers.

▲ Why thanksgiving and faith are vitally connected to prayer.

▲ The importance of Jesus' name.

▲ Why we do not have to pray for set amounts of time.

> Learning how to welcome God's activity and purposes into your life is much like learning how to be a child in the lap of God.

prodigal son on his way home to see his father. The son knew he had been wrong, so he rehearsed an entire *"I-know-I-don't-deserve-anything"* speech, hoping his father would at least give him a job with the servants. But the boy never even had a chance to start the speech—when his dad saw him at a great distance, he was so overjoyed to have him back home again that he smothered the son's speech with a tearful embrace that made it clear nothing else mattered. His son was home. Grieving was over. It was time to celebrate the future together.

What the father was interested in had almost nothing to do with what the son imagined would be the case. Sincere believers will often come to the realization that we have not lived as we should. Our prodigal nature will lead us to squander our spiritual inheritance—to strike out on our own in foolish pursuits that leave us bankrupt in heart and mind. Or perhaps less blatantly, we will conclude that we do not deserve to receive much from the Lord because we have not done well enough or tried hard enough.

LEGALISTIC TRAPS

We are tempted to approach so many things in the kingdom of God on the basis of what we think we know about where we stand with God, what we should be doing more or better and how we have blown it. That is why some truths in the kingdom of God are better understood from the inside out—understanding the heart of the truth before that truth is precisely defined and outlined as a behavior.

Read Luke 15:11–32. Why do you think we evaluate our own worthiness when we come to the Lord to ask for something in prayer?

_____

_____

What would the father of the prodigal son have felt if the son had insisted on "putting himself in his place"—even after the father wanted to celebrate their reunion?

_____

_____

Based on this story, how pleased is the Lord when we come to pray?

_____

_____

Prayer is one of the best examples of our human tendency to focus more on what we're not living up to, as opposed to something God offers to help us live life more abundantly. Mention the subject of prayer to most believers, and their first thought is, *You crummy Christian; you need to pray more.* Their attention focuses on an obligation or requirement to pray rather than on an opportunity to spend time with Jesus. If that legalistic lie does not knock them over, its opposite usually will: *You are too crummy of a Christian to pray at all.* Such thoughts of unworthiness push them away from conversation with the Lord and compound their sense of failure—of not living up to what they should.

The devil does not care if you crash to the right (*You are supposed to pray more*) or to the left (*You haven't been good enough to pray*). He just wants you off the road. He wants you to approach times of prayer like the prodigal son—feeling guilty for not coming sooner and more often and/or feeling too unworthy to come at all. The enemy of your life would love to have you begin prayer with a rehearsed speech to your heavenly Father, declaring how bad and wrong and unworthy you are. God will have none of that. He is just thrilled to have the time with you again and again.

When a kingdom key is more notable to us for its heaviness on our key chain than for the amazing number of doors it unlocks, we have missed something in our thinking about it. When it is more of a burden than a blessing, we have seen it incorrectly. What God has in mind for us is always cause for greater celebration, not greater condemnation. The spiritual principles and tools with which God wants us to grow familiar in our journey with Him are the same way, so we want to keep viewing them in light of why they make us rejoice, not how they seemingly point out our failings and unworthiness.

> The devil wants you to approach times of prayer like the prodigal son—feeling guilty for not coming sooner and more often and/or feeling too unworthy to come at all.

HOW TO PRAY

Without offering you a formula for the *exactly-correct-one-and-only-way-to-pray*, here are some helpful pointers (in no particular order):

1. Begin with praise and worship, focusing on God's greatness, His overarching authority in both realms of the cosmos and, most importantly, His arrangements for you to be His adopted child.

2. Feel free to bring each of your needs (the ones weighing on your mind) to Him without worrying that they are too small or that He is too busy to listen. Do not "nobly" avoid praying for yourself, but let Him deal with your long-range future needs without your worrying about them.

3. Acknowledge your own sins rather than trying to hide them. They do not disqualify you from praying, but they will cause problems for you if left unconfessed. Tell the Lord of your choice to forgive others, and leave their sins and yours in the same place—behind you.

4. Ask for strength to resist temptation and for deliverance from those "not good" spots in your heart that make you especially vulnerable to sinning. He already knows about them, and He wants to help you overcome what has been overcoming you.

5. Remember, prayer deals with the invisible, so it should mostly be done out of the sight of others, when we are alone—except when a group is together praying corporately about various concerns.

6. Repetition does not actually accomplish much—God hears you as well the first time you say something as He would hear you on the fifteenth time. But some matters bear ongoing prayer—where we continue to ask and seek in His presence. Repeating your prayer does not make it more likely to be heard and answered, but it can keep your heart focused on the Lord as your only answer.

7. There is no suggestion in the Bible that extra volume, perfect grammar or strange inflections in your voice will "aid" your prayers. Human emotion and enthusiasm are wonderful aspects of whom God has made us to be, but they are not what makes our prayers heard more attentively by God.

8. Ask the Lord to show you what to pray—and about what. Let Him bring things and people to your mind, in addition to what you pray about regularly. This is a good opportunity to pray according to Bible verses that come to your heart when thinking about those things or those people.

9. Believe in the Lord—His power, His promises, His willingness and His answers. Believe that He has taken care of what you talk to Him about, and hold on with faith to the answer that may not yet be visible in the natural arena.

10. Close every prayer with these simply incredible words: "In Jesus' name."

If you feel that you do not know how to pray, you are not alone. The disciples asked to be taught, and most believers have the same sense of uncertainty about praying effectively. But just because we need help learning how to utilize this most incredible privilege of being able to access the God of everything does not mean that we are going to have to "work hard at it" in the same way that we might have to study extra hard in an algebra class. God never intended us to struggle with prayer as some students struggle with math or language. You are not dense or saddled with a low spiritual IQ. Do not believe the lies of the enemy, or your own unkind voice, telling you that you will never "catch on" to prayer.

Question: The Bible presents us with several images of prayer that take away some of the fears we have of inadequacy—that it is too difficult for us to do well. Read the following verses in light of the suggested picture, and then put into your own words how they change your impression of praying:

"Now therefore, restore the man's wife, for he is a prophet, and he will pray for you, and you will live. But if you do not restore her, know that you shall surely die, you and all who are yours" (Gen. 20:7). *Praying is like "putting in a good word" for someone to the big boss because he listens to you.*

_____

_____

"In the morning, O LORD, Thou wilt hear my voice; in the morning I will order my prayer to Thee and eagerly watch" (Ps. 5:3). *Praying is like placing an order in a restaurant, then waiting for the food to arrive.*

_____

_____

"May my prayer be counted as incense before Thee; the lifting up of my hands as the evening offering" (Ps. 141:2). *Praying is like lighting a stick of incense, then letting the smoke ascend into the air until it fills the room with its fragrance.*

_____

_____

A FRIEND "HIGH UP" IN THE COMPANY

The saying goes, "It's not what you know, but whom you know that counts." If you have ever received backstage passes, free airline tickets, a special tour not open to the general public—all because of someone you knew who was "high up" in a business company— you have a good idea of what the Bible means by prayer. First and foremost, prayer is about special access. Prayer is a privileged opportunity, like preboarding an airplane along with the first-class passengers (even though you only have a coach ticket). We can get a hint about prayer by imagining that our lifelong best friend suddenly became wealthy.

Our relationship gives us hope that our friend will want to do something for us. We are not strangers desiring a handout. We are lifelong buddies who would love each other even if neither of us were rich. Knowing the friend is the basis upon which we legitimately anticipate help. Additionally, we contemplate the contrast between what our wealthy friend has (tons of money) and what we have (not enough money). Awareness of the huge differential inspires our thoughts of receiving assistance from our friend—we do not spend much time thinking about potential help from friends who are as poor as we are.

Think of how rich God is. He owns everything. Jesus has all authority in the heavens and on the earth, and nothing is impossible for Him. He makes a decision, and no one can question it. The more you understand the closeness of the relationship between God and you—how He feels about you, not just the other way around—and the more you grasp how wealthy and resourced the Lord is, the more you will believe that He is able to do exceedingly beyond your wildest hopes (Eph. 3:20–21).

> Now to Him who is able to do exceeding abundantly beyond all that we ask or think, according to the power that works within us, to Him be the glory.
> —Ephesians 3:20–21

> Prayer is a private audience with the Lord, an opportunity to ask any question, to wonder about any occurrence, to ask for help and provision from the richest, most powerful and most knowledgeable One in all of creation.

So it is with prayer. God has a lifelong relationship with us, not just as a friend, but as our loving Father. Our Father is extremely well-connected, and He has a limitless supply of everything, so it is not as though He is going to have to weigh our needs against what He can come up with or afford at this time.

Read Luke 18:1–8. Why does Jesus use the picture of an unrighteous judge in contrast to our loving Father in heaven?

_____

_____

Read verses 1 and 5 again. Why does Jesus tell us not to grow weary in prayer, but to persist in faith?

_____

_____

Prayer is a private audience with the Lord, an opportunity to ask any question, to wonder about any occurrence, to ask for help and provision from the richest, most powerful and most knowledgeable One in all of creation. What we are entitled to do while praying, and what eventuates as a result of our prayers, happens no other way and to no other people. We can do all things through the Lord—things that we have no hope of doing without Him.

So to be effective in our praying, we will need to learn some important lessons about this thing called prayer. What sort of activity is it?

PRAY ABOUT WHAT IS IMPOSSIBLE WITHOUT GOD

A first lesson we can learn about prayer is that it deals with what is impossible for us to accomplish on our own. With prayer we enter the arena of what we cannot do and cannot change, and where our only hope is in the Lord's intervention (Luke 18:27). As obvious as that may sound, it is such an easy truth to forget. Our tendency is to evaluate a situation—sizing up the possibility quotient and deciding what is likely to happen. If it is just a bit out of our reach or a trifle beyond our ability to change in our own strength, we add prayer like a little spin on a bowling ball. We can mistakenly treat prayer like added insurance, a little "extra [that] can't hurt." A spin might help us knock over more pins, but it isn't necessary.

In other words, if we are not careful to counteract this natural tendency, we will end up praying only about situations when we think there is a good possibility for something to happen all on its own—without requiring God's intervention. Thus, even when the Lord answers our prayer, it doesn't seem like that big of a deal because we already imagined that the situation could take care of itself. If we pray about circumstances and needs that are hopeless without Jesus' touch, we will actually see more answers, and our faith to pray for even more impossible situations will increase.

Read Luke 1:37 and 18:27. Prayer is asking God to do what only He can do in our life situations. Can you think of recent prayers you have offered up to Jesus that were not much more than "wait-and-see-if-it-will-work-itself-out" pauses with God's name attached to the waiting? Have there been needs that seemed too big to pray about? How has your thinking about prayer changed as a result of these verses?

_____

_____

Prayer accomplishes the impossible. Prayer is for those life situations when you are helpless and do not "have a prayer." That is one reason why Jesus almost always talks about forgiveness whenever He teaches His disciples about prayer. (Read Mark 11:23–26; Luke 11:1–4.) Nothing in your life will ever be more impossible than

> The things impossible with men are possible with God.
> —Luke 18:27

removing the guilt of your sin. In fact, the most difficult and costly miracle there will ever be already took place when Jesus' death forgave you and me for our sins. Casting a physical mountain into the ocean is child's play compared to God casting "all our sins into the depths of the sea" (Mic. 7:19).

Once when Jesus was talking to a large crowd of people gathered in someone's house, a paralyzed man was brought to Him (in an unusual way). Jesus told the man his sins were forgiven. (Read Mark 2:1–11.) The religious leaders said Jesus could not do that—only God had the power and authority to do something so incredible, so life changing. Their protest was based in their theology ("God would never forgive such a sinner"), but they actually understood a truth that we sometimes forget: No human being has the authority and the power to convert another person's spiritual condition on earth. It is impossible for us to change anyone's eternal destiny. However, to prove that He did have the capacity to forgive sins, Jesus healed the man and told him to walk.

Prayer accomplishes the impossible.

Affecting the natural world in which we live is easy for the One who made the worlds by speaking and the One who made a way for our sins to be removed. That is due to the fact that the spiritual world is always more difficult to change than things in the natural world. But human beings are usually unaware of how much the Lord accomplishes for them in the invisible realm of reality—and they are more impressed by observable miracles than they are by ones that last for eternity. Nevertheless, once you realize that the Lord decreed the worlds into existence and redeemed us by His grace, you understand that nothing is impossible for Him (Jer. 32:27).

God can do what no one else can do. That means we will be amazed at His extraordinary power, and unless we remember that He can do what is otherwise impossible, we will be timid in asking for His miraculous intervention. In each of the following biblical episodes, the Lord says He will do something unheard-of, something beyond the realm of natural plausibility.

Behold, I am the LORD, the God of all flesh; is anything too difficult for Me?
— Jeremiah 32:27

Question: As a way of practicing how to read your Bible for personal encouragement and direction, look up each passage below. Then outline the actual situation into which the Lord is going to introduce His rule, and describe a circumstance in your own life that parallels the situation faced by the people in the story.

Genesis 18:9–15

_____

_____

⌒

Zechariah 8:1–8

_____

_____

⌒

Prayer appeals to the almighty jurisdiction of the Lord over all the heavens and earth, and it taps His loving authority for the sake of His beloved children. We are asking, "Lord, let Your will be done—let Your authority, sway and dominion (over)rule—here on earth, as Your will is done in heaven." (Read Matthew 6:9–13.) Like the little girl who climbs up onto the lap of the big boss, we can come anytime, anywhere to our Father in heaven to ask for help and grace in our times of need (Heb. 4:16). We have almost no concept of what He can set in motion on our behalf—things that are not usually perceptible to our natural senses, things that we would never think of on our own (1 Cor. 2:9).

PRAY ABOUT WHAT IS INVISIBLE TO YOU

And that is our second lesson about prayer: It operates in the spiritual arena—accomplishing breakthroughs on the natural plane by first affecting things in the invisible dimension of reality. We must never lose sight of the fact that there are two dimensions of reality, two spheres in which we live and have our being. The spiritual realm is more real than the natural. Prayer deals not only with what is impossible for us, but also what is invisible to us. As we already learned, the physical universe was spoken into existence by the word of the Lord, so what we do see around us "was not made out of things which are visible" (Heb. 11:3).

Jesus taught His disciples to start their prayers with a simple acknowledgment of God as their Father *in heaven*—in the spiritual dimension where all the action takes place. He is the Lord of the heavens and, thereby, Lord of the earth. (Read Deuteronomy 10:14; Jeremiah 32:17.) The "eternal, immortal, invisible" God (1 Tim. 1:17), and His Son, Jesus, through whom "all things [were] created . . . visible and invisible" (Col. 1:16), invite us to ask for their intervention. God is not limited by natural circumstances as we are, and His answers to our prayer can just as easily involve calling into being "that which does not exist" as a rearrangement of the natural variables in our situation (Rom. 4:17).

Let us therefore draw near with confidence to the throne of grace, that we may receive mercy and may find grace to help in time of need.
—Hebrews 4:16

Eye has not seen, nor ear heard, nor have entered into the heart of man the things which God has prepared for those who love Him.
—1 Corinthians 2:9, NKJV

For our struggle is not against flesh and blood, but against the rulers, against the powers, against the world forces of this darkness, against the spiritual forces of wickedness in the heavenly places.
— Ephesians 6:12

Truly, truly, I say to you, unless one is born again, he cannot see the kingdom of God . . . That which is born of the flesh is flesh, and that which is born of the Spirit is spirit.
— John 3:3, 6

Flesh and blood cannot inherit the kingdom of God.
— 1 Corinthians 15:50

Truly I say to you, whatever you shall bind on earth shall be bound in heaven; and whatever you loose on earth shall be loosed in heaven.
— Matthew 18:18

And I say to you, ask, and it shall be given to you; seek, and you shall find; knock, and it shall be opened to you.
— Luke 11:9

. . . that God may open up to us a door for the word, so that we may speak forth the mystery of Christ.
— Colossians 4:3

And He healed many who were ill with various diseases.
— Mark 1:34

The real issues of our life are spiritual, and the struggles we have are not primarily against natural problems, but spiritual ones (Eph. 6:12). Whereas nothing in the physical world has the power on its own to affect spiritual reality, spiritual changes always bring about some shift in the natural world. Flesh and blood cannot enter the realm of the spirit (John 3:3–6), and neither can it inherit the eternal (1 Cor. 15:50).

Conversely, spiritual keys, like prayer, shape and influence how things turn out on earth. They can bind and loose (Matt. 18:18), they open doors (Luke 11:9; Col. 4:3) and they heal and deliver (Mark 1:34).

> Prayer is one of the "divinely powerful" tools of our trade that enable us to get at the spiritual, root cause and to affect scenarios in life.

Read Matthew 6:5–6. The Greek word for *secret* is *kruptos* [pronounced *kroop-tos*], meaning "concealed, hidden." The true dynamic of prayer happens in the sight of the Lord, not in the view of other people. Why do people worry about how they sound to others when they pray? Does this mean we should never pray publicly or aloud in a group of people? What is the main point Jesus is trying to make?

_____

_____

Prayer is one of the "divinely powerful" tools of our trade that enable us to get at the spiritual, root cause and to affect scenarios in life (2 Cor. 10:4). That takes some getting used to because we are so accustomed to walking by sight, not by faith (2 Cor. 5:7), and living our life on a natural level. We have been trained to do something (physical) about our problems and needs. We want to influence decisions and outcomes in life as a result of what we say or how we act. Praying about some situation does not feel like we are doing enough to our natural mind, and that explains why we tend not to pray much about problems we think we can basically handle on our own.

PRAY WITH FAITH IN GOD

That leads us to a third lesson about prayer: Since it is an invisible activity, and such a small one in comparison to the huge, impossibly large needs that face us, it is important to have faith. "Without faith [confidence and trust in, reliance upon, persuasion about what God has said] it is impossible" to receive from the Lord everything He wants to give you (Heb. 11:6). Faith specializes in the invisible and holds on to promises God speaks, even when the fulfillment of those words is nowhere to be seen (Heb. 11:1). Faith sees what your natural eyes cannot see. It is like a pair of infrared goggles that allow you to "see in the dark" what people without goggles cannot see. Faith is knowing, even at 1:30 in the afternoon, that the stars are still out there. Not seeing them does not nullify their existence.

Throughout your life you will find a difference between what the Lord says to you and what your circumstances say. Faith is a decision about *whom* to believe, not just *what* to believe. We pray in faith, making the simple but profound choice to believe that God is there, that He welcomes us and that He hears us. When we tell Him about the money we need for the kids' braces, about the job we lost or about the broken friendship we want restored, it is not as though He responds by telling us those situations are not real. They are real, and He knew about them even before we told Him (Matt. 6:32). Faith is not a pair of rose-colored glasses; it is not a game of make-believe or a religious term for clueless naivete.

Jesus promised He "will not leave us" to our own devices or resources (John 14:18; Heb. 13:5). Prayer is one of the ways that He assures we are not left on our own to deal with the true, and sometimes heart-wrenching, realities of a broken world. He says, "Have faith in God" (Mark 11:22). God doesn't say, "Trust Me; those problems do not exist." Rather, He says, "Trust Me; I can take care of them in ways you cannot imagine."

Read James 5:13–16. Why do you think the Lord encourages us to pray when we are suffering? What kind of prayer will restore someone to health?

_____

_____

Having faith in God and in His wonderful promises to care for us in life and to use us in ministry, we can be assured, ahead of time, that He is true to His words—what He promises is as good as delivered. (Read Mark 11:23–24.) It is like your boss taking you to dinner at an exclusive, members-only restaurant and telling you to order anything you want on the menu—ask for whatever you want, and it will be yours (John 15:7).

Your faith is not in what *you say* you want—as though, without being your boss's guest, you could get into the restaurant and make a fancy meal materialize on the table in front of you just because you repeat, "Beef brochette, beef brochette, beef brochette," several times each hour. No, the boss gets you in,

For we walk by faith, not by sight.
—2 Corinthians 5:7

Now faith is the assurance of things hoped for, the conviction of things not seen.
—Hebrews 11:1

For your heavenly Father knows that you need all these things.
—Matthew 6:32

If you abide in Me, and My words abide in you, ask whatever you wish, and it shall be done for you.
—John 15:7

and he is the only one who can arrange for the beef brochette to show up in front of you. The main point is to believe that because of what he invites you to do—pick anything on the menu—you will be granted your request, and you can start anticipating how good the entrée will taste even before the waiter brings it to your table. In everyday life, we order meals in a restaurant and wait for them in faith.

While it is important to verbalize your requests and speak in faith, some Christians place slightly too much emphasis on being able to speak things into existence—quite apart from having heard a prior invitation to do so by the Lord.

Read Philippians 4:6 and Colossians 4:2. Notice that both verses mention the importance of thankfulness in prayer. In light of what we are learning about faith, why is it important to be thankful when we pray? For what are we to be thankful?

_____

_____

PRAY WITH THANKFULNESS TO GOD

Our fourth lesson about prayer has to do with a grateful attitude. As in all kingdom enterprise, prayer is a way in which the Lord welcomes us to participate with Him in what He is fully capable of accomplishing all on His own. He delights in our delight, so like a mother letting a child help set the Thanksgiving table, God loves to share tasks with us. Prayer is our way of "helping" place the silver and china. We could not do it without Him, but He could easily do it without us. Keeping that in perspective—prayer is making the impossible possible—reminds us to be grateful.

Furthermore, mother's little Thanksgiving helper will need lots of help knowing where the fork goes and which side of the plate receives the butter dish. Oftentimes, the Lord will direct us in how to pray and what things to pray for. If we know that the Lord hears us when we pray, we also know that "we have the requests which we have asked from Him" (1 John 5:14–15). He will put the desires and requests on our heart to pray for. Not only does His Spirit teach us how to pray according to God's will, but sometimes He will even pray on our behalf beyond what we know to pray on our own (Rom. 8:26).

Answered prayer is simply one (more) expression of God's love for us. It is not some formulated occurrence that happens whenever

And in the same way the Spirit also helps our weakness; for we do not know how to pray as we should, but the Spirit Himself intercedes for us with groanings too deep for words.
                    —Romans 8:26

we happen to hit upon the right combination of words or postures. Prayer is not like a car that works one day but must be coaxed to run the next day. God likes us; He cares about our situation. God does not score our prayers like an Olympic judge deducting points for slips, hesitations and imperfect landings on the balance beam. He is more like the coach of an under-eight-years-old basketball team, scrimmaging his players at practice. Rather than being a stickler for details and calling every traveling violation or every foul, his basic bent is to smile and say, "Play on."

When it comes to prayer, since most of us worry about "getting it right," it is easy to fall into the trap of trying too hard or concentrating too much on external affectations—mannerisms, intonations of the voice—that *look* like praying.

▲▲
Answered prayer is simply one (more) expression of God's love for us.
▲▲

Read Psalm 38:9; 139:4 and Matthew 6:8. What do they tell you? If the Lord knows what we are going to ask before we ask it in prayer, do we need to worry about the exact way in which we pray?

_____

_____

It is not as though prayer is a game or that the crushing issues of real life are of no more concern to the Lord than a practice scrimmage. But learning to pray within the safe, encouraging and affectionate atmosphere of His love—remembering that He does the real work—is far more helpful than imagining He won't do any work unless we get our part exactly and always correct. Prayer is one of the most personal and powerful resources the Lord has given to us, and it is a gift to enjoy through what Jesus has accomplished on our behalf.

PRAY IN JESUS' NAME
In fact, that truth is the next lesson for us to be reminded of about prayer: Whatever we do in our life, we are to do "in the name of the Lord Jesus, giving thanks through Him to God the Father" (Col. 3:17). Jesus tells us to "ask the Father for anything," but to do so "in My [His] name" (John 16:23–24). Jesus is the name above "every name that is named" (Eph. 1:21). "There is salvation in no one else"—His is the only name in heaven or earth "by

which we must be saved" (Acts 4:12). When God reestablishes His complete rule over the new heavens and earth at the culmination of time, every knee will bow at the name of Jesus, acknowledging Him as Lord over all (Phil. 2:10).

The reason our prayers are heard by God is not because of what we are able to do, how correctly we have managed to live or how ingratiatingly we have said, "Please!" God hears our prayers only because we come in Jesus' name—in the privilege and authorization He has given to us. We are like young teenagers out shopping with Mom's credit card—her name is on the card because she has the good credit and she pays the bill. Our name, like that of a fourteen-year-old, is not found on any spiritual credit card, nor would our name written on an IOU note enable us to walk out of the store with a new pair of shoes.

When we pray, the name of Jesus empowers and "backs up" our request. Just as Jesus performed miracles in His Father's name (John 10:25), so we are to ask, in prayer, for breakthroughs and answers in Jesus' name. God our Father reaches into our world to heal people and to perform miracles in Jesus' name as a way of bringing glory—and recognition among people—to Jesus as the Savior of the world (Acts 4:30). Prayers to the Father in Jesus' name, answered by the power of the Holy Spirit, show the world just how completely "as one" the Father, Son and Spirit are. (Read John 14:13–14.)

The Lord's Prayer, which serves as a good model for all our prayers, begins with worship of His name ("Hallowed be Thy name"). God gives His name (and authorizes its use) only to His people as an expression of His very presence and power on earth. "In His name" is synonymous with "on behalf of Him and His authority, by virtue of what He has accomplished."

The Bible tells us many things about the name of the Lord. For instance, it is . . .

▲ To be praised "from the rising of the sun to its setting." (Read Psalm 113:3.)

▲ "A strong tower" of defense against the forces that try to destroy us. (Read Proverbs 18:10.)

▲ Not to be used "in vain"—as an empty expression of speech or to invoke any kind of unrighteousness. (Read Deuteronomy 5:11.)

Once again we are reminded about the difference between the relationship we get to enjoy with the Lord and the dead religion that is always trying to steal away that joy. Prayer works, not

---

That at the name of Jesus every knee should bow, of those who are in heaven, and on earth, and under the earth.
—Philippians 2:10

The works that I do in My Father's name, these bear witness of Me.
—John 10:25

Thou dost extend Thy hand to heal, and signs and wonders take place through the name of Thy holy servant Jesus.
—Acts 4:30

because we work to earn credits to "cash in" later, but because Jesus finished all the work on the cross "once for all" (Heb. 7:25, 27). And, interestingly, Jesus Himself daily comes before His Father in conversation and intercession—to "appear in the presence of God for us" (Heb. 9:24).

▲▲
No issue or need is too large or too little for us to bring before the Lord.
▲▲

Bottom line, the Lord loves to hear from us. Communion with Him is a two-way street, a dialogue, a sharing back and forth. As surely as He opens His heart and plans to us, so He longs to have us "pour out [our] heart" before Him (Ps. 62:8). He engages us in intimate, personal dialogue—wanting to hear about everything in our lives, from points of uncertainty like a pending job interview, to huge obstacles like an only daughter's leukemia. Prayer gives us freedom from worry and anxiety (Phil. 4:6–7). No issue or need is too large or too little for us to bring before the Lord.

PRAYER TIMES

God loves the free and open exchange He can have with us in times of prayer, much as parents enjoy talks they have with their youngster returning home on spring break from their first year at college. But we want to be careful not to think of prayer in set, required amounts, as though getting an answer from God is like buying a can of cola from a vending machine—it requires a certain number of quarters (minutes) before you can push the selection button. Sometimes we worry about how long we are supposed to pray—especially when we read Jesus' question to His disciples: "So, you men could not keep watch [pray] with Me for one hour?" (Matt. 26:40).

When Jesus asked that question, He was facing the culminating agony of His deepest testing. Jesus, in His utter humanness, was crying out for company and companionship. It was a question posed by His personal need, not a dictate meant by Him to establish a minimal time standard for real praying. He knew what it was like to have a willing spirit—but reluctant flesh—and that is why He told His disciples to pray that they would not often find themselves in situations where their flesh would be so sorely tempted to go against God's will. (Read Mark 14:32–38.) What we pray is more meaningful than how long we pray.

Setting aside a time each day to pray really helps to develop consistency. The complications of life will steal away your opportunities

> Be anxious for nothing, but in everything by prayer and supplication with thanksgiving let your requests be made known to God. And the peace of God, which surpasses all comprehension, shall guard your hearts and your minds in Christ Jesus.
> —Philippians 4:6–7

to pray, so it is a good idea to get your day started with prayer before the inevitable happens. Although it is certainly fine to pray just before you fall asleep at night, chances are you will fall asleep just before you pray. The spirit is willing, but the flesh is not always up for these conversations with God. You will be more fulfilled in prayer if you pick times (or physical positions) when your body is a bit more cooperative.

Pray all the time by offering up little sentences of thanks, quick "Go-before-me's" and other brief acknowledgments that you do not want to do this thing called life all on your own. Remember how very glad Jesus is to have you use the access He granted you. You can be confident that God wants you there with Him, and He looks forward to your times of prayer more than you do. An ongoing dialogue with the Lord throughout your days is quite precious to Him. One of the indications of a marvelous relationship between a daughter and her mother is that they can talk "on the go," spontaneously, as well as whenever they decide they "need to talk." God enjoys that kind of relationship with us. Not all prayer should be by appointment. That makes the relationship too stilted and artificial.

TALKING TO GOD

Though there are several different *types* of prayer mentioned in the Bible, they are each essentially just conversing with the Lord. For instance, 1 Timothy 2:1 uses different words to describe ways in which you will find yourself approaching the Lord in Jesus' name. Let's look at these:

Entreaties (*supplications*, KJV) — Requests about some specific need, especially when you are acutely aware of your inability to come up with the answer. You have been brought low by what you lack (wisdom, money, another chance, patience or strength), but rather than being humbled by your need, you choose to humbly ask for God to intervene.

Prayers—Earnest and, perhaps, more prolonged conversation with God to find His will and counsel for your life in general. You lay yourself before the Lord, with all your attention focused on Him, just as you would speak openly and deeply to a trusted counselor or best friend. You ask Him to tell you anything because your main desire is to freshly orient yourself and your whole life in the direction He prefers.

Petitions (*intercession*, KJV) — A series of questions posed to the Lord much like an interview with a famous or knowledgeable authority. You ask the Lord about anything of interest to you, and confer with Him about the state of your life, marriage, future or ministry. You have the chance to compare opinions with Him about the important and serious issues facing you, and when you are done conferring, there is little doubt where He stands on each matter.

Thanksgivings (*giving of thanks*, KJV) —Active expressions of gratitude and worship, telling the Lord how much you appreciate who He is and what He has done in your life. The thanks may be profoundly moving like a husband thanking his wife for seventeen good years of marriage or simple like thanking a friend for a ride home from school. It is a way you share your complete joy with Him, just as a seven-year-old screams in delight over a Christmas gift —the scream of delight delights a parent's heart.

LET'S TALK ABOUT IT

▲ How has your thinking about praying changed as a result of reading this chapter? How would you describe prayer (in your own words) to a friend who has never talked to the Lord?

_____

_____

▲ Why does God welcome our prayers?

_____

_____

▲ What happens when we pray? Think of a recent answer to a prayer that God brought to you.

_____

_____

▲ Two common lies about prayer are, "You crummy Christian, you need to pray more" and "You are too crummy to pray at all." Does either of these statements sound familiar in your mind when you approach prayer? What did you read in this chapter about prayer that changes those old ways of thinking?

_____

_____

▲ Why does Jesus almost always talk about forgiveness whenever He teaches His disciples about prayer? Is anything too hard for God?

_____

_____

▲ Why are thankfulness and faith important in prayer?

_____

_____

▲ Is there a formula we are supposed to follow when we pray to the Lord? Are our prayers to be short or long? Is there a correct time frame for our prayers?

_____

_____

▲ Think of an analogy to share with a friend about prayer. Finish this sentence (and explain why you finish it the way you do): "Prayer is like _____

_____."

YOUR TIME WITH GOD

Are you having a hard time coming up with what you need? Have you been brought low by what you lack (wisdom, another chance, money, patience, strength, etc.)? Ask the Lord to intervene. Ask God to show you anything that will help you surrender your life, and go in whatever direction He wants for you.

It is easy to be disheartened with long-term situations in our lives that seemingly have little hope for change. Can you think of an unresolved circumstance that you have stopped praying about? Will you consider talking with God about it again?

Set aside time each day to pray. Ask the Lord to show you what issues and needs to pray about—and how to pray about them. Let Him bring things and people to your mind in addition to what you pray about regularly. Believe in God—His power, His promises, His willingness and His answers. Believe that He has taken care of what you talk to Him about, and hold on with faith to the answer that may not be visible in the natural arena. You may want to pray these words:

Father, thank You for the way You love to be with me, talking and sharing with me. Thank You, Lord, for wanting to listen to me—even when I know so little about the bigger picture and when I understand only a small part of what is really going on. I am so glad that I may tell You what is troubling me, and as I do, I am aware that I am releasing all to You for a solution.

I am not giving up; I am giving myself over to You by being willing to let You work through me, through others and through the challenge itself. Thank You, God, for blessing me with life and blessing me throughout life. You have been so faithful to me—even when I did not realize it was You at work in my life.

Even though I know You know what I need before I ask You,

I still want to ask You to take care of the situations I set before You. Somehow, asking You directly like this helps me remember all that You do for me. I love coming into Your "office," and how You are never too busy to listen to me.

I do believe that nothing is impossible for You. Thank You, Lord. Praise You, Father. In Jesus' name, amen.

CHAPTER EIGHT

Obeying God

MOST OF US HAVE NEGATIVE ASSOCIATIONS WITH AT LEAST SOME FOODS. They do not agree with us, either because our body lacks the enzymes to digest them, or because our stomach "just can't handle them like it used to." As youngsters, our dislike of everything from asparagus to mushrooms made us "picky eaters"—difficult to please, and even more difficult to keep nutritionally balanced. We tended not to like what was "good for us," preferring to have deep-fried, rather than broiled, anything.

Fortunately, people do develop a taste for better foods. Now that we have discovered the marvelous flavor of mushrooms and asparagus, we cannot recall exactly why we did not like them. An expensive entrée of peppercorn steak along with crisply steamed vegetables smothered in bernaise sauce at a fine restaurant strikes us as an ideal meal, but when we were kids our commentary would have been just the opposite: "Yuck, I hate pepper, and what's this stuff on the carrots?" Sauces, spices and savors that would have turned our stomachs when we were six, seven or eight now turn our heads.

It's all about expectations. A kid who spots tiny bits of onion in the casserole is sure he is going to detect their terrible influence, no matter how much Mom says, "Just close your eyes; you won't even taste them." If you threw up after eating spinach, the two events became linked together in a subtle expectation that one event will more than likely follow the other. Just being told something is good for us does not make it taste good. In fact, most of us believe that if it is good for us it will not taste good. Vitamins and medicine taste bad, and we are slightly suspicious of anyone who really likes health foods.

So what happens? Why do we end up liking mushrooms? Usually it is by accident—we eat them without realizing it, and only later discover that they were an ingredient in the dish. Or we have no choice—it is one thing to pick mushrooms out of a meal at Mom's house, but quite another thing to segregate the mushrooms on our plate in front of a date we're trying to impress. Our culinary conversion begins with "That's not so bad after all," and moves to an eager anticipation of the next time we can have sautéed mushrooms. What we did not think we liked becomes something we want more of.

Hearing Mom say, "Eat your spinach—it's good for you," didn't have much impact when you had so many other options to choose from. But if she told you the same thing after the two of you were stranded on a deserted island where the only thing growing was wild spinach, you would be a lot more inclined to listen to her. It's the same in spiritual matters. We often listen better when our hearing is fueled by an urgent "need-to-know" interest.

A similar process takes place in learning to appreciate God's counsel to us. In the beginning, it is easy to think we do not like being told to *listen* to what God is saying to us. When someone told us to *listen* as kids, it was just a way of saying, "You are about to get in trouble." *Listen* meant "you are not listening." *Listen* usually preceded some sort of punishment, or at the very least it meant we had to stop doing or saying something we wanted. If words tasted like food, the taste of *listen* would be worse than liver; *listen* tastes boring, angry and fun-stopping to most kids—and to most adults. We want to get on with what we're doing, not wait to have someone tell us what to do.

Question: Why do you think people have a different interest in listening to someone in authority when they are going to be corrected (and punished) as opposed to when they need help and advice? To put it another way, why do the expectations we have about what we are going to hear change our attentiveness?

_____

_____

Read Isaiah 55:2–3. According to these verses, what four benefits come from listening to the Lord?

_____

_____

Read Jeremiah 13:11. This verse indicates that God gives us another benefit that comes to us as a result of listening to Him. What is it?

_____

_____

Oh that My people would listen to Me, that Israel would walk in My ways!

—Psalm 81:13

Pay attention to Me, O My people; and give ear to Me, O My nation; for a law will go forth from Me, and I will set My justice for a light of the peoples.

—Isaiah 51:4

Yet they did not listen to Me or incline their ear, but stiffened their neck; they did evil more than their fathers.

—Jeremiah 7:26

"LISTEN TO ME"

The loving, merciful and gracious God you are coming to know wants you to listen carefully to everything He says (Ps. 81:13). In the Bible, God admonishes us, more than almost anything else, to listen to Him. He wants us to listen to Him because it is the primary way He can bring blessing into our lives. The other voices we have listened to—our natural inclinations, various temptations—have not been able to deliver the satisfaction they promised. He wants us to know about His ways of life and how He has arranged life to work. He eagerly shares His truth with us as someone might offer to shine a flashlight on the dark path in front of us (Isa. 51:4).

But our natural, almost instinctive, reaction is to put our hands over our ears or our bottom—trying to block out what we think we don't want to hear, or trying to prevent the impending spank from landing squarely on our backside. Rather than inclining our ears to listen, we tend to stiffen in anticipation of punishment or in outright stubbornness (Jer. 7:26). God is not mad at us when He says, "Listen carefully to Me." He isn't trying to steal away our fun or let us know just how bad we have been.

Rather, the Lord who gave us forgiveness and freedom through the death of His own Son simply wants to increase the measure of good we experience in the midst of this broken world. He instructs us carefully like someone giving directions to an out-of-town visitor, because He wants our portion to be "goodness and mercy" all the days of our lives on earth (Ps. 23:6, KJV). It doesn't really accomplish much good if God tells us how to get to a place of blessing, and we do not pay attention to or follow what He says.

Your life with the Lord will not work very well here on earth without obedience. It was Adam and Eve's disobedience that introduced death into the world in the first place, and only Jesus' ultimate obedience to His Father has saved us from those consequences. (Read Romans 5:12–19.) It is one of the most fundamental truths in the kingdom of God—the more we obey God's words to us, the greater our joy and peace.

> It doesn't really accomplish much good if God tells us how to get to a place of blessing and we do not pay attention or follow what He says.

God does not get mad at us for disobedience, and neither does He love us less because of it. We are already forgiven for its eternal consequences, and it has no impact whatsoever on the strength or the nature of our relationship with the Lord. Through His obedience on the cross, Jesus has secured that relationship for us as God's children.

But disobedience does rob us of the blessings that God intends for us. By disobeying Him, we forfeit bits and pieces of His carefully designed scenario for our lives. And our rebellion against His ways does cause us to "miss" some elements of bounty in our life, just as we miss seeing something of interest when a tour guide tells us to look to the left, and we choose to look the other way.

"MUST WE" OR "MAY WE" OBEY?

As we have learned before, our culture has taught us poorly about the things of God. This is especially true when it comes to the concept of obedience. Too quickly in our minds we jump to an image of obeying that looks like an unhappy enlisted person saluting stiffly and going off to do Christian duty. Or we think of a harried servant who must add another impossible task to an already full schedule. Perhaps worse than that, we sometimes feel that obedience means doing things just because we have to, just because God says we do—as though He has laid out an obstacle course filled with arbitrary and distasteful "have-to's" to see who is really committed to His cause.

Nothing could be further from the truth. Though obedience usually does involve doing something as a result of what you hear, its primary meaning—the heart of obedience—is simply listening and paying attention to what God says to you. That is the meaning of *obey*—"to listen attentively and carefully so that you really hear what is being said."

Now here is the most important question to answer about obedience, and depending on how you understand God's favor and love for you and His total commitment to your well-being and joy, your heart will answer almost instinctively: Do we *have to* obey the Lord, or do we *get to* obey Him? *Must* we or *may* we listen to Him?

Jesus says that our "mouth speaks from that which fills [our] heart" (Luke 6:45). Since God's heart is completely full of love and affection for us, what He says to us in His Word and by His Spirit is an expression of that love. He tells us what He tells us because He wants the very best for us.

Read Psalm 81:8–16, and then answer these questions. When we are not keeping the Lord's words, what spiritual influence are we likely following (v. 9)?

_____

_____

▲ Do we *have to*
▲ obey the Lord, or
▲ do we *get to* obey
▲ Him? *Must* we or
▲ *may* we listen to
▲ Him?

What has God done for us, and what does He promise He will do for us if we listen to Him (v. 10)?

_____

_____

Why are we sometimes left to our own devices and choices? If we merely follow ourselves, how likely are we to be better off (v. 12)?

_____

_____

If we obey God, what does He promise to do to the things in life that oppose us (v. 14)?

_____

_____

His plea for our attention is another of the ways in which He seeks our best. He does not speak the same to everyone. Though everyone in the world can "hear" about the Lord when they listen to the majesty of creation, and even "hear" from Him in their conscience, for the most part, only His children get to receive specific words. It is one of the great privileges we have been granted.

PARENTAL ADVANTAGE

The secret counsel of the Lord will be yours, giving you the true insider's information about what choices to make (Ps. 25:12–14). This secret counsel from the Lord, being led by His voice and Spirit, will become one of the most distinguishing marks of your life. When people observe the way you live and the decisions you make, they will know there is something different about you. You have a perspective and a slant on life that they lack. You know things they cannot know because you are one of God's children— walking in His ways and listening to His counsel (Jer. 7:23).

Certainly that means you will have a different sense of right and wrong than others around you, but the main point of listening to God and obeying Him goes way beyond having a higher level of morality. As surely as people marveled at the uneducated disciples, but then perceived that they "had been with Jesus," so too will people be struck with your wisdom—a wisdom not of your natural abilities, but one that comes from being led by the Lord (Acts 4:13).

He plans to instruct and train you with His words the way that a good father does—"for our good" (Heb. 12:9–10)—so that you can become more and more like Him. Good parents talk to their children about much more than right and wrong. Loving mothers and fathers instruct their children about life and how things work—

Who is the man who fears the LORD? He will instruct him in the way he should choose. His soul will abide in prosperity, and his descendants will inherit the land. The secret of the LORD is for those who fear Him, and He will make them know His covenant.
—Psalm 25:12–14

But this is what I commanded them, saying, "Obey My voice, and I will be your God, and you will be My people; and you will walk in all the way which I command you, that it may be well with you."
—Jeremiah 7:23

Now as they observed the confidence of Peter and John, and understood that they were uneducated and untrained men, they were marveling, and began to recognize them as having been with Jesus.
—Acts 4:13

"This is how to draw an 'f' in longhand." "Share your toys." "Look both ways before crossing the street." And such parents also pass along invaluable lessons about relationships, how to handle money, the meaning of trust and other vitally important things.

To provide their children with the ultimate advantage for life, parents talk to their kids about life from a far more experienced and knowledgeable vantage point. Wise daughters and sons listen and take the words to heart, where they supply an endless stream of wisdom and counsel for the whole course of the children's lives. (Read Proverbs 3:1–2; 4:1–4, 20–22.)

KNOWING GOD'S "SECRETS"

God is a "revealer of mysteries." (Read Daniel 2:47.) He brings to light things that are normally hidden or out of sight to human perception and natural knowledge. In Matthew 13:10–11, Jesus says that only His disciples get in on the "mysteries of the kingdom." By mysteries, Jesus did not mean strange or bizarre doctrines; rather, He meant secrets that are known only to those who have been initiated into the kingdom of God by being born again. (Read John 3:3–7.)

The multitude received parables and proverbs, but Jesus' disciples heard the meaning of those parables. The Lord does not reveal Himself and His plans to everyone. That is what Isaiah prophesied about Jesus — "the arm of the LORD" would not be revealed to everyone, so not everyone would believe. (Read John 12:38.) In fact, the Lord hides some truth from unbelievers, and actively discloses truth to people who come to Him in simple, childlike trust. (Read Luke 10:21.)

As Moses puts it, "The secret things belong to the LORD our God, but the things revealed belong to us and to our sons forever." (Read Deuteronomy 29:29.) As believers in Christ, we are called "stewards of the mysteries of God" because we have been entrusted with His words for all of humankind. (Read 1 Corinthians 4:1.)

This is one of the most incredible facets of your new life in the Lord — you get to receive from Him all sorts of instruction about the things of life. His words will fill your mind with wisdom. They will warn you of false and treacherous ways. They will comfort and secure you; they will lead and guide you.

To obey God's words, to keep His counsel, simply means to pay very close attention to what He says and to treasure His words in your heart, guarding them carefully lest they get stolen or misplaced. You will discover that the enemy of your heart, as well as your own fallen nature, will do everything possible to steal away the treasure-laden words God deposits in your life.

The more attention you give to the Lord's words in your life, the

> For God knows that in the day you eat from it your eyes will be opened, and you will be like God, knowing good and evil.
> —Genesis 3:5

> There is no wisdom and no understanding and no counsel against the Lord.
> —Proverbs 21:30

more spiritual, emotional and personal abundance you will experience. The devil has always called God a liar, and his foremost ploy for getting humans to accept that accusation has been to convince us that God only gives commandments to withhold good things from us (Gen. 3:5). The enemy says, "God's words will deny you the full fulfillment you want." The truth is that there is no wisdom, no counsel, no understanding that goes against the leading and prompting of the Lord (Prov. 21:30).

THAT IT MAY GO WELL WITH YOU

As you are getting used to reading your Bible, try to get in the habit of looking for promises God makes to you. There are so many of them in the Scriptures, you almost cannot read even a short passage without encountering them. But even when we are looking for them, we tend to overlook promises that follow any kind of instruction. The instruction—what God tells us to do—sometimes obscures the promised blessing, just as the taste of mushrooms obscured everything else when we were kids. Stated or implied with every command from the Lord is a blessing for our happiness and well-being—though we may not recognize how good they taste.

The promise that most often follows the word *listen* is, "That it may go well with you." God wants us to obey His voice so that He can bring us into our full inheritance, much as personal lessons from a golf pro enable us to get all we possibly can from our swing. Why try and figure everything out on our own when God offers lessons for free? Paying attention to what the pro tells us, and adjusting our swing accordingly, will take strokes off our score.

One of the main metaphors you will encounter in the Bible is the picture of the Promised Land into which God called His people. It is, of course, an actual country where the tribes of Israel lived, but it also represents the full measure of spiritual life God wants us to enjoy. We are delivered out of captivity in *Egypt* and transferred into the "kingdom of His beloved Son," the *Promised Land* (Col. 1:13–14).

Question: Based on this understanding of the Promised Land, read Deuteronomy 4:39–40; 6:3, 18, and put into your own words what advantages we gain by being obedient to the Lord's counsel.

_____

_____

When a friend with a green thumb tells us which plants will do well in that dry, sunny corner of our garden, our friend is not trying to shame us or to point out the barrenness in that part of our life. The friend simply wants our yard to be as beautiful as possible.

Not only does the Lord love to talk with us just because He likes sharing His life, just as we enjoy conversation with best friends and loved ones, but He also wants to give us careful prompting for how to navigate our way through life with the least possible trauma and the greatest possible delight. Into the midst of a dangerously shattered cosmos that resembles the mangled insides of an earthquake-broken building, God gives detailed instructions for how to find our way safely out.

He is like an air traffic controller talking us down for a safe landing after we discovered both the pilot and copilot unconscious in the cockpit—and we are the only ones available to fly the plane. Not listening to the control tower has consequences for our safety and well-being, but that should not be misinterpreted as an angry threat from the controller. If you are installing some complicated software on your computer, it is important to follow the instructions. And if your friend is the only one who knows the directions to get to the stadium, it only makes sense to pay attention to those directions. Follow them and you get there; don't, and you won't.

▲▲▲

God speaks to us so that we can enjoy a blessing we might otherwise miss, but also that we can miss a terrible consequence that might otherwise come our way.

▲▲▲

In a sense, then, everything God tells us comes with consequences—either giving us the advantage or putting us at great disadvantage (Deut. 30:19; Josh. 8:34). He speaks to us so that we can enjoy a blessing we might otherwise miss, but also that we can miss a terrible consequence that might otherwise come our way. It is like finding yourself trying to diffuse a time bomb—we have all enjoyed the suspense in a movie of which color wire should be cut. The guessing and half-remembering are all part of a good plot. But what makes for a good movie makes for a lousy life. Having God whisper in your ear to cut the red wire is a lifesaver—unless you blow off His counsel and cut the blue one.

I call heaven and earth to witness against you today, that I have set before you life and death, the blessing and the curse. So choose life in order that you may live, you and your descendants.
—Deuteronomy 30:19

Then afterward he read all the words of the law, the blessing and the curse, according to all that is written in the book of the law.
—Joshua 8:34

KEEPING THE WORDS OF THE ONE WE LOVE

Jesus says, "If you love Me, keep My commandments" (John 14:15, NKJV). Some Christians have missed the heart of God for why He says this. They see "keeping" God's words as proving our love, or even more tragically, they misread the verse to say something like, "If you want Me to love you, you better keep My commandments." Such an understanding flies in the face of God's proactive love for us—a love that leaves little for us to do except to accept it. To feel that we must do things (obey) *for* His love (rather than as a response coming *from* gratitude for His love) eliminates the marvel and joy of unexplainable grace.

Whenever you feel that God is trying to take something from you, or get something from you—as proof or penance or payment—you can almost always count on the fact that you have misunderstood something. Jesus' words are a good case in point—first of all, they are a promise, not a demand. In effect He is saying, "Because of your love for Me, you will end up keeping My words." In the final analysis, our love for Jesus tethers our heart to what He wants for us, even though, like Peter, we will periodically deny Him by choices we make throughout life. (Read Luke 22:54–62.)

Because of the penetrating truth Jesus speaks to us throughout our journey, there will be times when His words create a confrontation between what we want or understand naturally and what God wants. Such conflicts are inevitable because we are flesh and blood, and we are still learning how to see things correctly. Whether it is something Jesus is showing us about ourselves, or something He is asking us to do, we will have to make a choice—will we keep walking with Him?

Read John 6:66–69. What made some people stumble over Jesus' words? Why did the disciples choose to stay with Jesus? What can you learn from that?

_____

_____

In those times when we are sorely tempted to forget His instruction, our love for Jesus gives us extra incentive and determination to keep His words. It is like a small girl who has become trapped in a dangerous spot as a result of a landslide—if she tries to move too quickly or in the wrong direction, the precarious ledge she is on will give way and hurtle her to her death. Panic seizes her; the many voices and noises disorient her. Finally, a father's calming voice tells her exactly what to do. He can guide her through the danger one step at a time because she is used to fastening onto his voice. All the love and connection from their history together serve to keep her attention focused on his words—when she would otherwise listen to the impulses of her frightened self.

THE MEANING OF DISOBEDIENCE

The connection between listening to God and loving God is so significant that we find it virtually everywhere in the Bible. He connects love so closely with His words because those words are expressions of His love. They are not arbitrary, unloving words spoken harshly or in disregard for us. His words are a manifestation of tender regard and affection for us. Since only His people are afforded the privilege of hearing His words, listening to Him and obeying Him identify us as His people (Deut. 4:7).

Does that mean that whenever we disobey the Lord and fall prey to carnal desires, we no longer love Jesus? Does He stand over us with a measuring stick evaluating the quality and extent of our love for Him on the basis of our sinlessness? Absolutely not. We have already seen that we are unable to keep God's words in our own strength. People who do not know the Lord do not care about what He says. We who love Him do care. And even in those times when we disobey His words and go against His counsel because of our sin, we are very aware of His words. We know we are doing wrong because it contradicts God's Word. We are mindful of our guiltiness because we acknowledge the truth of what He has said to us. If we did not "keep" Jesus' words, we would not acknowledge our sin as wrong, or we would not even care that it is wrong.

The sin that "indwells" each of us will do many wrong things. We know they are wrong, and we try our best to resist them because we do "pay attention to" God's Word. We have all broken the law by speeding (doing 45 miles per hour in a 35-mile-per-hour zone), and the whole time we are driving too fast, we know it (which is why we keep a vigilant eye out for patrol officers). We half expect to get caught, and we are prepared, ahead of time, to accept the consequences because we accept the authority of the speed limit sign. Violating the posted speed is very different from refusing to accept the speed limit: "I know I'm 10 miles per hour over the speed limit" is not the same as "Nobody can tell me how fast to drive."

For what great nation is there that has a god so near to it as is the Lord our God whenever we call on Him?
— Deuteronomy 4:7

DOING WHAT WE KNOW IS WRONG

Read Romans 7:14–8:1. As strange as it may sound, and as easily as it can become license for unrepentant hearts to do whatever they want to do, it still must be said: When we do what we know is wrong, and end up practicing the very things that we know we should not do, we are, in a profound way, agreeing with the Word of God, "confessing that it is good" (Rom. 7:16). In other words, we acknowledge that His Word is true and right; it correctly identifies the sin as sin. The reason that we know the activity is wrong is because the Bible says it is wrong.

That is why we do not want to do it; we agree with what the Bible says about its wrongness. We are "hearing" what His Word says, rather than dismissing its commentary on the activity. Since we want to "keep" His Word, there is a part of us that wants to avoid that wrong behavior.

As Paul experienced firsthand, our flesh is in bondage to sin — our natural inclinations are to go against the very truth of God. No matter how spiritual we ever become, our flesh will always be fleshy — and capable of "ordering us around" like a cruel taskmaster. Our inner person, the part of us that has been regenerated and born again in the Spirit, detests sin. It hates the sin that drags us around. Our inner self agrees with God's Word. Our flesh exerts its influence to get us to do something that we fully agree is wrong.

We wish we were stronger to resist sin's temptation, and many times we are. But on those occasions when we are not able to say no, we can see the evil that still resides in our flesh. It is very disillusioning to discover just how carnal we can be at times. Though we try to deny our fleshly longings, we do not always succeed, and that simply proves that there is a huge war going on inside of us.

If we just surrendered to our flesh and didn't care whether or not we were doing wrong, there would not be a battle raging between our conscience and our lust. If we did not pay attention to His Word that tells us the activity is wrong, we would not be troubled by doing it. But we do care, and that is why we feel so badly about doing wrong. How torturous it is — to be still so bound by sinful desires even while we are so in love with Jesus . . .

How does He view us? As hypocrites? As liars and spiritual con artists? No! He knows that we cannot save ourselves, and neither can we keep ourselves. He came to set us free for eternity, and He is pleased to be able to grant us forgiveness and freedom each day. Because of His grace, "there is no condemnation for those who are in Christ Jesus."

Throughout your walk with the Lord, you will feel like a divided person—your heart and mind want to keep the words of the Lord, but your flesh wants to follow the whispers of sin. Here the path gets very narrow, with steep and deadly drop-offs to either side. The falsehood on the left says, "You can do anything you want to do as long as you feel badly about doing it." The lie on the right declares, "If you sin, you obviously do not love God." The devil delights in human hearts hardened by the deceitfulness of sin ("Who cares; it's no big deal what I'm doing") and hearts pummeled with feelings of unanswerable guilt ("That's the last straw; you will never be forgiven or accepted by God after doing that").

THE SOWER'S WORD SEEDS

Jesus' ultimate purpose for coming to earth was to be the sacrifice of atonement that enables all of us to be forgiven for our sins and freed forever from their power to sentence us to eternal death. Jesus knew that freedom would only be accomplished by His death. Yet He also knew that His disciples would remain on earth after He was gone to carry out His ministry of bringing people hope and good news. Therefore, Jesus spent lots of time teaching His disciples about the kingdom of God—the rulership, dominion and authority of God reasserting itself in the midst of this rebellious planet. For instance, He explained that prayer is essentially inviting God's authority and will to override any life circumstance. (Read Matthew 6:9–10.)

The Lord wants us to learn how to function effectively in His kingdom. That is our earthly destiny and the source of our greatest fulfillment. That is why He wants us to listen to Him—He will be giving us careful tutoring about what to do or say that will change the broken people and circumstances around us. When Jesus explains the sower and the seed parable to His disciples, He impresses upon them that if they "do not understand this parable," they will not "understand all the parables [the rest of what He says]" (Mark 4:13). Why? Because this parable lays out one of the most significant struggles that goes on in our Christian journey—hearing and holding on to God's words. And it points out another vital aspect of obeying God—not only listening carefully to everything He says, but holding on to what we hear, guarding it and watching over it lest His words to us get stolen away or lost in the shuffle of life.

What sorts of things make it difficult for us to keep listening to the Lord's words and holding on to what He says?

First of all, if you do not really hear what the Lord says or pay attention to it, the enemy will snatch His words away before they have a chance to sink down into your heart. Since God's words are very small in comparison to all the other messages coming from the world, it is very easy to overlook them or to think that they are too small to make a big difference in how things turn out

▲ Prayer is
▲ essentially
▲ inviting God's
▲ authority and will
▲ to override any
▲ life circumstance.

It is like a mustard seed, which, when sown upon the soil, though it is smaller than all the seeds that are upon the soil . . .
—Mark 4:31

And these are the ones who are beside the road where the word is sown; and when they hear, immediately Satan comes and takes away the word which has been sown in them.
—Mark 4:15

They have no firm root in themselves, but are only temporary; then, when affliction or persecution arises because of the word, immediately they fall away.
—Mark 4:17

(Mark 4:31). If you attach little significance to what He says, His message will quickly disappear from your awareness, and you will be denied the benefit it would have brought you (Mark 4:15). It is like hearing about an easy-to-miss, out-of-the-way Italian restaurant, but not paying close attention to how to get there. When it comes time for dinner, you can't recall the directions, so you have to settle for a fast-food burger instead of cannelloni.

Similarly, when you merely enjoy God's words only so long as they are easy to accommodate—when nothing in your life circumstances challenge their truthfulness—they will evaporate without leaving any lasting fruit behind. It is fairly easy to get excited about what God promises to do for you, and when you are in a church service surrounded by enthusiastic friends and good music, God's Word sounds great! But all alone, in those seasons of testing when there is a price to pay for holding to His Word, you discover how deep the roots of His counsel have been allowed to go in your heart.

Rocks and roots do not do well together. Almost always, God's words are meant to bring about some sort of change in our life. Consequently, you will discover that His words bump up against hard places in your life. For instance, He will tell you to forgive someone, and it will not be easy—for any number of reasons (they are not sorry, they keep doing wrong, they aggravated an old, unhealed wound). Since the rocks in our soul, the hard, unmovable, impenetrable spots, are mostly made up of our conclusions about life, our heart will come up with many legitimate-sounding reasons why we cannot follow God's counsel.

That is when the rubber meets the obedience road. That is what faith is all about. Our loving Father will never ask us to do anything that jeopardizes us. His words lead only to life and fulfillment. Obeying Him means that we choose to believe what God says even in the face of contrary statements uttered by our own perspectives or by the world around us. God's words are meant to develop healthy root systems that tap into a deeper water supply than just what is on the surface in our situations (Mark 4:17). Words that bear fruit must have roots. Either the roots will weed out the rocks, or the rocks will disallow the roots.

Even when you recognize a whisper from the Lord and let it develop deep roots in your heart, you must always remember that there are other very strong plants growing in that same heart. Just like in your garden outside, there are weed seeds—incredibly hardy weed seeds—vying for the same moisture and nutrients needed by the planting of the Lord. If those other words are not pulled out from your heart, they will "choke the word" from the Lord, leaving it emaciated and "unfruitful" (Mark 4:18–19). Every gardener knows that if you want to plant a new lawn from grass seed, you better fumigate the soil and treat it with weed killer. Otherwise, no matter how many grass seeds you sow, the weeds will seize the moment and hijack the moisture and fertilizer for their own purposes. In this broken world, weeds have the advantage.

In other words, what you and I do in response to what the Lord says to us determines what those words do to us. Since the word of the Lord to us is most often faint, small or seemingly unrelated to the "big" need we face, it is easy to overlook or disregard His instruction. If we are not careful to give His words the weight they deserve in our lives, those words will not have the impact on our situation that God intended them to have. On the other hand, when we do pay attention to His whisper to our heart and follow His counsel, we will experience tremendous benefit and breakthrough. If we value God's words, they will enrich us. If we cultivate them, they will grow us (Mark 4:24). God's words produce good fruit in our lives.

FOLLOWERS OF GOD'S WORDS

When you received Jesus Christ as your Savior, you became one of His followers; that is, you follow His teaching and way of life. Similarly, as a disciple of Jesus, you are trained by His words and shaped by them. We cannot follow Him to the store in any literal way, nor can we be like the multitudes of old who physically followed Jesus, even into the wilderness, to be touched and taught by Him. The only way we can meaningfully follow Jesus on this earth is to follow His instructions for life in general and His specific promptings for our individual lives. That's what it means to follow in His ways; what Jesus meant when He said that His sheep hear and know His voice (John 10:4–5).

That sounds easy enough in some ways, but more often than not, Jesus' words and counsel run exactly contrary to everything we have ever been taught. To a natural person, the "things of the Spirit of God . . . are foolishness to him, and he cannot understand them" (1 Cor. 2:14). What God says rarely lines up with how we are used to thinking. Thus, if we want to "follow" the Lord, we must get used to turning a deaf ear to our old ways of thinking in favor of the new ways He offers us through His words (Mark 8:34). That is what Jesus means by "denying" ourselves; He says if we want to come after Him—line up and fit in with where He is going—we must deny and contradict the mental presumptions and patterns that have navigated life for us thus far. Over and over, the Lord says, "Trust Me—this is how things really work . . . " The last end up first. Give, and you end up with more. Greatness comes through servanthood.

> Take care what you listen to. By your standard of measure it shall be measured to you; and more shall be given you besides.
> —Mark 4:24

> When he puts forth all his own, he goes before them, and the sheep follow him because they know his voice. And a stranger they simply will not follow, but will flee from him, because they do not know the voice of strangers.
> —John 10:4–5

> In anyone wishes to come after Me, let him deny himself, and take up his cross, and follow Me.
> —Mark 8:34

The more you listen to the Lord, the more aware you become of the huge contradiction that exists between His words and the words you are accustomed to hearing. It is impossible to listen to both. It would be like trying to hear what is being said if two teaching tapes were accidentally dubbed over one another. Jesus keeps telling us to pay attention to His words, not to the instructions that come from our own heart. For instance, He tells us to "turn the other" cheek (Matt. 5:39), but our natural reaction to insult or injury is to get even.

The truth is, trying to "get even" only adds additional harm to our soul; it keeps us under the power of the one who offended or hurt us. By turning the other cheek, we ultimately free ourselves from being a victim. The conclusions we come to about what to say, think or do in life will be based either on our natural thoughts or on God's everlasting words (Matt. 24:35). The only sure foundation—the one that will stand up to the storms and pressures of life—is the words of the Lord. (Read Luke 6:47–49.) His words prompt us to act in a particular way; they direct us to adopt a posture toward things that face us; they align the details of our mind and heart to best fit in with what God wants to do for us and through us in every situation.

That is why one of the main jobs of the Holy Spirit is to "bring to your remembrance all that I [Jesus] said to you" (John 14:26). Jesus' words to us, which include all of Scripture and not just the Gospels, act as pathways to guide our steps through life. As you grow in the Lord, you will become better and better at hearing His voice and following His promptings. But for now, remember that listening to God involves two basic choices that you will make over and over—first, how eager and welcoming will you be to hear what He is saying; and second, how closely will you follow what He says?

It will help to realize that all His words are spoken out of love and compassion and kindness. His words are for our advantage and blessing. We can trust everything He says and believe that His instructions really work—even when our natural thinking tells us they won't. We are safe in His counsel, and even in those times when His love causes Him to correct us, what He says will produce good fruit in our future rather than shame about our past (Heb. 12:11). His voice can become the focal point for our attention in the midst of great stress or danger. And no matter how

> Heaven and earth will pass away, but My words shall not pass away.
> — Matthew 24:35

> Even in those times when God's love causes Him to correct us, what He says will produce good fruit in our future, rather than shame about our past.

> All discipline for the moment seems not to be joyful, but sorrowful; yet to those who have been trained by it, afterwards it yields the peaceful fruit of righteousness.
> — Hebrews 12:11

lost we have become, the Lord is always happy to hop in the car we're driving so He can give us detailed directions for getting back on track.

What an incredible privilege—to know the God of creation so intimately that He counsels us and guides us with His words (Ps. 73:24).

LET'S TALK ABOUT IT

▲ What does it mean to obey God and keep His words? How has your understanding about obedience changed as a result of reading this chapter?

_____

_____

▲ Why does God want us to listen to His words? What can we learn from God's secret counsel?

_____

_____

▲ God's counsel is like a child learning to develop a taste for "adult" foods. What is your first thought when God speaks to you? Do you feel in trouble? If so, ask God to begin to change the way His voice sounds to you.

_____

_____

▲ Why is loving God so closely connected to listening to God?

_____

_____

▲ Recalling what God has said to us in the past can strengthen our ability and confidence in hearing His voice. Think of specific things God has said to you recently. How did you hear His voice in those situations?

_____

_____

▲ What sorts of things make it hard to listen to God's words and hold on to what He says?

_____

_____

With Thy counsel Thou wilt guide me, and afterward receive me to glory.
—Psalm 73:24

▲ What does it mean to follow in Jesus' ways? What did Jesus mean when He said that His sheep hear and know His voice?

_____

_____

▲ What does Jesus mean by denying ourselves? What is the difference between Jesus' understanding of denial and what others or society says about denial?

_____

_____

YOUR TIME WITH GOD

It is exciting to realize that we get to receive counsel, instruction, advice and warning from the Creator of the universe. He instructs in the way we should go in order to bring more bounty and blessing into our life. Can you think of specific points of counsel Jesus has given you recently? Have you been following what He said? If you have, what blessing or good have His words brought into your life? If you have not been following His advice, will you acknowledge that to Him and ask Him, using your own words or those that follow, what you should do now?

Help me, Father, to be a better listener. Open my ears to Your voice only. I do not want to follow my own counsel, or that of any false influence. Help me to listen to You and to the wise counsel of others. The other whispers—my own thoughts and desires, things I hear from the world around me—sometimes drown out what You say to me. I want to be a more active listener and more responsive to what You say.

How often have I heard You speak but refused to listen, refused to acknowledge what You said and refused to obey and act upon it? Forgive me for turning a deaf ear to You so many times. I know You love me and only want the best for me. Forgive me for the times I have let myself think You were trying to withhold something good from me. That is a lie I do not want to listen to.

Plant Your seeds of life in my heart; let me recognize Your voice better and better. I do love You, Lord, and I want Your words. I welcome Your counsel and the sound of Your voice. Teach me from Your Word and alert me to Your truth for my life.

Speak to me, Savior. Thank You, Lord, in Your name, amen.

CHAPTER NINE

Changing Perspectives

IN MANY WAYS, LEARNING TO LINE UP THE PARTICU- LARS OF OUR WAYS WITH THE LORD'S WAYS IS LIKE LEARNING A NEW LANGUAGE. It can feel as if we're not making much progress in the beginning when we concentrate on simple vocabulary and basic phrases. And since the new language is so opposite from our natural language, we have to remember to think "backwards"—like putting adjectives behind the noun as the French do, instead of in front of the noun as the English do (example: *le tricot rouge*, not red sweater). Of course, once you learn a language such things make much more sense. So it is with the ways of the Lord; the more of them we learn, the more each of them makes better sense.

Unfortunately, some of the most important understandings for our walk with the Lord have become attached to religious-sounding words that obscure the truth God wants us to grasp. Words not only have definitions, but they have feelings associated with them— connotations that can actually overpower the words' dictionary meanings. It's troublesome enough for us to embrace spiritual truth because, even on the best day, we only see dimly into the realm of the spirit, and we are like young children trying to understand con- cepts far too advanced for our limited vocabulary (1 Cor. 13:11–12). That's why it helps so much to have the map of our Bible for our journey with God. But even with it in hand, we will not always see things as clearly as we would like to see them.

When that difficulty is compounded by an unintentional reli- giousness, either in ourselves or in others, which communicates essentially God's displeasure with our race and our need to make things up to Him, it can be very hard to discern what the Lord is trying to say to us about His way of life. Sadly, the world at large has been left with the idea that God still holds people in disdain and that He disapproves of almost everything about us. Because religion misses the whole point that God, by His grace and His work (alone), has done all that needs doing to fully restore and assure relationship between Him and us, it will try to yoke us back up to a bondage with reins such as "have to," "must," "should" and "you better."

IN THIS CHAPTER YOU WILL LEARN . . .

▲ Why repentance has such negative connotations.

▲ What it means to repent.

▲ Why repentance is the beginning of the "Good News."

▲ How repentance is a process, not a one-time act.

▲ Why God's kindness, not His wrath, calls us to repentance.

▲ How repentance is so helpful as a regular practice.

When I was a child, I used to speak as a child, think as a child, reason as a child; when I became a man, I did away with childish things. For now we see in a mirror dimly, but then face to face.

—1 Corinthians 13:11–12

There is, as we have seen, a dynamic interplay between forgiveness and obedience. Because we are forgiven (for everything for all time), we want to be more responsive to what the Lord tells us. But being more (or less) obedient does nothing to affect how forgiven we are. As simple and as redundant as that may seem, it holds the key to understanding many of the tools God offers to us for making our journey through this broken world. Whereas the Lord will encourage us to think a certain way—like giving preference to others—or to respond in a particular fashion—like turning the other cheek—in order to shower us with more blessing, religion will tell us to do what He says "or else!" Instead of gratitude and excitement, we get left with feelings of guilt, shame and unworthiness, and they become our motivation for doing what God wants us to do.

The balance between obedience and forgiveness shows up again and again in the Bible.

Read 1 John 1:10–2:2. Does God gain from our obedience, or lose from our disobedience?

_____

In light of His great mercy and love for us, why do you think He want us to pay close attention to His words?

_____

_____

Read Romans 6:16. Since "it was for freedom that Christ set us free" (Gal. 5:1), what slavery did He free us from? Can you see why He wants us to obey Him?

_____

_____

> One of the main challenges we have on our journey is to keep interpreting God's words to us on the basis of what He wants to do for us instead of what we might imagine He wants us to do for Him.

One of the main challenges we have on our journey is to keep interpreting God's words to us on the basis of what He wants to do for us instead of what we might imagine He wants us to do for Him. Otherwise, we will miss what He has in mind. We only see dimly, and we are always tempted to think of God as a demanding and exacting Judge. Therefore, many of the common terms Christians use to speak about the ways of the Lord get mired in half-truth and leave us with the mistaken impression that God is less than kind—or, at least, not that interested in abounding toward us.

REPENT FOR YOUR SAKE

Consequently, the cultural definitions and connotations we have for many biblical terms do not match with how the Bible defines them. This is a truth you will want to remember as you read your Bible—even though you think you know what a word means in your natural or religious vocabulary, it may not adequately express what God means when He uses it. *Repentance* is a perfect example of this discrepancy. Our culture views repentance as a terrible-tasting medicine, a very uncomfortable and humiliating experience we're supposed to endure periodically, like spending an entire day in the hospital, dressed in one of those three-quarter garments (with the missing tie), getting a complete physical. We look on repentance with as much anticipation as a root canal.

Being told to repent feels like being caught and sent to our room until we can admit to how bad we are. The tone of voice we hear when we think of repentance is probably angry, stern and hostile. We associate it more with browbeating than with anything uplifting. Repentance conjures up images of doomsday prophets carrying placards that announce the end of the world, of frustrated instructors who have nearly run out of patience with our persistent inability to perform adequately. When we think of John the Baptist—the primary biblical character associated with repentance—we picture a burly, bearded, caveman-looking person in animal skins, wagging his finger in people's faces and yelling, "Repent!"

The few real-life examples most of us have seen on street corners or at public gatherings of someone telling everyone else to repent have not helped us want to embrace this most marvelous provision of the Lord. Those who decry everyone else's sin and angrily demand them to reform communicate an "(I am) holier-than-thou" attitude that is completely out of sync with the gracious mercy of the Lord. Their call to repentance is shame based—they want us to realize how bad we are and admit to it. Such a notion of repentance focuses on our failures and shortcomings, as though the main point is to put our wrongs on display like so much dirty laundry. No wonder we feel like crossing the street to get away from their strident cries and angry demands.

Read the following passages and ask yourself if they "sound" like your impression of repentance. Answer the question after each verse.

Isaiah 55:3—What two things does God want to do for those who return to Him? _____

_____

Matthew 11:28—What does Jesus want to give to those who return to Him?

_____

John 5:40—What do people miss out on if they are unwilling to return to Jesus?

_____

John 6:65—Is coming to the Lord an obligation required or a privilege granted?

_____

John 7:37—Is Jesus extending an invitation or issuing a demand?

_____

THE BEGINNING OF GOOD NEWS

Our impression of repentance is far from favorable or inviting. And yet the Bible tells us that repentance is the starting point for the good news God wants us to know. (Read Mark 1:1–3.) The gospel message is that our life, and thereby our hope, are not finished. God has an extraordinary future for us. Where we are now, and what is true of our life at this point, is not the final story. Today is not forever; change is possible. Broken relationships, huge debt, dogged depression, hidden cravings, raging tempers, foul language, choking bitterness and paralyzing fears can all be changed in the name of Jesus. That is the good news. Our sins can be forgiven. Our brokenness can be restored.

> The law of the LORD is perfect, restoring the soul.
> —Psalm 19:7

And that's where repentance comes in. It surprises most believers to discover that the Lord, our Shepherd "restores [repents] our soul" (Ps. 23:3). The perfect Word of God does likewise (Ps. 19:7). Repentance is a spiritual activity that miraculously sets our face toward another future than the one we are doomed to get if we stay on our current path. Repentance is not a tool for condemnation about where we have been, but a welcomed invitation toward where God eagerly longs for us to go.

Read Luke 24: 46–47, which is what Jesus said to His disciples just before He ascended into heaven. How do you think the message of repentance would sound if Jesus had not died and been resurrected—if there was no forgiveness available to us from God?

_____

_____

John the Baptist was a messenger sent by God in order to alert people to the unimaginable opportunity He was sending them in Jesus. John was like an amnesty announcement from a government—telling everyone who is in the country illegally they will be exempt from prosecution and will receive their citizenship simply by coming to Jesus and admitting that they have been in the country illegally. The Lord does not want anyone to miss the opportunity to be recovered and restored, so He sent a messenger ahead of Jesus to get everyone ready to receive Him.

When the Bible says, "Prepare the way of the Lord," it is not an angry declaration, but an excited one; it isn't a threat telling kids they better straighten up their room or they won't get dinner, but an announcement that Grandma and Grandpa are coming to take everyone to dinner—so come inside and get ready. John did not come to tell people how bad they were—he came to tell them how different they could become. Jesus was coming to turn everything around and to put things back into their intended place.

▲▲▲
Broken relationships, huge debt, dogged depression, hidden cravings, raging tempers, foul language, choking bitterness and paralyzing fears can all be changed in the name of Jesus.
▲▲▲

John the Baptist went before Jesus as a forerunner, like Elijah, to "make ready a people prepared for the Lord" (Luke 1:17). Jesus calls him "Elijah who was to come" to restore all things (Matt. 11:14; 17:11). *Restoration* is one of the most central themes of repentance. In fact, *repent* [in Hebrew, *shuwb*] is translated "restore" in many verses like these in the Old Testament. It "returns" things to their original order and condition.

Read Deuteronomy 30:3. In His compassion God will gather us to Himself and give us relief from what through repentance?

_____
▬

Read Psalm 80:3. When we have been turned away from the Lord, what turns us back around so that His face can shine upon us again?

_____
▬

Read Jeremiah 15:19. When we repent to the Lord, what does He do to us?

_____
_____
▬

Read Jeremiah 29:14. How would you put the promises in this verse into your own words for your own life? When you repent, what does the Lord do?

_____

_____

Read Jeremiah 30:18. Is restoration an act of anger or compassion by the Lord? Since our repentance leads to our restoration, do you think it is God's compassion or His anger that leads us to repentance?

_____

For the most part, we do not need anyone to tell us how bad we are. Even though we try not to sin, we keep doing it, and that awareness of our failures stares us down day after day. Repentance is not God's way of rubbing our faces in our stuff so that we acknowledge its existence; rather, repentance is the kingdom way of asking God to fix what is wrong in our lives—as opposed to trying to fix things ourselves. Repentance is for real people with real shortcomings who long for full restoration.

The call to repent is not a warning to fix ourselves quickly before the Lord comes, but an opportunity to acknowledge where we are wrong and lost—where we desperately need His intervention and rescue. Repentance is our opportunity to send out a distress signal when our boat is taking on water and sinking. It is not a frantic redoubling of effort to bail the rising water more quickly.

> **Repentance is for real people with real shortcomings who long for full restoration.**

FETCHED HOME AGAIN

When we read about the throngs of people who eagerly traveled into the wilderness to repent and be baptized, we have to ask ourselves why. (Read Mark 1:4–5.) Why would so many people go through the hassle and inconvenience of traveling all that distance if they were going to get yelled at and shamed? It makes no sense; people avoid censure—they do not seek it out. If John's call to repentance was an angry, threatening shout, it is unlikely that anyone would be interested in participating. This biblical scene of swarms of folks racing to get a chance to repent is completely inconsistent with our cultural image of a soapbox doomsayer—and the feelings we have about repentance as a result of that image.

What did they experience that is different from what we associate with repentance? Why were they so eager to repent whereas we are so reluctant to do so? Perhaps some were just curious (about the details of their neighbors' public confessions), but curiosity alone or just "going along with the crowd" is not enough to explain why people went out of their way to repent.

The multitudes came from miles around because they were hearing from John a message of hope and forgiveness quite different from the religious condemnation they were used to hearing from the Pharisees. It is no accident that John "appeared in the wilderness." His message from God was directed to people's wilderness places where things are wrong, where they are crooked, where things are out of control. He wasn't bringing a message that told the multitudes they were hopelessly lost sinners who were not good enough to worship in the city temple—a message they heard daily from the Pharisees.

DESERT PLACES

The Bible is full of vivid imagery that communicates profound realities in our lives. Among the most telling of such pictures is the analogy of desert places—dry, desolate regions that drain away life rather than support it. In the Middle East there is quite a contrast between well-watered gardens and open stretches of rocky waste, between rivers and streams and dry canyons. No one survives long in the desert.

The wilderness, parched and empty, portrays a spiritual condition into which people fall because of their rebellion against the ways of the Lord. (Read Psalm 68:6.) Just think of the contrast there must have been in the minds of the people of Israel between the Garden of Eden, out of whose headwaters flowed four major rivers, and the vast stretches of desert all around them. (Read Genesis 2:10–14.) They were led through the wilderness to the Promised Land—a land that drank "water from the rain of heaven" (Deut. 11:11) and was personally watered by the Lord. (Read Psalm 65:10.) They had been told that if they walked in disobedience to Him, "there will be no rain and the ground will not yield its fruit." (Read Deuteronomy 11:17.)

One of the common phrases believers use to describe their spiritual condition—especially after making mistakes or getting caught up in the swirl of life on earth—is *dry*. What they mean by *dry*, as you will discover in your journey, is that they do not feel close to the Lord. Even though we all know He is always with us and that He never deserts us, we can sense desert sands encroaching on our lush garden. David felt like this at times:

O God, Thou art my God; I shall seek Thee earnestly; my soul thirsts for Thee, my flesh yearns for Thee, in a dry and weary land where there is no water.

—PSALM 63:1

In His mercy and grace, God converts our desert places into pools of water; He changes the empty, dry points in our life into rivers and streams.

He changes a wilderness into a pool of water, and a dry land into springs of water.

—PSALM 107:35

> *I will open rivers on the bare heights, and springs in the midst of the valleys; I will make the wilderness a pool of water, and the dry land fountains of water.*
>
> —ISAIAH 41:18

God's coming is often described as "like the spring rain watering the earth" (Hos. 6:3). He "comes to rain righteousness" on us when we "sow with a view to righteousness" (10:12). The gospel message is essentially His promise to restore our righteousness out of the desert waste places of our unrighteousness by pouring out His Spirit: "For I will pour out water on the thirsty land and streams on the dry ground; I will pour out My Spirit on your offspring, and My blessing on your descendants" (Isa. 44:3). The Lord comes into our rebellious, dry places and fills them with rivers of His Spirit.

When we have gotten ourselves lost in the wilderness (the foolish choices we made, all the opportunities we had to get back on the path but chose not to take), we feel guilty. That sense of guilt can often mislead us into trying hard to find our own way back home. Instead of taking the time and energy to collect wood for a signal fire on a mountaintop to call for help, we tend to chase another rabbit trail, hoping it will get us back where we should be. Repentance calls for rescue while we are lost—in the midst of our out-of-control state when we are helpless to help ourselves. It is a flare we send up so the search party can find right where we are and return us to where we belong. One of the literal meanings of *repent* is "to fetch back home." God uses our repentance to bring us home.

People who misunderstand repentance wrongly conclude that they are supposed to wait until they have stopped sinning before they come to the Lord to repent. They think they must wait until they are out of the woods for good before they can legitimately ask for forgiveness and rescue. Instead of sending up the flare, they tell themselves, *You got yourself into this mess; you're going to have to get yourself out.*

Or they take it one step further and conclude the only way to prove to God that they are deeply sorry for what they have done wrong (again) is to somehow find their way home without His help: "Don't bother God with your excuses and your whining. Just turn your life around now." That sounds very noble and religiously correct, but it completely misses the heart of God and His gracious provision for our real life.

Read the story of the leper Naaman in 2 Kings 5:1–14. As a mighty general, Naaman was prepared to do any feat of strength or valor to gain God's favor and healing. When the prophet told him to do a simple, easy thing in order to have his flesh restored (repented back to its intended condition), Naaman was furious. Why?

_____

_____

~~~

KIND CALLING

In the kingdom of God, the simple, (too) easy things are usually the means by which God accomplishes His desire in our lives. Repentance is one of those easy-sounding activities, and our own pride will try to prove our valor and sincerity to God, just as Naaman did. Try to remember the words of Naaman's servant: "My father, had the prophet told you to do some great thing, would you not have done it? How much more then, when he says to you, 'Wash, and be clean'?" (v. 13).

Remember that we are saved by grace, not by our own goodness or by our own effort (Eph. 2:8–9). It is the "riches of His [God's] kindness" and His "forbearance and patience"—not His anger or frustration—that lead us to repentance (Rom. 2:4). It is so difficult for us to shed our religious notions about God and His intentions for us. If we do not remember how fondly He thinks of us and how much He wants us to be with Him all the time—no matter what we have done or how badly we have gotten ourselves lost— we will fail to make use of this wonderful gift called *repentance.*

Repentance is pictured in the Bible mostly as a gift, a mercy, a boon "granted" by God (Acts 5:31). It is not a line He draws in the sand—it is not a precursor to the punishment He would prefer to give us. It is a huge mistake to view repentance as a chance to prove ourselves to God—even though we have done wrong, we're going to try to "make it up to" Him by showing Him how disgusted we are with ourselves.

A subtle temptation we all face in our spiritual life is to try to "take over from here"—to appreciate what God did for us prior to today, but to assume the burden for keeping ourselves straight from this point forward. We try "being perfected by the flesh," rather than continuing on in the Spirit (Gal. 3:3). In other words, we attempt (vainly) to behave well enough in order to be good enough to repent enough of the bad things in our life. It feels dishonest to tell the Lord about our wrongs *before* we correct them. We mistakenly presume that we should wait until we're out of the woods—no longer lost—before we repent of having been in them.

For example, we get trapped by the incorrect conclusion that only after we have successfully resisted the temptation to rage is it acceptable to repent of our deep anger. That is one of the primary

> For by grace you have been saved through faith; and that not of yourselves, it is the gift of God; not as a result of works, that no one should boast.
> —Ephesians 2:8–9

misconceptions that keeps us from wanting to repent. After all, repentance draws attention to various habits, thoughts, behaviors and attitudes that do not belong in our lives. They aren't what we know they should be (our clue for repentance), and we have already tried as much as we know how to stop them—without lasting success. If we imagine that repentance is our promise never to do again what we have been doing wrong, it only makes sense that we must wait until the temptation has been fully conquered before we can legitimately repent.

> God doesn't say, "Change! And then you can legitimately repent." No, He says, "Repent. Then you will be able to change."

First we want to get our sin under control, then we can repent of it. Before we are prepared to offer God a guarantee of our hard-fought victory over a sin, we do not want to bring the sin to His attention. But that is like waiting until your house is sold before you engage the services of a real estate agent. Or wanting to know a song before you try singing it; being well again before visiting the doctor. Such notions are backwards. Like the Sabbath or the Bible, repentance was designed to serve us, not the other way around. God doesn't say, "Change! And then you can legitimately repent." No, He says, "Repent. Then you will be able to change."

MERCIFUL CONVERSION

Repentance is essentially a process of conversion, exchanging one reality for another, converting something into another thing. When you travel to a far-off country, your first order of business, after you collect your luggage from the carousel, is to convert your money to the currency of the nation you are in. Otherwise, your money is worthless—not accepted. The exchange process is fairly simple—place as much money as you want to convert on the bank counter, and the teller will replace it with Swiss francs, Norwegian kroner and so on. Any money you leave in your wallet and choose not to put on the counter doesn't get converted.

God's ways and thoughts are not like ours; our two worlds operate under two completely foreign governments and economies. Earthly money will get us nowhere in God's kingdom. Through repentance, we take the currency of the world—wrong thoughts, feelings, desires and actions—and exchange them for the currency of the kingdom in the same way we convert dollars for Dutch guilders. Repentance converts our sin; it exchanges our unrighteous deeds for the righteousness found in "more than abundant" supply in Jesus (1 Tim. 1:14).

The Lord is so wonderfully willing to *make* that exchange. He waits eagerly for us to bring Him a wrong thought so that we can watch Him convert it into a correct thought (His). Without conversion—an exchange from one currency to the other—our thoughts and ways will not be able to match up to His. Our iniquities are like filthy garments, but the Lord in His gracious love exchanges our rags for rich raiment (Isa. 64:6; 61:10). He takes our sins away and clothes us in "festal robes" (Zech. 3:4).

Of course, the ultimate and eternal conversion of our life happens when we accept Jesus' sacrificial atonement for our sins. It is not as though unrepented sins withstand His forgiveness and remain as a blot on our record. It is important to see the parallel between ongoing repentance in your daily life and the once-for-all-time conversion you experienced when Jesus initially came into your life. That *eternal conversion* transformed you into a new person, completely freed from the power and consequence of sin (2 Cor. 5:17). *Ongoing repentance* speeds up the change process here on earth in the meantime.

Question: Repentance is like a great head start on the big change that will happen to you when your earthly life is over. Read 1 Corinthians 15:51–52 and 1 John 3:2. If you are going to get changed before you end up with your eternal reward in heaven, what do you think is the point for changing before then?

_____

_____

A CHANGE PROCESS

This is why repentance is so useful in our walk with the Lord—and why the enemy of your heart wants to discourage you from repenting. Repentance and change go hand in hand; the more that we repent of wrong attitudes and behaviors, the more they will change. The process is not always instantaneous. In other words, the self-pity or covetousness you acknowledge and repent of today may show up again tomorrow, and the next day, and the next. As you continue to repent, time and time again, it can almost feel like hypocrisy—"I continue committing the very sin I supposedly repented of yesterday (or a few moments ago)." Feeling guilty for your sin *and* for your hypocrisy, you will be tempted to stop repenting; at least then you will only have to feel guilty for your sin.

This is when we must follow Jesus' encouragement to keep on repenting and put our confidence in what God can do for us, not

> For all of us have become like one who is unclean, and all our righteous deeds are like a filthy garment.
> —Isaiah 64:6

> He has clothed me with garments of salvation, He has wrapped me with a robe of righteousness.
> —Isaiah 61:10

> Therefore if any man is in Christ, he is a new creature; the old things passed away; behold, new things have come.
> —2 Corinthians 5:17

The time is fulfilled, and the kingdom of God is at hand; repent and believe [put your trust] in the gospel.

—Mark 1:15

Peter said to Him, "Lord, why can I not follow You right now? I will lay down my life for You." Jesus answered, "Will you lay down your life for Me? Truly, truly, I say to you, a cock shall not crow, until you deny Me three times."

—John 13:37–38

what we can accomplish ourselves (Mark 1:15). The gospel is an incredibly simple message: *Any time and every time you realize that you are doing something wrong, and confess it to the Lord, He forgives you. Absolutely. Without question or hesitation.*

Though He tells you to "sin no more" (John 8:11), He does not insist on your assurance that you will never do that wrong again. In fact, since He knows your future, He knows you will commit the sin again—just as Jesus told Peter he would—even though your honest sincerity wants to protest that you will always remain faithful and dedicated (John 13:37–38). Jesus forgave Peter, and He forgives us. Absolutely. Without question or hesitation.

Question: Jesus told us to forgive our fellow humans for any and every offense they commit against us—not just once or twice, but over and over again. Read Matthew 18:21–22. How many repeat offenses does Jesus say we should forgive a person?

_____

A COMPASS

Every time we repent, we receive forgiveness. God never reaches His limit of tolerance. We cannot exhaust His supply of mercy. In exactly the same way, every time we repent, we get changed—even if only slightly. Imagine a person who has no sense of direction whatsoever and who, consequently, gets turned around and headed the wrong way continuously while trying to cross a desert. Each time he pulls out his compass and reorients himself in the proper direction, he is repenting. The more times he reads the compass, the quicker he will find his way across the desert.

While it is frustrating to discover that according to the compass he is heading southeast (again) when he should be going north, the alternative—not reading the compass—almost guarantees he will remain lost.

After having to turn around perhaps hundreds of times, thanks to the compass, his sense of direction will improve, and he will come to the end of the desert. The devil wants to make you feel guilty about needing to check your compass so often. He will chide you for pulling it out: "Didn't you just repent about your lying yesterday? Do you think God will let you repent again so easily and so soon?" Remember the compass—even if you had to use it just twenty minutes ago, it will still give you a true heading.

DIFFERENT CONCLUSIONS

Repentance is not a promise on our part that we will never do something again. It is, instead, a straightforward acknowledgment that what we have done (or are doing) is wrong. When we repent, we reconsider the course of life we have been following—we concede that we have come up with the wrong answers. It is like getting back a math test along with the invitation from our teacher to correct our work for full credit. By reworking the problems the teacher has marked wrong, we have the opportunity to end up getting everything right on the test. That was the point of spelling pretests in elementary school—by showing us which words we spelled incorrectly, the pretest brought us to repentance and changed the way we spelled those words on the test that counted for a grade.

All of us imagine that how we think is the right way to think. If we thought we thought incorrectly, we would change our thinking. So what we end up doing has its own kind of logic. We are unforgiving toward someone because they deserve it after what they did to us. We worry about money because we need more. We watch a nasty movie because it will satisfy us. We make a joke at someone's expense because it will make us popular. We sin because of what we think it will do for us—how it will advantage, fulfill, protect or empower us. Almost no one does wrong just to do wrong, and even if a person's only goal is to "be bad," it is usually because the individual perceives that such behavior will give identity or some other personality commodity to use to gain something for themselves.

Repenting is coming to the realization that our thinking has been backwards. Instead of *giving to* us, our sins have been *stealing from* us. Rather than offering us more and better bits of the "good life," they have been killing us. For example, think of someone who is being lazy and foolish by not being diligent to record ATM cash withdrawals in his or her check register. Eventually the person will realize that the foolish practice of laziness comes at too high a price (too many bounced checks and overdraft charges). Realization is at the root of repentance. When the monthly bank statement comes, the person will be better served by changing his or her records to match the bank's records, not the other way around.

Or putting it in other words, the opposite of repentance is telling God He should change His ways or His Word to line up with how we choose to live. An unrepentant heart insists that God is wrong— a repentant heart confesses that we are wrong. You may not be able to accomplish the complete change in your thoughts or actions just yet, but the process of repentance begins with the humble and needy admission that you, not the Lord, are out of line.

CONFESSION AND REPENTANCE

And that explains why confession is such an important aspect of repentance. Essentially, *to confess* means "to openly agree with someone." We confess to (agree with) the Lord that His way is right and that our way is wrong.

So how do we repent? What does it mean in practical terms? When you come to the realization that you are doing something wrong—in your heart, mind or actions—you bring that realization to the Lord in confession. There are three important parts to confession—not that they have to be followed as some sort of formula—but complete confession involves openly agreeing with the Lord that:

1. "I am doing it"—no one else is responsible for making me do it.
2. "It is wrong"—there is no justification that can make this wrong right.
3. "I do not want to keep doing it"—I want to live another way than I have been living.

Jesus made it clear that He did not come to congratulate people who had managed to keep themselves from getting lost in sin, but He came into the world "to call . . . sinners to repentance" (Luke 5:32). "If we say that we have no sin" in our life, "we are deceiving ourselves" and calling Jesus a liar (1 John 1:8, 10). Of course, we are supposed to avoid sinning, yet when we do sin, Jesus is there for us as our "Advocate" (1 John 2:1). When we "confess our sins," His faithfulness prompts Him to forgive us—to separate us from the power those sins have to manipulate us and from the penalty that those sins justly warrant (1 John 1:9). His faithfulness neutralizes our unfaithfulness, and His righteousness washes away our unrighteousness.

The forgiveness and cleansing He does in our life is complete with each confession—just as it was complete when we first confessed Jesus as Lord. There isn't a residue left over for us to scrub out on our own. This is critical to remember when it comes to the frequent instances for repentance in our daily life. Each of the many times we commit a particular sin, like fantasizing or lusting, the Lord wants us to confess so that He can restore us and get us back on the right track. But we do not have to repent numerous times over each individual time we sin. Christians tend to get stuck repenting repeatedly over single incidents and not repenting after each incident.

In chapter 12 we will look at repentance and forgiveness between people—acknowledging that making things right with the Lord is not exactly the same as, and in many ways easier than, restoring right relationship with other people.

> Christians tend to get stuck repenting repeatedly over single incidents and not repenting after each incident.

REPENTANCE AND RESTORATION

The angels in heaven celebrate with joy whenever someone repents (Luke 15:7). Is that because of some smug self-satisfaction they have when a sinner realizes the angels had it right all along? Are they happy because a human is now groveling and squirming with embarrassment? No. They celebrate like the shepherd who finds his one lost sheep, or the woman who finds the coin she had lost, because what was missing and out of place has been restored to where it has always belonged. (Read Luke 15:4–6, 8–9.) Remember, you and I belong with the Lord; that is why He made us.

When John the Baptist challenged the Pharisees to "bring forth fruit in keeping with" their supposed repentance (Matt. 3:8), he was not telling all of us we need to prove that we are really repentant. He was warning them against the presumption that their spiritual ancestry was all they needed and that they could come and watch everyone else who needed to repent. Fruit does grow from repentance, but we cannot force the fruit by means of our fleshy efforts to "be better."

We are called to repent because repentance leads to marvelous spiritual developments in our life.

Read Acts 3:19. What does the Lord send our way after we repent?

_____

ᴧᴧᴧ

Read 2 Corinthians 7:9–10. True repentance takes away the impotent regret people feel about the wrongs they have committed and replaces it with a life-giving resolve for their future. Can you put in your own words the difference between the "sorrow of the world" and "repentance without regret"?

_____

_____

ᴧᴧᴧ

Read 2 Timothy 2:25. Repentance leads to greater what?

_____

ᴧᴧᴧ

Repentance is not a dreadful requirement, an angry cry of condemnation we're to heap upon ourselves. It is, rather, an invitation God extends to us to free us from the daily stuff of our lives that is out of alignment with His ways. The Lord urges us to be "zealous" for and earnestly desire opportunities to repent because they will lead to us being trained, shaped and taught by Him (Rev. 3:19).

> I tell you that in the same way, there will be more joy in heaven over one sinner who repents, than over ninety-nine righteous persons who need no repentance.
>
> —Luke 15:7

Repentance is a chance to reorient ourselves as often as we need to in order to stay on track.

Jesus, who came to "destroy the works of the devil" (1 John 3:8), wants to lead you and me to repentance over and over again, until those places where the enemy has fastened his hateful grip in our heart and mind are loosened and broken up. True repentance is another of the marvelous and miraculous provisions God grants to us to get everything of our lives rearranged according to His original plan for those whom He loves so dearly and so deeply.

LET'S TALK ABOUT IT

▲ Why do you think people have such a difficult time acknowledging when they do something wrong? Are there things about the admission of being wrong that are particularly troublesome for you?

_____

_____

▲ How has your thinking about repentance changed from reading this chapter? Describe in a few sentences God's concept of repentance. What is God looking for in your heart when He asks you to repent?

_____

_____

▲ What is the difference between wanting to be right and wanting to have been right? Which of the two perspectives is most likely to lead someone to repentance?

_____

_____

▲ Why is repentance the starting point for the good news God wants us to know? How is repentance a process of conversion, exchanging one reality for another?

_____

_____

▲ What are some attitudes, thought patterns or behaviors you have that you know do not line up with God's way of thinking or living? Where are things in your life out of control? Would you like to receive intervention and rescue from the Lord?

_____

_____

▲ What happens when you repent? How can you build a large bon-fire to let the Lord know where you are so He can rescue you?

_____

_____

▲ To confess means to openly agree with someone. What are the three important parts to confession or openly agreeing with God?

_____

_____

YOUR TIME WITH GOD

The forgiveness of God is one of the greatest gifts a person will ever receive from God. As you consider all of the principles you have learned in this chapter, willingly bring your mistakes and fail-ures—your sins—to our loving heavenly Father and ask for His gift of forgiveness to help you rearrange your life according to the awe-some design for which He created you. You will be glad you did! Use the following prayer to make your commitment to God afresh.

Dear Father in heaven, I am doing this; it is wrong, and I do not want to keep doing it. I want to live another way. Free me of the daily stuff in my life that is out of alignment with Your ways. Thank You for giving me the chance to stay on track and for rearranging my life to Your original plan, no matter what I have done.

I openly acknowledge where I have allowed myself to turn off from Your way. I have done and spoken wrong things. I want You to know that I agree with You about them and about the poison they have put into my system. Forgive me, Lord. Purge me of their evil.

Lord, thank You that You so easily exchange the wrongs in my life for more of You. Even though I feel frustrated with myself or ashamed for things I know are wrong, I know You always approach me with kindness and forgiveness. Thank You that You are the God of infinite compassion and mercy, and no matter how often I seek forgiveness, You forgive me each time.

Lord, I ask that I would more willingly participate in the process of change that happens when I repent and seek forgive-ness from You. Thank You that repentance is just one of the avenues through which You long to change me for good. In Jesus' name, amen.

CHAPTER TEN

Being Baptized With the Spirit

IN THIS CHAPTER YOU WILL LEARN . . .

▲ How the Father, Son and Spirit work together.

▲ Who the Holy Spirit is and what He does.

▲ Why participation and cooperation with the Spirit are exciting.

▲ The difference between receiving and being baptized in the Spirit.

▲ What it means to pray in the Spirit and to prophesy.

▲ How to be baptized with the Spirit.

SCIENCE FAIRS FOR ELEMENTARY SCHOOL YOUNG-STERS ARE QUITE A MIXED BAG OF THE INGENIOUS AND THE MUNDANE. This probably reflects the parents' bent toward or away from the scientific more than the kids'. The subjects of study range from the need of plants for light to the relative conductivity of different materials. Most projects have been recycled from previous years, and only once in a while is one truly noteworthy. But what makes science fairs delightful to attend, aside from the fun of spotting the same basic experiment we ran a few decades ago, are the many reminders about facts and forces of the material world that we take for granted or have simply forgotten about.

Take, for instance, the three states in which all matter can exist—solid, liquid and gas. No science fair would be complete without a poster board display of snapshots and charts faithfully recording the temperatures at which water and other substances (like shampoo or chocolate) become gaseous, liquid and solid. Though the physical appearance of the elements takes different forms, their molecular composition remains constant—everyone knows ice, steam and water are really just H_2O by any other name. Yet no one would confuse steam with ice. Most likely, one of the snapshots on the poster board will be a chunk of ice melting in a pot of boiling water that is emanating steam—three states with the same essential composition. It is not always easy to differentiate the exact moment when H_2O is all ice (completely frozen) or when to call H_2O steam because the steam keeps distilling on the lid of the pot.

Something of the same can be said about the triune God with whom you now have relationship. There is no exact earthly analogy by which we can explain the nature of perfect oneness between God the Father, Son and Holy Spirit. How they can be one and yet distinct is a great mystery, but not one to stumble over. In a way, it is as simple as how Jesus puts it—seeing one of the One is the same as seeing another one of the One (John 17:21–22). Likewise, we are baptized in the name of all three of the One (Matt. 28:19)—not as though appeasing three separate gods and making sure not to leave any one of them out of the equation, but rather as a declaration of the fullness and completeness with which the one true God attends to everything in all of creation. In Jesus "all the fullness of deity dwells in bodily form" (Col. 1:19; 2:9–10).

While on earth, Jesus perfectly manifested the Father to His disciples—"He has explained Him" (John 1:18). Jesus was the "touchable" expression of the invisible God in the material world. Jesus did nothing on earth acting on His own initiative apart from His Father. What He saw and heard from His Father became what He Himself did (John 5:17; 8:38). They were and are of one accord. Their unity and oneness do not require them to merge into one entity, but to be in complete agreement toward the same purposes. Your eyes, for instance, work as one—unless there is something wrong. They can function independently of one another (to take a vision test for your license), and there is a difference between your left eye and your right, but together they offer you a (preferably) single view. Though your eyes are plural, they are a single characteristic of your features.

WHO IS THE HOLY SPIRIT?

The Holy Spirit is not a vague force or a misty, shadowy power; He is a distinct and knowable persona like both the Father and the Son. So, who is the Holy Spirit, and what is He like?

First of all, He is the Spirit of God. Just as the Father and Son "are one" (John 10:30) and yet distinct in their respective roles in creation and in our lives, so too is the Holy Spirit one with, yet distinct from, the Father and the Son. The Holy Spirit expresses everything that we need to know about the Father and the Son. The Spirit, like Jesus, has existed from the beginning with God, as God. (Read John 1:1–3.) The Spirit was the one who moved upon the emptiness of the world at creation (Gen. 1:2). When we receive Jesus by faith into our hearts, it is actually the Holy Spirit who enters as Jesus' representative "in our hearts as a pledge" from God (2 Cor. 1:22; 5:5).

▲▲

The Holy Spirit is not a vague force or a misty, shadowy power; He is a distinct and knowable persona.

▲▲

Three scriptures talk about the Holy Spirit as a pledge from the Lord. Another translation for "pledge" is "down payment." A down payment says, "I am going to buy this property; hold it in escrow until you receive the full payment. I'll be back with the rest of the cash." Having the Spirit in our spirit is the best guarantee we could have about God's ultimate interest in and plans for us. See what else these three scriptures tell us.

> That they may all be one; even as Thou, Father, art in Me, and I in Thee, that they also may be in Us; that the world may believe that Thou didst send Me. And the glory which Thou hast given Me I have given to them; that they may be one, just as We are one.
> —John 17:21–22

> Go therefore and make disciples of all the nations, baptizing them in the name of the Father and the Son and the Holy Spirit.
> —Matthew 28:19

> My Father is working until now, and I Myself am working . . . I speak the things which I have seen with My Father.
> —John 5:17; 8:38

> And the earth was formless and void, and darkness was over the surface of the deep; and the Spirit of God was moving over the surface of the waters.
> —Genesis 1:2

Read 2 Corinthians 5:4–5. For what purpose were we prepared? In other words, what has been God's plan all along, and how does the Spirit's presence in our lives assure us of that plan?

_____

_____

Read 2 Corinthians 1:21–22. When were we anointed by the Lord? What is the proof of that anointing?

_____

_____

Read Ephesians 1:13–14. When did we receive the Holy Spirit, and on what basis was He given to us?

_____

_____

> I am the way, and the truth, and the life; no one comes to the Father, but through Me.
> —John 14:6

Some of the older Bible translations refer to the Holy Spirit as the Holy *Ghost*, a term that has only made Him seem mysterious and slightly scary, especially since He is not talked about as much as the Father and the Son. He is the lesser known of the Trinity because He constantly brings us to the Father and the Son, just as Jesus brings us to the Father (John 14:6). His is the work and the voice with which you are most familiar, even though the Spirit is speaking the words and doing the works of the Father in your life.

Jesus took what He knew from the Father and shared it with His disciples. He did not do or teach things that He came up with on His own. In the same way, the Spirit works in and through us according to what He sees and hears from God—"He will not speak on His own initiative" (John 16:13). As you will learn in your journey with the Lord, the secret to true ministry is doing and saying what we are prompted to by the Spirit, rather than just doing and saying whatever we think of on our own.

> One of the main assignments of the Holy Spirit is to assure us of our connection with our Father in heaven.

> And because you are sons, God has sent forth the Spirit of His Son into our hearts, crying, "Abba! Father!"
> —Galatians 4:6

> However, you are not in the flesh but in the Spirit, if indeed the Spirit of God dwells in you.
> —Romans 8:9

One of the main assignments of the Holy Spirit is to assure us of our connection with our Father in heaven—to convince us that He is our Father (Gal. 4:6) and that we belong to Him (Rom. 8:9). By the power of the Spirit we are translated from mere flesh and blood to spirit beings, alive and in lasting relationship with the Lord. Jesus says that individuals must be *born again*—"born of the Spirit"—or they cannot enter the kingdom of God (John 3:5–7).

Because the Spirit is so integrally tied into relationship with God, those who do not know and receive the Lord "cannot receive" Him (John 14:17). He is a total stranger to people who claim to be "close to God" without receiving Jesus into their heart. Without the Holy Spirit, we cannot be "related" to God, our Father. The adoption is complete only when the Spirit takes up residence in a person's spirit.

Read John 14:16–17. How long will the Holy Spirit be with us?

_____

For what reason does Jesus want us to have the Holy Spirit?

_____

_____

Why do you think the world cannot accept the Holy Spirit?

_____

_____

Do you think we are, at times, tempted to miss His work or His presence because we are evaluating situations naturally?

_____

WHAT DOES THE SPIRIT DO?

The primary work of the Holy Spirit is to communicate to all the world, in an understandable manner, what Jesus is really like and that He is the sum total of God's message to every person (John 16:14). The Spirit woos individuals to Jesus and enables them finally to come to the place where they can say, "Jesus is Lord" (1 Cor. 12:3). He does this partly by convicting people of sin (John 16:8), and partly by "pour[ing] out" the love of God into their hearts where it gels into an undeniable reality (Rom. 5:5). Confronted with their own wickedness and by God's tender mercy even in the face of their wickedness, people respond to Jesus' offer of complete forgiveness.

The Holy Spirit is called *parakletos*, a Greek term meaning "helper, advocate, nearby aid giver, the called-alongside-One." Jesus, who is "seated" at the "right hand" of His Father in heaven (Eph. 1:20; Col. 3:1), does not want us to be left "as orphans," all alone on earth (John 14:18). That is why He gives us His Spirit— to keep us in immediate touch with Him and the Father. The Holy Spirit is in the closest possible proximity to the deepest and most profound aspect of our being—our spirit. That is what assures our

He [the Holy Spirit] shall glorify Me [Jesus]; for He shall take of Mine, and shall disclose it to you.

—John 16:14

And He, when He comes, will convict the world concerning sin, and righteousness, and judgment.

—John 16:8

For who among men knows the thoughts of a man except the spirit of the man, which is in him? Even so the thoughts of God no one knows except the Spirit of God. Now we have received, not the spirit of the world, but the Spirit who is from God, that we might know the things freely given to us by God.
— 1 Corinthians 2:11–12

communion with God. The Lord wants us to get in on the incredible oneness and unity between Father, Son and Spirit. (Read John 17:11, 21–22.)

Almost every aspect of our spiritual life and ministry reinforces the value God places on communion between Him and us. And that is where the Holy Spirit concentrates much of His work—enabling us to be in one accord with the Father and the Son. Even though we might try our best to line up our life with God's way, we simply cannot do so with the limitations of our natural abilities, strength or insight. How exciting that God is not just a distant Creator, but one who actively involves Himself in our lives. God never intended to have us try to follow Him on our own like a nuclear physicist with a class of eighth-grade students. He knows we will not be able to stay with Him without some very special tutoring. He wants to lead, teach, prompt and strengthen us supernaturally. And God does that mostly by His Spirit.

Because of the Spirit, we can understand what the Lord wants us to know. The Holy Spirit knows everything God thinks and feels (1 Cor. 2:11–12); He searches "the depths of God" and discloses those hidden truths to us, God's children. By learning from the Spirit we become capacitated to do and say and know things that would otherwise be incomprehensible to us. That is why He is named the "Spirit of truth" (John 16:13)—He discloses to us the way things really are, the way God decrees them to be.

▲▲

By learning from the Spirit we become capacitated to do and say and know things that would otherwise be incomprehensible to us.

▲▲

Look at the following verses in light of what we have learned about truth—that, as far as it relates to spiritual matters, truth is not something we can figure out on our own; it comes to us only on the basis of revelation from God.

Read 1 Corinthians 2:9–10. For whom are these wonderful secrets prepared?

_____

How does God reveal these things to us?

_____

In a way, the Spirit is like a construction manager who moves a trailer onto a newly purchased piece of property housing a dilapidated building. He erects a sign announcing a soon-to-be-renovated store.

The old structure does not yet look like much, but everyone realizes—through seeing the sign and the resident manager—that there really is going to be a new store someday. That renovated "store," envisioned years before by the Lord who purchased the land, will be in process for the rest of our lives. Following the blueprints drawn by God, the Holy Spirit oversees the transformation of the old building into the new; He restores us to be more and more like what we were intended to be (1 Cor. 6:11).

The metamorphosis accomplished by the Spirit is known as *sanctification*—a progressive replacement of old and broken fixtures, a repairing of damaged siding and flooring, a repainting of faded walls, and a rewiring of all switches. Inside and out our old place gets a makeover, including the garden where the Holy Spirit plants and tends an incredible array of fruit trees (Gal. 5:22–23). So, along with the change in our old attitudes, thoughts and behavior, the Spirit of God produces new ones like patience, joy and self-control. And by the way, there are no building codes or regulations that relate to fruit trees.

PARTICIPATION WITH THE SPIRIT

In a very real sense, almost everything that God does in or through us is done by the Holy Spirit. Some things He does completely for us—not requiring any sort of active participation on our part—but most of what He does calls for our partnership and cooperation. He doesn't invite us to work with Him because He needs our help, as though He is short of something. He is not stuck in the sand somewhere, in need of being pulled out by us so that He can get on with His work. It is not as though He says, "If you don't do your part, I'm not going to do mine—so there!" He is neither petulant nor perturbed; He isn't looking for someone to stick with the chores or to do the prep work before He paints the living room.

Quite the contrary. His whole reason for wanting to share ministry with us is to reinforce just how much God loves us. Like a proud father wanting to add our name to the family business, He enjoys filling us in on all the details of His whole operation. Since you and I are destined for an eternity of working side by side with the Lord, cooperation with the Holy Spirit here on earth is a lot like driver's training—the Spirit "talks us through" the ins-and-outs of ministry and life situations so that we grow familiar with how things work in the kingdom of God.

The Holy Spirit enables us to proclaim the gospel to others with power and anointing, and He will give us words to speak as

And such were some of you; but you were washed, but you were sanctified, but you were justified in the name of the Lord Jesus Christ, and in the Spirit of our God.
—1 Corinthians. 6:11

But the fruit of the Spirit is love, joy, peace, patience, kindness, goodness, faithfulness, gentleness, self-control; against such things there is no law.
—Galatians 5:22–23

well as wonders to perform. (Read Mark 13:11; Acts 1:8.) Along with these external, miraculous manifestations, the Holy Spirit wants to do an internal transformation in our personalities and character so that they too bear witness of the Lord. (Read Ephesians 3:16; 1 Thessalonians 1:5.) Internal transformations that enable us to live a truly spiritual life and external manifestations that empower us to minister to others are trademarks of the Holy Spirit at work in our lives.

Read Hebrews 2:4. Why do you think God uses miracles to bear witness to our words?

_____

_____

> My sheep hear My voice, and I know them, and they follow Me.
> —John 10:27

As we learned earlier, all true ministry is a response to a leading or prompting from God. The Holy Spirit sensitizes us to Jesus' voice so we can discern it more readily (John 10:27). But the key to what the Holy Spirit wants to accomplish in our lives has to do with our cooperation with Him—allowing Him to guide our steps. That is the very nature of what we call *inspiration*—being inspired by, *in-spirited* (literally, *God-breathed-into*)—being led to say, think or do what would otherwise not come into our minds to do. Jesus wants us to receive miraculous capabilities and empowerment to fully carry out His assignments to us for those around us.

In concert with the Holy Spirit, we receive revelation beyond even the most sincere natural ability—supernaturally knowing and doing things. In a similar fashion to how the Spirit came upon Mary so that she could give birth to the "Son of God" (Luke 1:35), we are welcomed (of course, not to the same degree or with the same result) to receive supernatural seeds of revelation and truth from the Spirit. Speaking or doing what the Spirit prompts us to say or do will give a measure of life and rescue to other people.

But we must have a fundamental willingness to cooperate with the Spirit and volunteer freely like Mary, saying, "Let it be according to the Lord's will." The centrality (to our whole Christian life) of learning to function in cooperation with the Holy Spirit leads us to one of the earliest, tangible experiences with the Spirit available to a believer in Jesus. That experience is referred to as the baptism in the Holy Spirit.

KNOWLEDGE AND LOVE

One of the expressions you will hear on your journey with the Lord is "sound doctrine." The word for *doctrine* simply means instruction and teaching. Good, healthy doctrine teaches people the ways of God, and it informs them of His purposes and His truth. Without sound doctrine the church can be "tossed here and there by waves, and carried about by every wind of doctrine" by false but impressive people (Eph. 4:14) and by "their own desires" (2 Tim. 4:3). Sound doctrine nourishes the church and provides a basis for correcting people who get off base about the truth of God. (Read 1 Timothy 4:6; Titus 1:9–11.) The only source of good doctrine is the Bible. (Read 2 Timothy 3:14–17.)

Good doctrine is very important, and we have an earnest desire to help other believers. Consequently, there is always a danger of letting our sincere beliefs become dogmas that divide the body of Christ rather than develop it. We all see dimly into the realm of the kingdom, and we live in a broken world. Therefore, our journey is a walk of faith—we are still learning along the way—and it behooves us to maintain a posture of graciousness and love toward others in the family of God who do not see things exactly as we do.

In fact, the Bible tells us that if we think we know anything (conclusively) to such a degree that our knowledge places us above others, then we have not yet known as we ought to know. Why? Because knowledge tends to make people "arrogant" (self-assured, superior feeling). Love, on the other hand, "edifies" and encourages others (1 Cor. 8:1–2). That is why Paul says, "The goal of our instruction is love" (1 Tim. 1:5).

Therefore, regardless of the issue we're discussing with fellow believers in Christ, our primary interest ought always to be to "preserve the unity" in the body by actively "putting on love," the "perfect bond of unity" (Eph. 4:3; Col. 3:14).

BEING BAPTIZED WITH THE HOLY SPIRIT

Just as there is no earthly analogy that can adequately express all the wonder of the Trinity and the fullness of the Godhead, neither do we have a precise way of picturing the wonder of being baptized in the Spirit. In a way it is like a river that overflows its banks and thereby enriches the surrounding soil with nutrients and minerals that would not get there otherwise. The ground is fertilized in a unique way—not the only way, but a distinct way that is available to every believer.

As a result of the floodwaters, the softened earth is more receptive to the deposit of spiritual seed than would normally be the case. When we are baptized in the Spirit it is as though He overflows the banks of our spirit and inundates our soul—our mind, will, emotions and conscience. That is why being *baptized* in the Spirit is sometimes referred to as being *filled* with the Spirit.

> When we are baptized in the Spirit it is as though He overflows the banks of our spirit and inundates our soul—our mind, will, emotions and conscience.

RECEIVING THE HOLY SPIRIT INTO YOUR LIFE VS. BEING BAPTIZED IN HIM

So what is the difference between receiving the Holy Spirit and being baptized in the Holy Spirit?

If you have acknowledged Jesus as your Savior, the presence of the Spirit in your life as an identifying mark is an indisputable fact. (Read Romans 8:9, 16; Galatians 4:6.) Indwelling and possessing our spirits, He engages in all sorts of housecleaning in the attics, basements and back sheds of our minds, wills, emotions and behavior. The Holy Spirit helps us grasp spiritual truth. Without Him, we have no relationship with the Lord. This may sound a bit redundant to what has been said already, but it cannot be emphasized enough—the Holy Spirit lives within every believer's spirit.

Jesus told His followers, "Receive the Holy Spirit" (John 20:22), and they did. But several weeks later, He announced to those same disciples: "You shall be baptized with the Holy Spirit not many days from now" (Acts 1:5), and so they were on the day we now refer to as Pentecost, when they were manifestly empowered by the Holy Spirit in the upper room. (Read Acts 2:1–4.) From this simple example we see that it is one thing to *receive the Spirit* in your life, and another to be *baptized in Him*. While the two happenings can easily occur at the same time, and often do, they are not identical to one another, as we see in some instances in the life of the early church. (Read Acts 10:47; 19:5–6).

The presence of the Spirit gives you (spiritual) life. The baptism in the Spirit gives you miraculous, *available-no-other-way* (spiritual) empowerment to share that life with others. This is why Jesus told His disciples to take the gospel into all the world, but only after they received "[miraculous] power" by being "baptized with the Holy Spirit" (Acts 1:5, 8). Though it is not an exact parallel, it is a bit like the difference between what the Lord wants to do *in* you, as opposed to what He wants to do *through* you.

The Holy Spirit in a believer's life is like having a water well on his or her property. Being baptized with the Spirit is like having a powerful water pump put in that well or, due to some seismic shift of the underground water table, suddenly having that well become a gushing spring, enabling the person to irrigate many more acres of crops.

Or think of the difference between air and wind—you could not live without air, and there could be no wind without air, but the wind is an additional activity and force by which the air is set in motion to move other things. The Lord wants us to be more than alive in His Spirit; He longs for us to experience His Spirit like a mighty, rushing wind—not just a presence—moving us to mightily impact life around us.

Does that mean that there are now fewer rocks in the soil or that it has fewer weed seeds? No. Are spiritual seeds better cared for by someone who has been baptized in the Holy Spirit? No. Can that person be as carnal—and even more so—than he or she was before their experience? Yes. Being baptized in the Spirit doesn't make you more obedient or more faithful or more special than anyone else, or more than you were before. It is not a guarantee of spirituality, or proof against lies of the enemy. Just as we can have a Bible and not read it, or not let the words sink into our heart, so too can people be filled with the Spirit but not make full use of its provisions and enablements.

What does being baptized in the Spirit capacitate us for? Why does the Lord want us to be baptized in the Spirit? You might say that the baptism with the Holy Spirit "spreads" the Spirit's presence throughout your natural faculties—just as a water pump spreads water further into the fields than a well alone is able to. As the Spirit overflows us and permeates (in-spirits) our conscious thoughts, feelings, impressions and so forth, we become more able than we were to receive promptings from Him.

It is like having a more powerful radio receiver or a much larger satellite dish—the spiritual reception is vastly improved from what it was before. That is how and why the fullness of the Spirit enables us to participate more actively in the miraculous. It heightens our awareness and sensitizes our soul to His movings and to His whispers.

That's the point for being baptized with the Holy Spirit—it is not a point for theological contention with fellow believers—not a point of pride between the *have-beens* and the *have-not-beens*—but a miraculous ministry point for the sake of other people. It is another reminder that though God can do whatever needs doing without us, He chooses to work in us and through us by His grace and by His Spirit. As with all matters in the kingdom of God, this supernatural gracing can only be appreciated and understood by viewing it in light of God's ever-welcoming, ever-ennobling love and His ever-active compassion for the broken people of the world.

As an isolated fact, experience or theology, the baptism in the Spirit cannot be fully comprehended. It is only when we face the real challenges of loving ministry toward other people that the need for additional empowerment becomes apparent. In other words, being baptized in the Holy Spirit only makes sense when you understand that God wants to capacitate you for ministry to other people in ways that go way beyond your natural powers—as sincere as they may be.

SUPERNATURAL AFTERMATH

Being baptized with the Holy Spirit is like a gently falling leaf suddenly encountering a vast, rushing wind that buoys and propels the leaf in ways it could not do on its own. Though the leaf was already drifting as an entity of both earth and air, the rushing wind can carry it far beyond the edges of the tree. When we are moved upon and baptized in the Spirit, we become like that leaf, wondrously transported to scenic spots of understanding and to revelational places of insight far beyond what would otherwise have been the case.

Like people swimming in a fast-flowing river, we get turned and positioned by the movement of the water. In the river we are capable of moving in ways that would be impossible and unnatural for anyone just standing on the riverbank. Indeed, the very actions just to tread water while drifting down the river would be foolish mannerisms and postures on dry land.

That is why in the Scriptures we generally see supernatural manifestations accompanying the experience of being baptized in the Holy Spirit. Not weird or spooky or old-fashioned or religious demonstrations, but certainly spiritual ones. The wind carrying the leaf cannot be seen by the natural eye, but its effects on the leaf, and how it moves, can be (John 3:8). People in the river can do things that are not possible outside of the river.

In like fashion, there are usually indications in a person's life after he or she has been baptized in the Holy Spirit. Probably the most common of the supernatural capabilities that follow in the aftermath of being baptized in the Spirit are:

1. The ability to pray in a language unknown to your natural mind
2. The ability to receive (and speak) revelation unknown to your natural mind

It is unwise and unnecessary to make some kind of hard-and-fast rule about the signs that must accompany the baptism with the Holy Spirit—our job is not to run a spot test on others to see if they have met our criteria. When people are first converted and receive the Holy Spirit as the seal of their redemption, they do not always experience a physical or emotional sensation. Not all fall to their knees or weep or cry out to the Lord—but many do.

Being forgiven and restored back to full relationship with the Lord is the most spiritual and moving experience we will ever have in our lives. But that spiritual experience manifests more or less differently in everyone's life. So it is with being baptized in the Spirit. Not everyone will evidence the experience the same.

Many believers unknowingly opt out of their rightful inheritance and dismiss a miraculous grace-gift from the Lord because they do not want to experience anything supernatural—like being able to pray in a language their mind never learned or being alerted to facts and understandings their mind could never know on its

> The wind blows where it wishes and you hear the sound of it, but do not know where it comes from and where it is going; so is everyone who is born of the Spirit.
>
> —John 3:8

own. The enemy of our soul wants to make us nervous about the things of the Spirit intersecting our daily life. Though he has lost the war of keeping you and me from believing in a miracle-working Savior, he is still fighting to convince us not to let things get out of (our natural) control and become too "spiritual"—beyond our natural perception.

In a very simple but profound way, the baptism in the Holy Spirit and the supernatural enablements that come with it bring us back to the most central themes of our walk with the Lord—*grace* (being empowered and enabled by God) and *faith* (choosing to act upon the words and promptings of God). Our journey with Him is a series of one decision after another to allow Him to lead us and to accomplish things in our lives by His power, instead of trying to do things all on our own. When our natural inclination is to go left, His direction is usually to go right. When we think, *No way!*, He quietly reminds us that He is the way. What strikes us as foolish and meaningless, He uses to accomplish His great purposes.

▲▲▲

The baptism in the Holy Spirit and the supernatural enablements that come with it bring us back to the most central themes of our walk with the Lord—*grace* and *faith*.

▲▲▲

PRAYING IN THE SPIRIT

One of the best examples of this is praying in an unknown language, or as it is also called, *praying in the Spirit* or *speaking in tongues*. On the Day of Pentecost when the disciples received the promised enabling and empowering of the Spirit, the most immediate consequence was their sudden ability to declare "the mighty deeds of God" in languages they did not know or understand (Acts 2:11). When bystanders ridiculed them, Peter explained that this phenomenon was an outpouring of God's Spirit, as prophesied by Joel (Joel 2:28–29). Isaiah also spoke of how God would one day speak to people, who relied too much on their natural abilities, "through stammering lips and a foreign tongue" (Isa. 28:11).

When you are baptized in the Holy Spirit, you receive in your spirit a language with which to speak and pray beyond the limits of your natural understanding. Your mind does not know the language, but your spirit does; thus, while you are praying in the Spirit, your mind does not know what you are praying. (Read 1 Corinthians 14:14.) The words sound strange to you because you did not acquire them through study the way you learned French in

> And it will come about after this that I will pour out My Spirit on all mankind; and your sons and daughters will prophesy, your old men will dream dreams, your young men will see visions. And even on the male and female servants I will pour out My Spirit in those days.
>
> —Joel 2:28–29

school. Though the "unknown" language makes no sense to your ears, it does to the people or to the angelic beings whose "natural" or native language it is.

DOUBTS ABOUT THE REALITY OF YOUR SPIRITUAL LANGUAGE

Your mind is used to being in charge, so when the unlearned, spiritual language bypasses your conscious thinking, your mind is a bit offended — and hypervigilant to discredit this foreign language. Consequently, it will call the language into question. If your mind is like most, it will suggest three possibilities for why it has been passed over, why it does not know what you are saying:

1. "This is not a real language; it is made up — just a bunch of sounds without any real meaning."

2. "These words are copying what someone else said; it mimics another language — just a bunch of empty sounds with no meaning."

3. "These are silly sounds I made up long ago when I was a kid; I forgot them when I got older — just a bunch of make-believe sounds and childish gibberish."

Doubts will always assail us in ministry, and that is one reason why partnering with the Holy Spirit in this most basic way — speaking the words that He gives to you by faith — will mature you for receiving other words and assignments from Him for the sake of others. Do not be afraid. Speak as the Spirit gives you utterance . . .

When you pray in the Spirit, you are actively cooperating with the Holy Spirit as He directs and leads your prayers—usually dealing with issues or needs in our lives that are too profound or too ill-defined for us to "pray as we should" (Rom. 8:26). Very quickly, we run out of words for expressing praise to the Lord and for talking to Him about all the deep stuff in our lives. That is when it is so wonderful to be able to bypass the limitations of our natural vocabulary in order to pray and praise with spiritual words "not taught by human wisdom" (1 Cor. 2:13). The Bible says that when we pray in the Spirit, we are speaking "mysteries"—truths that cannot be uttered by naturally taught tongues (1 Cor. 14:2).

Since the Spirit is interceding for us while we pray in the Spirit, He knows how to line up our requests with God's will, and what sorts of matters need praying about in our lives—weaknesses and vulnerabilities about which we are probably unaware (Rom. 8:27). As a consequence, praying in the Spirit strengthens and develops us (1 Cor. 14:4). It is one way of "building yourselves up on your

He who searches the hearts knows what the mind of the Spirit is, because He intercedes for the saints according to the will of God.

— Romans 8:27

One who speaks in a tongue edifies himself.

— 1 Corinthians 14:4

most holy faith" (Jude 20). And because our conscious mind is not that engaged in the praying, we can be "praying at all times in the Spirit" throughout our daily activities (Eph. 6:18).

Being able to pray in the Spirit is not a goal to pursue for its own sake, but a kind of gateway through which to move out in more faith. In order to pray in the Spirit, you have to step out and speak with your own lips and vocal cords. The Spirit gives you the words (the "utterance"), but you have to say them (Acts 2:4). The Spirit does not make your mouth move as though you are in some kind of trance. Instead, He invites you to believe that you know a language that your mind says you do not know. And as surely as you speak your native language without thinking ahead of time of the words that will spill from your lips, so He welcomes you to begin praying and speaking in your supernatural, non-native language.

PROPHESYING

Spiritual ministry always requires faith—not necessarily because the problems confronting us are so large, but because the activity is always something the Lord is achieving, and we are simply getting in on what He is already up to. Apart from the Lord, on our own initiative or in our own wisdom, we "can do nothing" of any lasting spiritual value (John 15:5). In concert with the Holy Spirit who discloses what the Lord is doing, we become (very) junior partners with the Lord in ministry. It should not surprise us to discover that God has lots to say to His kids, whom He loves so much. He thinks about us all the time (Ps. 139:17–18); He watches us continually, looking to see what counsel we might need (Ps. 32:8).

Along with the privilege of being able to speak to God in words that go beyond what we know on our own, we are also granted the capacity to hear words in our native language that inform us about things that are beyond what we could know on our own. When God gives us such revelation (*prophecy*), it is meant to be spoken to other people (*prophesied*). Whereas praying in the Spirit builds us up and edifies us personally, prophesying edifies and encourages others (1 Cor. 14:3–4). Prophesy expresses the heart of God for particular people at specific times in their lives and draws their attention to what He is doing in them or what He wants them to do.

Generally, when you are receiving a prophetic word, you will see some picture in your mind—either a static image or a short clip. Two other things will accompany that picture. First and foremost, your mind will be alerted to and reminded of at least one verse from the Bible. (When you are just beginning to learn how to prophesy, to be sure that this word is from the Lord, it is always better if two or three verses come to mind.) All prophecy must be

> How precious also are Thy thoughts to me, O God! How vast is the sum of them! If I should count them, they would outnumber the sand. When I awake, I am still with Thee.
> —Psalm 139:17–18

> I will instruct you and teach you in the way which you should go; I will counsel you with My eye upon you.
> —Psalm 32:8

> But one who prophesies speaks to men for edification and exhortation and consolation. One who speaks in a tongue edifies himself; but one who prophesies edifies the church.
> —1 Corinthians 14:3–4

in line with the Bible, and if a word cannot be supported by Scripture, it isn't a word from the Lord. Most likely, it is born out of someone's enthusiasm or human spirit.

Second, when you get a picture and some Scripture, you also "know" instantly what the picture means—or how you can put the picture into nonvisual words. It is not wrong to explain the picture, giving its details, but a prophetic picture means something—it is a message from the Lord to someone. It is not just a photo or a painting.

When we perceive the faint whisper of what the Lord reveals to our understanding and speak it as a word of prophecy, the people to whom we give the word will be encouraged, built up and drawn closer to Him. That is the goal and the point. In a sense, prophesying is like giving others the results of a verse search God kindly did for them through the Bible—it highlights the key elements of His truth for their situation. And sometimes—especially for people who do not yet acknowledge the reality of God in their lives—a prophecy is so poignant and penetrating, it convinces them of God's present and active existence (1 Cor. 14:24–25).

▲▲

When we perceive the faint whisper of what the Lord reveals to our understanding and speak it as a word of prophecy, the people to whom we give the word will be encouraged, built up and drawn closer to Him.

▲▲

So much more could be said about prophecy and speaking in tongues as ministry, but as purely supernatural capabilities, utterly impossible with only our native abilities, they serve as fabulous reminders of the work of the Holy Spirit. We must be vigilant against the temptation to "wear" the baptism in the Spirit, speaking in tongues or prophesying like badges or medals on our chest. Supernatural enablements are not decorations for past glories in our lives. They are (only) amazing tools to be used for the sake of other people—and the whole time we are making use of them, they are a reminder that it is the Lord, not us, who is doing what needs doing by His grace.

> But if all prophesy, and an unbeliever or an ungifted man enters, he is convicted by all, he is called to account by all; the secrets of his heart are disclosed; and so he will fall on his face and worship God, declaring that God is certainly among you.
> —1 Corinthians 14:24–25

SIMPLE, PRACTICAL HELPS FOR BEING BAPTIZED IN THE HOLY SPIRIT AND PRAYING IN THE SPIRIT

Begin by praising God for your existing relationship with Him and for the presence of the Holy Spirit in your spirit.

Ask Jesus to baptize you in His Spirit. He is very happy to do so.

Believe that the instant you asked to be baptized, you were—just as you received forgiveness the moment you first asked for it in Jesus' name.

Accept the reality of a language your spirit now knows—even though your mind will tell you it doesn't know what you're talking about.

Begin to pray in that unknown language. Do not wait for something to happen to you or for God to make your mouth move involuntarily. Note: You might sense, visualize or "hear" strange words or syllables. You might also have an urge to speak an unknown phrase.

Resist the temptation to doubt the validity of what you pray. Note: You might think you have just "made up" the language or copied the sounds you heard someone else pray. The words might sound like something you used to say as a kid—sounding childish or silly.

Keep praying as the Spirit gives you the words. Do not listen to the few words you get first, and then just repeat those words (that your mind has now heard you speak).

All of this works much better by having someone lay hands on you and pray for you.

LET'S TALK ABOUT IT

▲ How has your thinking changed about the Holy Spirit as a result of reading this chapter? Are you more comfortable with and more open to His work in your life now?

_____

_____

▲ What are some trademarks of the Holy Spirit at work in someone's life? Can you think of areas in your life that have been transformed by the work of the Holy Spirit in you? Thank God for the things that He has done.

_____

_____

▲ What is the secret to true ministry? Ask the Lord to open your ears and eyes to what He is doing in your life—and what He wants to do through you by the power of the Holy Spirit.

_____

_____

▲ What is the difference between receiving the Holy Spirit into your life and being baptized in Him? Do you have any fears or uneasiness about being baptized in the Spirit? What did this chapter say about that?

_____

_____

▲ What are the most common supernatural capabilities that follow being baptized in the Spirit? Must we insist on everyone having them?

_____

_____

▲ How does baptism in the Spirit bring us back to the most central themes in our walk with God—grace and faith?

_____

_____

▲ What happens when you pray in the Spirit? What are the most common lies that tell you your spiritual language is a counterfeit? Did you hear any of those lies when you were first beginning to pray in the Spirit?

_____

_____

▲ What is prophecy, and why is it important to share it with others? How do you know that you have a word from the Lord?

_____

_____

YOUR TIME WITH GOD

Are there issues or needs in your life that are too hard and difficult to put into words? Ask the Holy Spirit to meet you where you are. To do this, praise God for your relationship with Him and for the presence of the Holy Spirit in your spirit.

Accept the existence of a language your spirit knows—even though your mind tells you it doesn't know what you are talking about. Begin to pray in that unknown language. Resist the temptation to doubt the validity of what you pray. Keep praying as the Spirit gives you the words. You may want to begin your prayer time using the following prayer.

Thank You, Lord, that You love me and that I have a relationship with You. Thank You that from the moment I invited You into my heart, Your Spirit has been with me. Thank You for all the things Your Spirit has already done to change and transform my life. Thank You that You give me everything I need in my life to do me good.

Holy Spirit, guide my steps. Sensitize me to Jesus' voice so I can recognize it more readily and be empowered to carry out His assignments to me for those around me. I invite Your prompting, God, for me to say, think or do what would otherwise not come into my mind to do.

I confess Jesus as my Savior, and I want to be as fully empowered as I can be by the Holy Spirit to minister to others. And now, Lord, I ask that You would baptize me in Your Spirit— that You would overflow my spirit and fill me completely, through and through, with Your Spirit. Sensitize my understanding so that I can "hear" the spiritual language You have given to me. I will speak what You give. In Jesus' name, amen.

CHAPTER ELEVEN

Warring Spiritually

A GREAT MANY MORE THINGS AFFECT US THAN WE MAY THINK, AND WHAT WE THINK WE HAVE PIN-POINTED AS THE CAUSE OF SOMETHING OFTEN TURNS OUT NOT TO BE THE CULPRIT. For example, the virus we suspected of creating our sore throat actually was some bacterium. Similarly, who knows if a headache is due to lack of sleep or caffeine, to stress, to an allergic reaction or to the flu? Migraines are anyone's guess. Business leaders or entertainers may attribute their successes to certain factors—in retrospect—but even they know they do not really know how they did it. There are just too many elements and variables floating around in the world.

Every time, for instance, you step on the bathroom scales and wish you weighed less, you stand in the mix of several converging forces that have had a part in bringing you to where you are—the tempting lure of last night's cheesecake and the manifestly weak power of your will, the too tightly packed schedule that has made regular exercise nearly impossible, simple heredity, the addition of years and a slowing metabolism and, of course, gravity. At such times it is comforting to remember that you do not really *weigh* anything at all.

You actually have no intrinsic weight or heaviness, even though you do have mass. It's just that gravity has a hold on you—and won't let go. On the moon gravity is not as much of a problem. Your one hundred sixty-five pounds here on earth would be a mere twenty-eight pounds there, and between here and there, your weight would disappear altogether. Weightlessness is not due to a change in your fundamental composition; it is caused by the loss of gravity, not the loss of appetite.

Gravity is an excellent example of the many invisible powers that affect our daily lives. Though it is the main villain behind the nasty fall you took when you missed the step on the stairs, it is so much a part of the "givens" in the world that you would hardly think to include it in your explanation to a friend about the bruise on your arm. All you think to say is, "I wasn't paying attention to where I stepped."

There is a lot going on in life. And not all of it is going our way.

Because of your earnest desire to "walk in a manner worthy of the Lord" in all respects in your life, you want to embrace everything He wants for you (Col. 1:10). In loving and grateful response to Him, you will want to prosper spiritually (3 John 2). Yet there will be times when you will puzzle over why you cannot make the progress on your journey you would like to make. You will find yourself stymied and bogged down as though you are dragging an iron ball on a chain. You will wonder why obeying Him feels suddenly like swimming against the current of a mighty river. You will even question your own sincerity and faith when you seem unable to stop doing stuff that you know is wrong.

THE NATURE OF EVIL

The Bible tells us about several specific forces and dynamics in the world that are dead-set against us and diametrically opposed to God's purposes in our lives. It is not as though we want to give undue attention to them or to focus exclusively on them and then react in fear to their existence. "God has not given us a spirit of fear" (2 Tim. 1:7, NKJV), and because of His greatness and power, we have no need to be "alarmed by our opponents" or to back down from any kind of spiritual antagonist (Phil. 1:28).

Read 1 John 4:4. We know from this verse that even though forces of evil sometimes seem more powerful than the Lord, He is always greater in might, majesty and dominion. Why do you think people sometimes lose sight of His greatness?

_____

_____

If you have no clue about the contrary spiritual forces that press in on you and grab hold of you as gravity weighs down your physical frame, or if you inadvertently dismiss them from the equation of how life turns out, you will fall into one of several traps laid for you by the hater of your soul. You will have little answer for self-condemnation, and even less of an answer to free other people from what ravages them. If, on the other hand, you attribute every wayward step in your life to forces beyond your control, you land in other snares—self-defensiveness, irresponsible immaturity and spiritual impotence. Your own choices are responsible for much of what you end up with in life—but they are not solely responsible for all the outcomes you face.

More than we may realize, we are caught in the midst of a great struggle between good and evil, between God's way and all other ways. Our culture has an incomplete and inadequate definition of

Beloved, I pray that in all respects you may prosper and be in good health, just as your soul prospers.

—3 John 2

evil. We tend think of it primarily in extreme terms—like serial murderers, grotesque satanic rituals or swindlers who prey on the elderly. But evil exhibits itself in many other ways without looking garish or immoral. For instance, cancer is evil. So is bitterness. Even "funny" little remarks that cut and criticize are evil. Evil can be obvious like a violent temper or invisible like envy and self-pity.

The Bible portrays evil not as a frightening, horror-movie-type power filled with suspense or terrifying images of dark dealings and savage, blood-dripping creatures who stalk human beings. That is how Hollywood misleads the world. Real evil is not so dramatic—or fascinating in its embodiment. Evil itself rarely generates Halloween-style horror, though it does drive people to do frightening and horrific things. Instead, evil produces misery, wretchedness, despair, pain and loss. What the Bible describes as evil are the hurtful and heart-wrenching impacts on God's dear children—all the grief, distress, affliction, sorrow and trouble brought into our lives.

The true nature of evil has almost nothing to do with the beings and powers that Hollywood suggests wield it. The forces of evil are not like characters in a dramatic sci-fi novel empowered by energies that call for motion picture special effects. They are unremarkable in themselves—almost as featureless as a virus or some bacterium. Evil itself is the emptiness and wrongness brought by those creatures to a lonely and frail old man in a dingy convalescent home, strapped to an oxygen mask as he waits out the remaining weeks of his cancer-ridden life. Evil forces are like mosquitoes—evil is what happens when the malaria they carry wastes away a child's life, cutting off her smile and her days. Evil is a thing of loss, destruction and death—abject and utter desolation.

That is because evil opposes everything of God's desire for us. Evil attempts to counter the increase God longs to give you; it protests the Lord's creative and restorative work in the lives of His people. Evil is the lost future and lost relationship that always accompany death—nothing more, but nothing less.

> **What the Bible describes as evil are the hurtful and heart-wrenching impacts on God's dear children—all the grief, distress, affliction, sorrow and trouble brought into our lives.**

LIFE AND DEATH (RE)DEFINED

Most people think of death as the ending of someone's physical life—when he or she stops breathing and when brain function has stopped completely. Such a physical concept of death makes it difficult to understand many Bible verses because they are not talking about the cessation of life, just its distortion. Death has a far more fundamental and spiritual meaning.

Death cuts people off from the life experiences they would otherwise have enjoyed in God's original plan, and death cuts them off from the relationships they have had. Death robs people of their connection with others and with their intended future. When death came into the world through sin, it caused Adam and Eve to lose their God-intended future (without labor in the garden) and their closeness to the Lord. (Read Genesis 3:8, 19, 24.)

Read the following verses and apply the spiritual definition of death to them. Do they make more sense to you now?

For the wages of sin is death, but the free gift of God is eternal life in Christ Jesus our Lord.

—ROMANS 6:23

. . . but now has been revealed by the appearing of our Savior Christ Jesus, who abolished death, and brought life and immortality to light through the gospel.

—2 TIMOTHY 1:10

Then when lust has conceived, it gives birth to sin; and when sin is accomplished, it brings forth death.

—JAMES 1:15

Eternal life is not just life that goes on forever and ever. Rather, it is life without death—life that never suffers the loss of relationship or God-ordained future. It will be life with nothing missing, nothing wrong. In other words, it will be life as God always intended it to be—full of joy, satisfaction, fulfillment and, most of all, relationship fully restored and secured between Him and us. That is why the Bible defines eternal life in terms of relationship with the Lord . . .

And this is eternal life, that they may know Thee, the only true God, and Jesus Christ whom Thou hast sent.

—JOHN 17:3

. . . and why eternal life is in Jesus—because only in Him do we have the forgiveness of sins and deliverance from all residue of evil (death):

And the witness is this, that God has given us eternal life, and this life is in His Son. He who has the Son has the life; he who does not have the Son of God does not have the life.

—1 JOHN 5:11–12

The Hollywood version of evil will make us run in fear; a true realization of evil will motivate us to intervene and do something to put an end to the suffering it is creating. A horror flick does nothing but make us jumpy in the dark; a documentary of starving children in Uganda moves us to compassion and action. Hollywood points to garlic and a hand-held cross to ward off evil; God points to sour wine and the cross-held hands of His Son to destroy it once and for all—"It is finished!" (John 19:30). The two versions of evil have almost nothing in common.

Question: The sensationalist picture of evil causes people to draw back in dread. A true sense of evil makes people want to intervene. Why do you think that the enemy wants people to have a picture of evil that is scary, creepy, suspenseful, dark and laced with grotesque images of horror?

_____

_____

THE NATURE OF WHAT OPPOSES US

So, what are some of the forces of evil that beset us on our journey with the Lord? The Bible presents us with four basic categories of death-dealing, loss-bringing, hope-stealing evil. Let's take a look at each.

The world

Perhaps most obviously, even to people who do not believe in the Lord, evil can be seen in the world around us. In fact, one of the most-asked questions you will encounter wonders how a good God could create a world filled with so much evil. The fact that this is not how He made it may escape them, but the evidence of evil is irrefutable— not ghosts and goblins, but poverty, war, crime and misery. Truly we live in the midst of a derelict and ailing world that is filled with every manner of heartache and anxiety. People suffer and die as a matter of this world's present course—a course that was never intended by God.

> The trajectory of the world courses against God's way, against everything that is lasting, good, satisfying and joyful.

This diseased atmosphere that surrounds us, this total environment of wrong-ending-up, is what the Bible calls the *world*. Long ago when mankind abnegated their rightful role as stewards of this planet and gave it into the hands of the devil, the *world* was captured in futility. (Read Genesis 3; Romans 8:20.) Now, like a bound hostage, it lies stretched out "in the power of the evil one," Satan (1 John 5:19). The trajectory of the *world* courses against God's way, against everything that is lasting, good, satisfying and joyful. Like a stolen car driven by a heedless teen, the *world* careens wildly on a ruinous course, plunging toward death and carrying us all with it.

So the days containing our lives are evil in their effect (Eph. 5:15–16), and though we do our best to make our way against the stream of "this present evil age" (Gal. 1:4), the *world* affects us far more than we realize. The *world* loves to be loved, and it offers things to please our eyes and our ego so that we will follow it as fish go after a spinning lure. It boasts of its prowess like a tournament knight, and with bawdy humor and suggestive poses it promises what it can do for us (too).

In the following verses the word *evil* refers to the influence or effect it has on other things, not an intrinsic wickedness. In other words, it is not evil in itself—as though it was made that way—but harmful, vicious, calamitous, hurtful and deadly to other things (like us).

Read Galatians 1:4. Give some examples of "bad things that happen to good people." If people do not know about the vicious effects of the world, whom do they usually blame for the bad things that happen in life?

_____

_____

Read Ephesians 5:16. Left to themselves, our days will follow the general course of the world that is away from God's intention. How can we "turn our days around" to redeem them and make the most of our time on earth?

_____

_____

The *world* is what people call "the good life"—the sense that the future is before you, and there is nothing you cannot do if you just put your all into it. It is like a dazzling infomercial where a self-made millionaire is offering to share secrets for making it big. It is hard not to believe what the *world* says—especially when the backdrop pictures look like everything we ever wanted. The *world* has a lure all its own and a course of life that leads surely to destruction. The way may look good to us, and even seem reasonable, but the end "is the way of death" (Prov. 14:12).

The flesh

Used in the Bible both as a metaphor for physical, nonspiritual elements like our earthly body *and* for our sinful nature, the *flesh* sets itself against the Spirit of God and desires exactly the opposite of what He wants (Gal. 5:16–17). The key component of the *flesh* is desire—craving, longing, lusting—demanding what it wants,

> Therefore be careful how you walk, not as unwise men, but as wise, making the most of your time, because the days are evil.
>
> —Ephesians 5:15–16

> But I say, walk by the Spirit, and you will not carry out the desire of the flesh. For the flesh sets its desire against the Spirit, and the Spirit against the flesh; for these are in opposition to one another, so that you may not do the things that you please.
>
> —Galatians 5:16–17

when and how it wants, regardless of the consequences. The *flesh* is like a spoiled nine-year-old—it sets its mind on something it wants and becomes "hostile toward God" in its rebellion if it is told no (Rom. 8:6–8). It likes to be in charge of us.

Like a bratty kid, only with far more developed capabilities, the *flesh* brings "corruption" and ruin (Gal. 6:7–8), either by throwing a tantrum when it is denied or by breaking anything it gets its hands on and has its way with. All on its own—and certainly without our permission—the *flesh* can generate jealousy, flaming tempers, drug and drinking problems, immorality, quarrels and more (Gal. 5:19–21). It offers us a tainted picture of reality by rationalizing what it wants (spell that d-e-s-e-r-v-e-s) or by fanaticizing a resistance-free scenario of pure pleasure.

▲▲▲

The flesh is like a spoiled nine-year-old— it sets its mind on something it wants and becomes "hostile toward God" in its rebellion if it is told no.

▲▲▲

Though our spirit is more than "willing" to follow the Lord, the *flesh* that surrounds it is very "weak" and sickly when it comes to spiritual pursuits (Matt. 26:41). Not remarkably, when we deny the *flesh,* like with fasting, it rises up like an angered rhino and charges right at whatever discipline has dared to cause it discomfort. The *flesh* is like a slave-trader who offered to befriend us, then sold us to sin so that it could have its way with us. Just as people moving past middle-age complain about their bodies "betraying" them— such as when a knee gives out—our flesh will inevitably let us down and give out under the weight of temptation.

Read Romans 7:14–15, 18. Ask yourself, "Who seems to be in charge of whom?"

_____

_____

This "old nature" of ours was forever ruined by the Fall. Our constitutional makeup, the way we are now wired, is to prefer wrong over right the way that Adam chose the fruit over obedience. The *flesh* "cannot please God" because nothing good (as opposed to evil) resides in it (Rom. 8:8). It is irredeemably evil—so far beyond reform that the Lord warns us to be ever vigilant against it and to set up safeguards to control and disable it (1 Cor. 9:27). Though our flesh is out on parole, it cannot be trusted alone with our valuables.

Now the deeds of the flesh are evident, which are: immorality, impurity, sensuality, idolatry, sorcery, enmities, strife, jealousy, outbursts of anger, disputes, dissensions, factions, envying, drunkenness, carousing, and things like these, of which I forewarn you just as I have forewarned you that those who practice such things shall not inherit the kingdom of God.
— Galatians 5:19–21

I buffet my body and make it my slave, lest possibly, after I have preached to others, I myself should be disqualified.
— 1 Corinthians 9:27

The force of sin

Most people understand that a sin is something wrong that we do, think or say. But it is surprising to learn that sin is not only an act or an episode; it is also a force, like gravity, that does things to us. When we do something against the will of God, it is a sin—a violation, a trespass across boundaries He has established to keep us safe and satisfied. We are responsible for having done it—it was our choice like Adam's and Eve's. But part of the reason we succumbed to the temptation is because of the power of the *force of sin* that acts like a strong, prevailing wind, blowing us off course.

Very early on, God warned humankind of the *force of sin* that had "entered into the world" through the door opened by Adam and Eve's disobedience (Rom. 5:12). It was like a malignant infection spreading death and misery everywhere. The Lord admonished us to exercise dominion over it because it will wait in ambush, "crouching at the door" and seizing every opportunity to overwhelm us (Gen. 4:7). The *force of sin* is like a giant spider that has spun a web across the likely paths of our mind and heart. Knowing about our weakness in the *flesh* and the allure of the *world,* the *force of sin* lays the strands of its entanglement where they are most liable to catch hold of our liabilities. It is the ultimate opportunist.

The *force of sin* "so easily entangles us" because the wrongness and waywardness of evil keep casting it in our direction like some huge trapper's net (Heb. 12:1). If we simply hold still and let things happen without actively working to push the netting away from ourselves, the mesh of its web will wrap us round about so the spider can suck our life juices dry. The spider's sting is death— "the sting of death is sin"—cutting us off from what God intended for us (1 Cor. 15:56). Even knowing that danger, we still make poor choices that put us more at risk or under its influence.

As proof of its utter evilness, the *force of sin* actually takes advantage of the law of God, using the holy and righteous commandments from the Lord as a means to deceive and kill us (Rom. 7:7–8). As soon as we hear of something forbidden—like a sign telling us not to stand too close to a cliff's edge—the *force of sin* begins pushing us in that very direction with thoughts like, *Why? I wonder how close I can get. It's probably not that dangerous for capable people like me.*

▲▲▲▲▲▲▲▲▲▲▲▲▲▲▲▲▲▲▲▲▲▲▲▲▲▲▲▲▲▲▲▲▲▲▲▲

The *force of sin* develops a progressive control in our lives that increases with the sins we commit, making each of us a "slave of sin."

▲▲▲▲▲▲▲▲▲▲▲▲▲▲▲▲▲▲▲▲▲▲▲▲▲▲▲▲▲▲▲▲▲▲▲▲

What shall we say then? Is the Law sin? May it never be! On the contrary, I would not have come to know sin except through the Law; for I would not have known about coveting if the Law had not said, "You shall not covet."
—Romans 7:7–8

Even though we each have our own responsibility and culpability for our sins, the Bible explains that sometimes it is the *force of sin* that is causing us to sin: "For sin, taking opportunity through the commandment, deceived me, and through it killed me . . . Therefore did that which is good become a cause of death for me? May it never be! Rather it was sin, in order that it might be shown to be sin by effecting my death through that which is good, that through the commandment sin might become utterly sinful . . . But if I do the very thing I do not wish to do, I agree with the Law, confessing that it is good. So now, no longer am I the one doing it, but sin which indwells me" (Rom. 7:11, 13, 16–17).

The *force of sin* develops a progressive control in our lives that increases with the sins we commit, making each of us a "slave of sin" (John 8:34). A vicious cycle ensues—a sin puts you somewhat more under the influence of the *force of sin*, which in turn preys upon the vulnerability caused by that sin. One bad choice to step off the edge of that snowy mountain can create an avalanche that carries us with it, until it buries us beneath the weight of lots more than we bargained for.

The evil spirited

Though our western and scientific culture scoffs at the existence of a spiritual dimension of reality beyond the very limited limits of physical measurement and observation, we know exactly the opposite. This tangible world only exists because it was formed out of the spiritual realm (Heb. 11:3; Ps. 33:6). The unseen world is more real than what we behold on this planet with our eyes (2 Cor. 4:18). Hence, the primary sphere of our struggle against evil will not be natural, but supernatural; as the Bible says, we wrestle [mostly] against the *evil spirited* schemes and "spiritual forces of wickedness" in the heavenlies (2 Cor. 2:11; Eph. 6:12).

▲▲▲

Like traces of toxic chemicals seeping from
a waste site causing deformity, disease
and death, the *evil spirited*
weave their way into the human psyche
and the human condition. They bring
emptiness, confusion and sadness.

▲▲▲

Jesus Himself was confronted by satanic temptation. (Read Matthew 4:1–11.) It seems preposterous to imagine that we won't be. Two of the primary proofs He offered about His kingdom authority were casting out evil spirits and healing all who were

> By faith we understand that the worlds were prepared by the word of God, so that what is seen was not made out of things which are visible.
>
> —Hebrews 11:3

> By the word of the Lᴏʀᴅ the heavens were made, and by the breath of His mouth all their host.
>
> —Psalm 33:6

> We look not at the things which are seen, but at the things which are not seen; for the things which are seen are temporal, but the things which are not seen are eternal.
>
> —2 Corinthians 4:18

"oppressed" by demonic presences (Acts 10:38). The *evil spirited* are exactly that—beings whose entire identities and assignments are against God's marvelous ways and truth. They are not spooky-scary evil from a Hollywood movie set, but they are like weed seeds of ruin, grief, adversity, barrenness, disappointment and pain wanting to plant themselves everywhere.

Just as there are myriads upon myriads of angels sent out by the Lord to minister and "render service" to us (Heb. 1:14), so the devil has a far lesser number of the *evil spirited* hosts who do the opposite—they afflict and burden people with sickness, worry, unbelief, false beliefs, addiction, depression and many other kinds of unexplainable emotional wretchedness or torment of the mind. Like traces of toxic chemicals seeping from a waste site causing deformity, disease and death, the *evil spirited* weave their way into the human psyche and the human condition. They bring emptiness, confusion and sadness.

On the cross, Jesus not only purchased our salvation from sin's death grip, but He also "disarmed" hell's minions and broke up the works of the devil.

Read Colossians 2:15. Upon returning home from war, it was common practice for victorious generals to parade their vanquished foes through the city streets for all to see. In light of that, can you put this verse into your own words?

_____

_____

Read Hebrews 2:14. *Render powerless* means "make entirely idle, bring to naught, make of no consequence." What did Jesus' death accomplish with regard to our enemy?

_____

_____

Read 1 John 3:8. Can you think of three analogies of substances or things that seem solid and strong, but that can be "destroyed"?

_____

_____

Whereas Jesus laid down His life to free us from the death brought by evil, the devil's only agenda is to afflict our life with every possible kind of loss, heartache and brokenness (John 10:10–11). The "serpent of old who is called the devil and Satan" is a liar whose primary activities on earth are deception and accusation. (Read John 8:44; Acts 13:10; Revelation 12:9–10.) How he

> The thief comes only to steal, and kill, and destroy; I came that they might have life, and might have it abundantly. I am the good shepherd; the good shepherd lays down His life for the sheep.
>
> —John 10:10–11

hates the people of God—we who will occupy a higher place in the cosmic order than the place he abandoned so long ago because of his foolish vanity.

THE NATURE OF WHAT CHAMPIONS US

In the face of such foes, what are we to do? Are there ways to conquer these forces of evil, or must we be their victims as long as we live on earth?

God is our champion—the One who fights for us against oppressive foes we could otherwise not defeat (Isa. 19:20). In fact, He is called our "dread champion" (Jer. 20:11), who will disgrace our persecutors and foil their schemes. Once again, we see this consistent theme throughout our journey with the Lord, that He does for us what we cannot do for ourselves. This is the most important lesson to remember about warring against the unseen enemies in our life—"the battle is the LORD's" (1 Sam. 17:47; Ps. 62:1–2), and "if God is for us, who"—really—can be "against us" (Rom. 8:31)?

Let's revisit each of the four categories of evil we confront in life, to see what the Bible offers us as antidotes to their influence and effects.

The world

God made the *world*, and "He will judge the world in righteousness" (Ps. 9:8; 89:11). Even though the *world* has fallen under the sway of the enemy, God has a prior claim to it. He sends us into the *world* to preach, not out of it to hide. (Read Mark 16:15; John 17:18.) Though we will have difficulties in the *world*, Jesus promises to give us His peace and His victory (John 14:27; 16:33). Through the cross, the *world* is "crucified to me" (Gal. 6:14). In God's eternal plan for His creation, the *world* is "passing away" (1 John 2:17)—soon to be replaced by "a new heaven and earth" in which no wrongness exists (2 Pet. 3:13). The whole point of heaven is that it replaces our current living situation (the *world*) with one that is fixed on the same course as God.

Read 2 Peter 1:4. Where does the "corruption" come from in the *world*, and what tool helps us escape that?

_____

_____

And it will become a sign and a witness to the LORD of hosts in the land of Egypt; for they will cry to the LORD because of oppressors, and He will send them a Savior and a Champion, and He will deliver them.
—Isaiah 19:20

Peace I leave with you; My peace I give to you; not as the world gives, do I give to you.
—John 14:27

These things I have spoken to you, that in Me you may have peace. In the world you have tribulation, but take courage; I have overcome the world.
—John 16:33

Read 1 John 5:4–5. What weapon is most effective against the *world?*

_____

The flesh

We know that the *flesh* has little to offer us spiritually—it "profits nothing" (John 6:63), and it is very weak, very susceptible to sin. (Read Romans 6:19.) But Jesus did come in the flesh and live without sin (John 1:14), and we are told to clothe ourselves in Him and "make no provision for the flesh in regard to its lusts" (Rom. 13:14). If we walk by the Spirit—being led and prompted by Him—we will be far less likely to "carry out the desire of the flesh" (Gal. 5:16).

Read Galatians 5:13. As an antidote to serving our own flesh, what should we do?

_____

Read 1 Peter 4:1–2. For what purpose should we "arm" ourselves to counteract the force of flesh in our lives?

_____

_____

The force of sin

The deceitfulness of the *force of sin* can be resisted by intentionally striving against its suggestions in a way that will make you feel as though you are dying because of not getting what it tells you that you must have (Heb. 3:13; 12:4). The good news, of course, is that Jesus condemned the *force of sin* to the very death penalty it had sought to put on us, and the Holy Spirit works aggressively to "convict the world" of it (John 16:8). Additionally, since we are born of God, our spirit has already been put completely off limits to the influence and the touch of the *force of sin* (1 John 3:9).

Read Romans 6:12–13. What do you think it means to "present" the parts of your life "as instruments of righteousness to God"?

_____

_____

Read Hebrews 11:25. What choice can you make that will prevent the *force of sin* from reigning in your life?

_____

_____

... lest any of you be hardened by the deceitfulness of sin.
—Hebrews 3:13

You have not yet resisted to the point of shedding blood in your striving against sin.
—Hebrews 12:4

No one who is born of God practices sin, because His seed abides in him; and he cannot sin, because he is born of God.
—1 John 3:9

The evil spirited

To begin with, let us remember that God is the "LORD Most High" of the heavens and the earth, who rules "over all the earth" (Ps. 97:9), and Jesus is His "Son" (Luke 1:32). The conflict between good and evil should never be misinterpreted as though it pits two equals—God and Satan—against one another. The devil is not God's counterpart in any manner. He is merely a created being—made by God, an angel like Michael or Gabriel—who was exiled to earth away from God's presence because he chose not to live out God's high purposes for him in the courts of heaven. (Read Ezekiel 28:14–17.)

Satan's rebellion was a prototype for ours; he sinned against the Lord, and he fooled Adam and Eve into doing likewise. But the fact that we sin against the Lord certainly does not make us His equals, and neither does Satan's ongoing rebellion against the King of kings put him on a level with God. Although the devil is no match even for God's angels, and although his doom is fixed, we— in our own strength—are no match for him and his ploys. We cannot rely upon our native intellect, physical strength or any man-made ritual to overpower him.

Jesus called Satan "the ruler of the world" (John 16:11), meaning that, for the time being anyway, the devil was permitted jurisdiction over the earth and all of its inhabitants.

This was not always the case, nor did God ever intend it to be so. Originally, God had given Adam and Eve complete dominion over the world, equipping His children to steward the creatures and the resources of our planet with wise creativity under His ultimate authority (Gen. 1:28). But when Adam and Eve allowed the enemy to control their thoughts ("Has God *really* said . . .") and ultimately their actions (when they ate the fruit forbidden by God), they unknowingly gave up their stewardship authority and left it to be seized by Satan. (Read Genesis 3:1, 6.)

In the Book of Revelation, God outlines His plan for overruling Satan and the authority he seized in the coup against humanity. God, our Father, is going to re-create everything anew without any lingering or future traces of death, sorrow, pain or unrighteousness. Until that time—when Jesus returns to the earth to set things right—we who call Him Lord are commissioned to "occupy" the world like elite Special Forces' operatives. Stationed behind enemy lines, we are to prepare inroads for His kingdom coming. Like Jesus, we are to go about "doing good, and healing," rescuing and delivering anyone who has been "oppressed by the devil" (Acts 10:38).

When we choose to identify with Jesus in His death, we also receive power to reign in the authority that His new life has over

> And God blessed them; and God said to them, "Be fruitful and multiply, and fill the earth, and subdue it; and rule over the fish of the sea and over the birds of the sky, and over every living thing that moves on the earth."
>
> — Genesis 1:28

death and sin. Our spiritual authority over evil rests solely upon Jesus because He is the One who "disarmed the rulers and authorities . . . having triumphed over them" through the cross (Col. 2:14–15). Thus, when we, or those we love, are bullied by our own *flesh,* by the *force of sin,* by the *world* or by the *evil spirited,* we can say, "I may be weak on my own, but in Jesus' name and authority, I say *no* to you!" Few other words strike as much fear into the heart of the enemy of our race. When we resist the devil like that, he vanishes from the scene, shunning our presence (James 4:7).

▲▲▲

When we are bullied by our own *flesh,* by the *force of sin,* by the *world* or by the *evil spirited,* we can say, "I may be weak on my own, but in Jesus' name and authority, I say *no* to you!"

▲▲▲

THE WEAPONS OF OUR WARFARE

We have been anointed with power and with His Spirit. Thus equipped and taught through God's Word, we take the "ministry of reconciliation" into a dying and desperate world where evil has broken people's lives and stolen their hope (2 Cor. 5:18). The armor of God *and* our willingness to suffer for the sake of others enable us to endure and defy the pressures coming against us from the *evil spirited,* from the *world,* from the f*orce of sin* and from our own *flesh.*

The "weapons of our warfare" are spiritually powerful beyond any natural ability, and they are specifically designed to break down the points of assault against our soul (2 Cor. 10:1–6), much in the same way that antibiotics attack invading elements in our bodies. Just as a good diet and exercise can help prevent *some* bodily illnesses, so certain regular activities—talking to the Lord, reading His Word, worshiping, being in fellowship with other believers, repenting—can make us less vulnerable to *some* spiritual ailments caused by the *world,* the *flesh,* the *force of sin* or the *evil spirited.*

In fact, we learn that warring spiritually is essentially adopting a stance of firm resolve to keep trusting in the Lord when it seems that life is not working. It is seeking the kingdom of God as our first priority, resisting the lies that say God does not care or is unable to do anything about our painful places. When we suffer on this broken planet, when our cravings go unsatisfied, when our hearts get blown toward wrong choices, when we find ourselves inexplicably bound by compulsions or tumbled in confusions, we know the battle has been joined.

Submit therefore to God. Resist the devil and he will flee from you.

—James 4:7

Question: From the viewpoint of victory, looking back at our struggle here on earth, what specific tools has the Lord given us to withstand and push back the powers that assail our friends and us?

_____

_____

What are *some* of the effective countermeasures we have at our disposal?

_____

_____

The name of Jesus

His name is the most powerful name in all of creation. When we use it to pray or to speak against any force or situation, we are calling upon His authority, His right and capacity to overrule everything else. The name of Jesus is so far beyond any other name that it is like a having a four-wheel-drive vehicle in a cross-country race against horse-drawn "chariots" (Ps. 20:7), or like having an industrial strength fire extinguisher to put out a candle. (Read Psalm 118:10–12.)

The name of Jesus enables us to bring healing to the sick, freedom to those tormented by evil spirits and salvation to any who will believe. (Read Acts 4:10; James 5:14–15; Acts 16:18; 2:22.) In the name of Jesus we will "perform miracles" (Mark 9:39), and our lives will be attended by a steady flow of the miraculous that capacitates us to do what is not naturally possible (Mark 16:17–18).

"Whatever you ask of the Father" in the name of Jesus, He hears us and grants our requests (John 15:16). We become His deputized agents, conducting kingdom business on His behalf, doing what He did—"doing good and healing all" from the powers of evil (Acts 10:38). The Lord's name is both an offensive weapon you will be prompted to use to make great headway against evil, and also a defensive one—"a strong tower"—in times when you feel discouraged (Prov. 18:10).

The Word of God

When Jesus resisted temptation by the devil in the wilderness, He quoted Scripture at the enemy. He said, "It is written . . . " (Read Matthew 4:1–11.) Jesus used the authority and the truth of His Father's Word to turn back the half-truths and lies of the "father of lies." Even though all authority was given to Jesus by His

> And these signs will accompany those who have believed: in My name they will cast out demons, they will speak with new tongues; they will pick up serpents, and if they drink any deadly poison, it shall not hurt them; they will lay hands on the sick, and they will recover.
> —Mark 16:17–18

Father, Jesus still chose to rely solely on the Word of God to turn away temptation. Interesting that the One who is the word of God made use of the Word of God to overcome evil.

God's Word is the everlasting truth upon which everything in all of creation is based. (Read Psalm 119:160; John 17:17.) Every one of His words is like an already-tested "shield" that can protect us from any volley of evil arrows launched at us (Prov. 30:5). In the face of the many afflictions, difficulties and fears that will confront us on our journey of faith, we can speak the truth of God's Word and confess its reality over and above the natural reality we see. By holding onto His promises, we have a sure foundation with which to withstand any storm.

Spending time regularly in His Word is probably the best way to stay close to the Lord, "following" the truths it quickens to us and "waiting eagerly" for Him to instruct us. It is a way to seek His wisdom for facing the evil at hand (Isa. 26:8).

The fear of the Lord

To *fear* does not mean to tremble in dreaded anticipation of what God is going to do to you. His "enemies" tremble, not His kids (Joel 3:16). The fear of the Lord is remembering that He has the final say in everything, and that all the particulars of life will be judged according to His rules—no one else's. It is realizing that no matter what it seems like, His ways and "judgments" are totally reliable and correct—"righteous altogether" (Ps. 19:9).

The fear of the Lord gives us wisdom about what is right, and it gives us the extra incentive we often need to choose that right when our *flesh* and the *world* lure us in another direction. (Read Psalm 111:10; Proverbs 16:6.) Evil forces make things wrong and wretched and empty—the fear of the Lord is essentially realizing the link between evil forces and the deathly misery they cause.

Even when we are so strongly tempted to follow the *world* or to obey our *flesh* in order to get what we think we want, the fear of the Lord enables us to realize the true outcome of going that way. We will turn back because of how much we really hate what evil does to ourselves and to others. (Read Proverbs 8:13; 14:26–27.) That is how the fear of the Lord keeps us and makes us less likely to be hassled by evil forces. "The fear of the LORD leads to life" (Prov. 19:23).

Worship and praise

Warfare and worship are linked together in the Bible far more than most believers realize. With the high praises of God in our mouths and a sword in our hands, we will bind the very powers of

Indeed, while following the way of Thy judgments, O LORD, we have waited for Thee eagerly; Thy name, even Thy memory, is the desire of our souls.
—Isaiah 26:8

> The LORD is my strength and song, and He has become my salvation; this is my God, and I will praise Him; my father's God, and I will extol Him.
> — Exodus 15:2

> Be Thou exalted, O LORD, in Thy strength; we will sing and praise Thy power.
> — Psalm 21:13

evil that have sought to capture us. (Read Psalm 149:6–9.) When we feel powerless in the face of evil coming our way, we get to put our attention on the Lord (instead of the evil), and as we worship Him with song, He sets ambushes against the oncoming powers of wrongness. (Read 2 Chronicles 20:12, 17–19, 21–22.)

In praising and extolling God, we experience an increase of His power brought to bear upon our situation, much in the same way that someone waving their arms and shouting draws the attention of a rescue team (Exod. 15:2; Ps. 21:13). Someone forced at gunpoint to drive past a police checkpoint will try to send little signals that something isn't right; worship acts as that sort of attention-getter. Notice how some praise words like *magnify* and *extol* are pictures of increase. Though God is always the same, worship increases our sense of just how big He is in comparison to our foes.

Paul and Silas sang songs of worship to the Lord when they were locked in prison, and as they did, an earthquake shook their cell and set them (and others) free. (Read Acts 16:25–26.) This and many other examples in the Bible show us that praise has a unique capacity to release people and circumstances from the enslaving grip of evil. Very frequently, as we praise the Lord in the midst of difficult circumstances, He changes them. And even when the situation remains the same, we get changed to His glory.

Resisting the devil

As a finite being who can only be in one place at a time, Satan, the accuser, the liar, searches for prey "like a roaring lion" (1 Pet. 5:8). He and his hordes of emptiness want to devour God's people; they take aim at our faith with fiery darts—points of accusation against the loving goodness and power of God—trying to get to us when our life circumstances are causing us to suffer. The enemy knows we do not like pain of any sort. We do not want to suffer. And so, after a protracted season of pain, or when our suffering reaches intolerable levels, the devil will try to get us to turn away from God's truth.

> Making the choice to keep believing in the Lord's rescue is one of the most powerful weapons in our spiritual arsenal.

Resisting him will cause him to "flee" (James 4:7). The way we resist the devil is to keep entrusting ourselves to the Lord—to realize that our "brethren who are in the world" are suffering along with us (1 Pet. 5:9). We do not use garlic or crosses; instead, we kneel at the foot of the cross where Jesus suffered and repeat His words: "Into Thy hands I commit my spirit" (Luke 23:46). Bottom line, the devil tries to convince us that God *will not* or *cannot* take care of us. Making the choice to keep believing in the Lord's rescue is one of the most powerful weapons in our spiritual arsenal. The cultural quip, "The devil made me do it," is spiritual capitulation. But one of the most foe-terrifying spiritual war cries that can ever be uttered is, "Though He [God] slay me, I will hope in Him" (Job 13:15).

The armor of God

Using the imagery of a Roman legionnaire, the Scriptures paint a detailed picture of several implements for our struggle against the schemes and the world forces of evil. (Read Ephesians 6:10–17.)

▲ *Truth*—the way that God has made things, His way, what He decrees about everything. The truth of God's Word sets us free from the lies and temptations of the *evil spirited*, the *world*, our *flesh* and the *force of sin*. (Read John 8:32, 44.) When things seem to be slipping, when aspects of your life are coming undone, call out for God's truth to be a belt holding things up.

▲ *Righteousness*—the goodness, soundness and exactly-the-way-it's-supposed-to-be-ness of God's life. We have been made eternally righteous through Christ, but the more we line up our daily life with Him, the less vulnerable we will be. Our heart is easily fooled into justifying itself, but when you sense something isn't quite right, ask God to highlight the wrong with His righteousness.

▲ *Repentance*—acknowledging the wrong direction we've been going and turning around. By confessing our way-wardness, we get cleansed from the easily infected residue that acts like a magnet to draw trouble our way (1 John 1:9). No matter how many times you must turn back around to walk the right way, keep doing so.

▲ *Faith*—believing whatever God has said to us in His Word about our situation. All the forces of evil try to get us to take matters into our own hands or to listen to words (thoughts, emotions, circumstances) other than the Lord's. (Read Romans 10:17; 2 Corinthians 5:7; 1 Thessalonians 3:5.) When you feel hopeless or confused, go back to the last words you heard the Lord speak to you—and hold to them like to a shield.

> If we confess our sins, He is faithful and righteous to forgive us our sins and to cleanse us from all unrighteousness.
> —1 John 1:9

▲ *Salvation*—not only eternal deliverance from the power of sin and the "domain of darkness," but also freedom from evil-spirited bondages in our mind, will and emotions. (Read 2 Corinthians 1:10; Colossians 1:13.) Miraculous elimination of demonic hindrances through the ministry of deliverance is an incredible resource in our lives. In those areas of your life where you encounter confusion or compulsion, ask God to deliver your thoughts from evil.

▲ *Scripture*—specific and timely Bible verses quickened to us through prophetic words, teaching, counsel and reading. God e-mails His words to us in order to heal and rescue us. (Read Psalm 107:20; Matthew 8:8, 16). If you picture Scripture as a sword, you will understand how to use it to parry the thrusts of the enemy—and how to strike down his lies.

▲ *Prayer*—asking for the intervention of God's kingdom will in our life situations, "Thy kingdom come" (Luke 11:2). Jesus taught us to pray for God's will to be done—not as a fatalistic "Whatever!", but as a resource to call upon in the day of trouble. (Read Psalm 50:15; Nahum 1:7.) Very often prayer is a running dialogue with the Lord, whispered throughout the day in moments of challenge or celebration.

▲ *Praying in the Spirit*—allowing the Holy Spirit to intercede for us when we do not know how to pray. (Read Romans 8:26.) A language unknown to our natural minds, and not directed by our empirically oriented senses, is better suited for spiritual warfare than a limited vocabulary of natural words. Both as a regular part of your devotions each day and in times of focused battle, pray with your spiritual language.

Our planet does live under the control and "power of the evil one" (Eph. 2:2; 1 John 5:19), but he will be brought to final judgment and cast forever into the "lake of fire" (Rev. 20:10). The ending of the story has already been told. Our struggle on earth merely turns the pages toward that end. There are still casualties, and the overall picture is that of a war fought by a furious and desperate enemy who knows he has but "a short time" before lasting and total defeat (Rev. 12:12). He will be "crushed" by the Lord (Rom. 16:20), and Jesus, who had already seen "Satan fall from heaven" (Luke 10:18), "rendered powerless" the devil when He died on the cross and removed our vulnerability to all the barren brokenness of death (Heb. 2:14–15).

God's inexorable implementation of His plan is to have "all rule and all authority and power" subjugated to Jesus (1 Cor. 15:24–28), until that final great day when "every tongue" of every creature will declare Him Lord (Phil. 2:10–11). We are going where all human history is heading, to an already prepared victory banquet—and life without the slightest vestige of evil or death—in heaven. (Read John 14:2; Matthew 22:4; Revelation 19:9.) No matter what the nature of the forces seeking to hinder God's ultimate purposes in our lives—be they spirits, powers, death or any other created thing—we are assured of conquering them overwhelmingly through Jesus (Rom. 8:38–39).

As you grow in understanding from what you read in the Bible and what you learn from fellow believers, you will find yourself better able to discern and detect the nature of what assails you (2 Cor. 2:11; Heb. 5:14). Knowing your foe is helpful, but knowing what God has given to you is even more important. The Lord "trains [our] hands for war" (Ps. 144:1–2), and He uses us to tell others, "The kingdom of God has come near to you" (Luke 10:9), but He is always the One who fights for us, rather than us fighting for Him.

▲▲

Knowing your foe is helpful, but knowing what God has given to you is even more important.

▲▲

LET'S TALK ABOUT IT

▲ In what ways can the spiritual realm press into the natural world? As a result of reading this chapter, how has your thinking changed in terms of the various causes there are for how life turns out?

_____

_____

▲ What is the nature of evil? How does the Bible describe evil, compared with how Hollywood depicts it?

_____

_____

▲ What are the four basic categories of death-dealing, loss-bringing, hope-stealing evil the Bible presents us with?

_____

_____

For I am convinced that neither death, nor life, nor angels, nor principalities, nor things present, nor things to come, nor powers, nor height, nor depth, nor any other created thing, shall be able to separate us from the love of God, which is in Christ Jesus our Lord.
—Romans 8:38–39

. . . in order that no advantage be taken of us by Satan; for we are not ignorant of his schemes.
—2 Corinthians 2:11

Solid food is for the mature, who because of practice have their senses trained to discern good and evil.
—Hebrews 5:14

▲ Is it accurate to describe the conflict between good and evil as an equal battle between the devil and the Lord? Why or why not? What does it mean to have God as our Champion?

_____

_____

▲ We have been given several spiritual weapons with which to resist and defeat the forces of evil. To review some of those powerful tools, answer the following:

What does the name of Jesus enable us to do?

_____

_____

▲ Why is quoted Scripture so effective in the face of temptation and lies?

_____

_____

▲ What does it really mean to "fear the Lord"?

_____

_____

▲ How are worship and warfare linked together in the Bible?

_____

_____

▲ In what specific way does the Bible encourage us to resist the devil?

_____

_____

▲ The enemy will try to trap us with lies in our thoughts and situations to try to convince us that God is not who He says He is. Are there recurring lies or thought patterns that the enemy taunts you with? How can you use the weapons of spiritual warfare described in this chapter to fight against them?

_____

_____

YOUR TIME WITH GOD

In this chapter you have learned about our enemies—the formidable foursome we face in the *world*, the *flesh*, the *force of sin* and the *evil spirited*. Formidable, that is, except when confronted with the incredible, supernatural power that is available to us through the Holy Spirit and the armor of God. We do not have to fear that foursome—instead we can call upon our great God to fight for us and bring the victory. Prepare for spiritual battle—and for total victory—by praying this prayer:

> Lord Jesus, I lift up Your Name in my life. You are my righteousness and my strength. In You alone I find salvation and truth. I invite You to reign and rule in everything that concerns me. Thank You that in You I can find healing, provision and freedom from torment.
>
> Father God, thank You that there is nothing in the spiritual or natural world that is greater or more powerful than You. You are God Most High. You conquer any spiritual force that sets itself against me. Help me each day to be alert to resisting the enemy's plan for destruction in my life and the lives of others. Thank You that knowing You is the most important thing I can do to fight against the enemy.
>
> Help me, Lord, to keep trusting in You when it seems life is not working, to keep seeking Your kingdom and Your ways as my first priority. Help me to resist the lies that say You do not care or that You are not able to do anything about my painful places. With You, Lord, I am safe no matter how my flesh may tempt me, how the world may blind or dazzle me, how the evil spirited may oppose me or how sin may crouch at my door.
>
> Keep me, and teach me how to keep Your Word and way. In Your name, Jesus, I pray. Amen.

CHAPTER TWELVE

Loving and Forgiving Others

IN THIS CHAPTER YOU WILL LEARN . . .

▲ The distinguishing characteristic of believers in Jesus Christ.

▲ How to love unlovable people, and why loving people is connected with loving God.

▲ About the new commandment from Jesus.

▲ Why love is a choice of behaviors, not a feeling.

▲ How legalism destroys relationships.

▲ What forgiveness is — and is not.

▲ Why forgiveness is also a choice about people, not a feeling about them.

LIFE IS FULL OF DEDUCTIONS—NOT OF THE IRS VARIETY, BUT CONCLUSIONS WE COME TO ON THE BASIS OF LITTLE DETAILS WE SPOT IN PEOPLE AND THINGS AROUND US. When we notice the droopy, half-mast eyes of a three-year-old and the frozen moments in the midst of her play, we correctly surmise that it is time for a nap. The gaggle of geese heading north again gives us hope for hotter days not too long from now. A photo of a dark-eyed woman in a grass skirt was probably not, we guess, snapped in Iceland. Based on no more than the colors of their clothes, we know whether those three guys a few seats over from us at the football game will root with us or against us.

We can tell a lot from just a little. And we communicate volumes with the smallest snatches of words and actions.

That explains why most religions of the world ask their devotees to express their piety in little ways that set them apart from everyone else. It could be a ritual like daily prayer or a pilgrimage to a holy site, or an article of clothing such as a turban, a hidden garment or a saffron robe. Other religious observances take the form of a bodily emblem like a spot of ash or a tattoo, or of a strict dietary limitation—avoiding meat or fasting for designated periods. Within religious circles, the more advanced and devoted adherents are given special significations like titles, vestments or privileges—something that says to all around, "Here is a truly spiritual person; ask this one for wisdom."

Religious activities and symbols exhibited by a god's followers do more than just identify those people with their god. The religious exercises also declare something about the nature of that god in terms of which attributes it prizes most highly. Since a god can ask anything of its devotees, what it wants of them and how it wants them identified are clues to what the god is really like. Generally speaking, what is most true of a god is what the god longs to have be most true of its followers. They decree, "You shall be like me."

So what marks a believer in Jesus Christ? What are the telltale signals alerting everyone around us to the fact that we have surrendered our life to Him? Is it an article we are to put on like a cross? An item to carry with us wherever we go, like our Bible? A regular exercise like attending church each week? How will any except our closest friends and family know that we are disciples of Jesus? What is the most meaningful attribute that communicates not just the reality of our relationship with Him, but also what is most true of Him?

PROMINENT FEATURE IN THE MIRROR

Jesus, God's only begotten Son, gave His followers a very simple answer to that question: "Love one another, just as I have loved you" (John 15:12). He said, "By this all men will know that you are My disciples, if you have love for one another" (John 13:35). Not surprisingly, He wants us to be distinguished by exactly the same quality that most characterizes God Himself. As we have learned, "God is love" (1 John 4:16), and love is the key to all of His thoughts, words and actions throughout all time. He is the originator of love—"love is from God" (1 John 4:7). He has set His affections on us, and He wants us to communicate that same action toward others. Since love is God's most prominent feature, His children will bear that resemblance to Him.

Question: Why do you think people equate "being godly" with "being morally good," but not necessarily being very loving? When you imagine a truly spiritual person, do you think of a kind, gentle, loving individual—or something else?

_____

_____

Read 1 John 4:20–21. Is it sometimes easier to be "good" than it is to love people who are not necessarily lovable? Why does it seem easier to love God than to love people?

_____

_____

Read 1 John 4:16. What is it about God's love for you that enables you to believe it? How has He shown "proof" of His love? Is it possible for us to "prove" our love for others in a similar way?

_____

_____

Jesus explained to His disciples that the love with which He cherished them was a perfect copy of the love He had first received from His Father (John 15:9). He was like His Father in all ways; He manifested the glory, the radiance of God, so that in seeing

> Just as the Father has loved Me, I have also loved you; abide in My love.
>
> —John 15:9

And the Word became flesh, and dwelt among us, and we beheld His glory, glory as of the only begotten from the Father, full of grace and truth.
— John 1:14

And He is the radiance of His glory and the exact representation of His nature, and upholds all things by the word of His power.
— Hebrews 1:3

But when the kindness of God our Savior and His love for mankind appeared, He saved us.
— Titus 3:4–5

Now may our Lord Jesus Christ Himself and God our Father, who has loved us and given us eternal comfort and good hope by grace, comfort and strengthen your hearts in every good work and word.
— 2 Thessalonians 2:16–17

Jesus, people could see the Father (John 1:14; Heb. 1:3). The miracles Jesus performed and the teachings He shared were not His; the Father abiding in Him took the initiative and did them through Jesus. (Read John 5:30; 8:28; 12:49; 14:10.)

Even more than the miracles or the teachings, the primary reflection of God through Jesus was (and is) love. Jesus lived out the very patterns of grace, mercy and kindness—and desire for restored relationship—that were true of God's love for all mankind (Titus 3:4–5). On earth Jesus reflected the Father's love as a mirror duplicates the one who gazes into it. This simple truth has profound implications for each of us when it comes to manifesting the one true mark of a believer—loving others.

▲▲

On earth Jesus reflected the Father's love as a mirror duplicates the one who gazes into it.

▲▲

As with all other aspects of our life with the Lord, He does for us what we cannot do on our own. Even His commandment for us to love others is fulfilled by His grace doing the work. God wants to shine through us. He simply wants us to hold the mirror of our life up to Him so that it angles a clear reflection of His love to everyone around us. When we "see" someone in the mirror, it just means that the mirror is angled properly to return his or her reflection. Mirrors are not pictures—they are incapable of projecting an image of their own. So, one of the first secrets we learn about loving others "like" Jesus first loved us, is to do exactly that—imitate the manner and ways of His love.

LOVING WITH THE LOVE OF THE LORD

It is not as though we have to muster the capacity to love others from within ourselves. Rather, just as God loves us, so we (should) love others, or, put in more practical terms, how we love others will be a true reflection of what we claim to know about the comforting and hope-giving love from God (2 Thess. 2:16–17). Being recipients of Jesus' love, surrounded always by His favor and delight, gives us hope for being able to love others.

Although it takes practice, the principle for loving others as God loves us is fairly simple. When you find verses that describe any attribute of God's love for us, like these that follow, begin to "do" that quality to and for the people around you. Think of the "doings" as focused steps to follow. At the end of the trail, you will have loved others as Jesus loves you.

Read 2 Thessalonians 2:16–17. Can you see the specific acts of love in this passage—offer people comfort, give them hope and strengthen their hearts?

_____

_____

Read Ephesians 4:32. What are the three acts of love found in this verse? Can you put them in your own words?

_____

_____

Read Deuteronomy 7:7. What sort of people ought to draw your attention? Whom should you pick out in a group—the most or the least "popular"?

_____

_____

Read Deuteronomy 10:15. In this example, loving like the Lord is as simple as choosing someone around you to be loving toward. How can you engage in purposeful acts of love?

_____

_____

On our own we sometimes find it difficult to love the people around us. Individuals get on our nerves, do foolish and hurtful things to us, get in our way or act boorish, selfish and clueless. What's more, they have tempers, lusts, fears, agendas and hurts just like us. That is a volatile combination—others' stuff and ours do not mix well just as nitro and glycerin do not mix. So, how are we to love unlovable people who, like ourselves, have a great many rough edges and as yet unrefined qualities?

Natural love is generally a response to something about someone else—the way the person laughs, how thoughtful or clever that person is. We are attracted by their attractiveness, and we want to be with them because we want to be close to what we like about them. Conversely, if something about them bothers us—the nasal whine in their voice or the suffocating conceit of their self-centeredness—we do not want to be around them. Some people simply bug us, and we stumble over things in their life that are not the way we want them to be.

But that is not the way God loves—God loves us because of what is true about Him, not because of what is true about us. If He based His desire to be with us on how desirable we were while locked in our sin, we would still be estranged from Him. He did

> ▲ God loves us
> ▲ because of what
> ▲ is true about
> ▲ Him, not because
> ▲ of what is true
> ▲ about us.

But God demonstrates His own love toward us, in that while we were yet sinners, Christ died for us.

—Romans 5:8

not wait for us to be rid of all our bad things before He would love us; He loved us first by looking beyond our stuff when we were still sinners (Rom. 5:8). In His heart, He created a separation between us and our evil deeds so that He could remove the separation between us and Him.

WHAT'S WRONG?

The thought of loving certain people makes us recoil. Our natural reflex is to draw back, perhaps politely and without drawing a lot of attention to our snub of them, but determinedly to remove ourselves from having to be gracious, loving and kind to people we cannot tolerate. Our justification is that no one could like the person—he or she is obnoxious, bossy or strange. We even feel a bit discerning, able to spot the wrongs and distortions in the person's personality, character or lifestyle.

The catch is that God, who sees more than we do, has no difficulty whatsoever loving that person. Does He see the person's issues and the way he or she behaves? Absolutely! So, what enables Him to love the person in spite of the person? The answer is a bit unsettling, because it is so contrary to how we are used to thinking. God can easily love people (like us) with major issues and personality quirks—broken, malformed humans—because He Himself has no such issues.

"The Lord is one," we are told, meaning that He is complete, perfect, self-contained and whole without any missing parts (Deut. 6:4; Mark 12:29). In other words, there is nothing wrong with Him—"The Lord is [absolutely] righteous" (2 Chron. 12:6). That is why He can love anyone and everyone—there isn't anything wrong in Him to react unjustly to the wrong in people. He will judge the world, and He does set Himself in opposition to pride, sin and evil in the world. But that judgment is not unloving. He never loses sight of or affectionate interest in any person.

Would it surprise you to learn that the main reason we struggle with loving others is not so much because of the things that are wrong in them, as much as with what is carnal in us? Trusting them is another issue; so is foolishly ignoring toxic elements in their personality. But being able to love others comes mostly from rightness *in us*, rather than rightness *in them*. The more whole you become as a child of God, the better able you will be to love unlovable people.

Look at the following verses, and see the way they connect righteousness with spiritual attitudes of love:

Gracious is the Lord, and righteous; yes, our God is compassionate.
—Psalm 116:5

The Lord is righteous in all His ways, and kind in all His deeds.
—Psalm 145:17

If you ask the Lord to help you love people as He does, He will get to work almost immediately—adjusting your heart, mind, will and perspective.

As you and I grow in the Lord and experience His gracious love firsthand again and again, His love actually begins to imprint itself on our soul so that we become better and better able to actively love others. The healing we receive from our loving Father in heaven makes it easier to react to people and to embrace them the way God does instead of how we naturally would. It is almost like having our hearts turned into tracing paper—as they get laid down over the portrait of God's love, our hearts can then be pencil-marked and faintly sketched to increasingly resemble that image of His loving heart.

Few experiences on your journey with God are more exciting and satisfying than finding yourself reacting in supernatural love toward people from whom you would naturally recoil. The *after-the-fact* recognition of what just happened (or even better, the *right-in-the-middle-of-it-happening* realization) will cause you to celebrate—far more than you used to rejoice when those people left the room. It is a taste of the victory and transformation God is working in your soul. Nothing tastes quite as good as love.

THE NEW COMMANDMENT

On several occasions Jesus was asked to summarize what God longs for and what obedience to Him really entails. Jesus boiled it down to two basic commands—the two things that God cares most about, that most explain what He is like: "You shall love the Lord your God with all your heart, and with all your soul, and with all your mind, and with all your strength . . . You shall love your neighbor as yourself" (Mark 12:30–31). God wants loving relationship to be the foremost focus in our lives because it has always been the principle concentration in His! Everything about everything in the kingdom of God distills down to one tremendous truth—God wants all of His children to enjoy a happy, safe and fulfilling eternity, forever reconnected to His limitless and overflowing love.

Why does He link our loving Him with loving others? Is He like an exasperated carpool mom trying to handle an eternal drive with squirrely children fighting in the back of the van—"Can't you kids just get along?" Or does He know something about what it really means to love Him—something that we as humans would forget or choose to overlook? Jesus ties the two loves directly together, so much so that, as we have seen, no one can say they love God if they do not love other people. The real test of just how much we love God is in how able we are to love people.

So, Jesus said, "A new commandment I give to you, that you love one another, even as I have loved you, that you also love one

> ▲
> ▲ The real test of
> ▲ just how much we
> ▲ love God is in
> ▲ how able we are
> ▲ to love people.
> ▲

another" (John 13:34). This simple teaching was a fresh beginning place for all the things that the disciples would learn, a new foundation upon which all other spiritual truth would be based. It was a way to encapsulate the essence of maturity in His kingdom—the understanding that was to precede all knowledge, all ministry and all true significance on their journey of faith.

The danger for us as believers is to separate the truth of God from the love of God—when they are supposed to be one and the same thing. That is why the apostle Paul would later write about what it really means to be a significant spiritual person, informing us that whatever else we may know, say or do, if we do not have this kind of love, our words, actions and knowledge are empty as far as God is concerned:

> *If I speak with the tongues of men and of angels, but do not have love, I have become a noisy gong or a clanging cymbal. And if I have the gift of prophecy, and know all mysteries and all knowledge; and if I have all faith, so as to remove mountains, but do not have love, I am nothing. And if I give all my possessions to feed the poor, and if I deliver my body to be burned, but do not have love, it profits me nothing . . . For now we see in a mirror dimly, but then face to face; now I know in part, but then I shall know fully just as I also have been fully known. But now abide faith, hope, love, these three; but the greatest of these is love.*
> —1 CORINTHIANS 13:1–3, 12–13

It is the "new commandment" that freshly summarizes our calling as believers. "He who loves his neighbor has fulfilled the law" (Rom. 13:8). In other words, how God wants us to live in the midst of this broken world is not best understood as a long list of specific dos and don'ts, but as a heart of love that "does no wrong" to a neighbor (vv. 9–10). Love is proactive in behavior and positive in tone. The more that we come to love people with the same sort of love with which we have been loved by the Lord, the more spiritual we truly are.

The danger for us as believers is to separate the truth of God from the love of God.

Loving others is like a direction-giver sitting in the information booth in a hospital lobby; when you need to know what to think or do, loving God with your whole self *and* loving others like yourself will give you the best answers.

LOVE IN ACTION

Love, then, is to be the signifying mark of our spirituality—true maturity in Christ is measured by the degree to which we love other people. If such a love is to differentiate us from other people in the world and classify us as Jesus' disciples, it cannot be an invisible quality like an emotion or a feeling. Otherwise, no one could see it. And this fact, along with the relative impossibility of forcing ourselves to generate loving feelings for people whom we find unsavory, gives us a clue that the Lord is not talking about love as an internal emotional response, but as something outward and visible.

We are learning that love does stuff—it accomplishes things in our life and in the lives of others—it is active, resourceful and spiritually strong. More than we might imagine, it is the primary focus of God's work in and through our lives.

Read Romans 13:8. What is the only thing we should owe anyone?

_____

Read 1 Corinthians 8:1. What affects people the most (for the good), love or knowledge?

_____

Read 1 Corinthians 13:8. What is the quality that outlasts every other spiritual activity and quality?

_____

Read 1 Corinthians 16:14. What is the motive for everything we do in ministry?

_____

Read 1 Timothy 1:5. What is the goal of all teaching and doctrine? Is it fair to evaluate the quality of someone's teaching on the basis of how it helped us to love other people more?

_____

Loving others Jesus' way actually means doing things to and for them, more than feeling things about them. Spiritual love is a choice of actions, not the whim of emotions. It is how we deal with people, not how we feel toward them; love manifests itself in "deed and truth," not words (1 John 3:18). Spiritual love triggers "good deeds" and very particular behavior toward others (Heb. 10:24). That is how we knew Jesus loved us—"He laid down His life for us" (1 John 3:16).

> ▲ Love is to be the
> ▲ signifying mark of
> ▲ our spirituality—
> ▲ true maturity in
> ▲ Christ is measured
> ▲ by the degree to
> ▲ which we love
> ▲ other people.

Let love be without hypocrisy. Abhor what is evil; cling to what is good. Be devoted to one another in brotherly love; give preference to one another in honor.

— Romans 12:9–10

Walk in love, just as Christ also loved you, and gave Himself up for us, an offering and a sacrifice to God as a fragrant aroma.

— Ephesians 5:2

If He had only loved us from afar, with hopeful thoughts about our future or our condition, we would never have known it. He did something to make His love real, and we are to do the same— acting out our love for people.

For instance, when we give preference to others, putting their needs or concerns above our own, we are loving them (Rom. 12:9–10). "Preferring" can be acted out in several ways. It may be as simple as choosing to go to the end of the potluck line, or becoming known at your work as the one person who is always willing to fill in for someone when they have a family crisis or a need to switch work days. Such behavior gets noticed.

Managing to bear up under and put up with somebody's stinky attitude—long after they have been given up on by everybody else, "showing forbearance in love"—is another example of love in action (Eph. 4:2). So is any decision to disadvantage yourself for the sake of another person—like selecting the smallest piece of pie, offering to stay after the event to clean up or volunteering to drive someone home even though they live out of your way (Eph. 5:2).

Not all love actions are sacrificial in nature. Think of just a few of the things God does for us because of His love, and you begin to get an idea of how joyous and fulfilling it is to love others:

▲ Extending mercy to people who do not deserve it (Read Ephesians 2:4.)
▲ Creating a place that meets the needs and aspirations of others (Read Genesis 1.)
▲ Treating strangers like part of the family (Read 1 John 3:1.)
▲ Performing acts of kindness (Read Titus 3:4.)
▲ Rescuing others out of tight or awkward situations (Read Deuteronomy 7:8.)
▲ Promoting and believing in others—even when they are untried (Read 2 Chronicles 9:8.)
▲ Being invitingly kind, and thereby drawing people in from a distance (Read Jeremiah 31:3.)

The more we mirror God's loving behavior toward us by how we treat and deal with people around us, the more we will reflect His love to them. Seeing how we are toward them gives them a beginning understanding of how God feels about them. As an invisible God who shuns any idol or any attempt by His followers to create a material representation of Him in stone, wood or precious metal, the Lord relies on us to be His portrait to a lost world.

How grievous it must be to Him to have His followers mostly known throughout the world as the people who tell everyone how wrong or bad they are. The church sometimes stands closer to the Pharisees than it does to the sinners, and members of the body of Christ are capable of having a better memory for wrongs suffered than many baseball enthusiasts have for batting averages. When we become more feared as the *confronters* than sought out as the *consolers*, noted as the finger-pointers instead of the hand-holders, then we have given the name of the Lord a bum rap.

Such an understanding leads us to one of the most essential ingredients in our love for others—the aspect of God's love that is the most responsible for securing our relationship with Him. In the mirror of our life, our friends and acquaintances are supposed to see *loving forgiveness.* It should be the single most prominent feature of our dealings with all other human beings. Without that feature, we present a distorted message to the world—a message that is exactly opposite to the one we cherish so dearly for ourselves.

AVOIDING LEGALISM

In giving us His all-purpose commandment—to love one another—Jesus was correcting a misconception that many religious people have. Religion says that our main job is to believe and do the correct things, to get and stay "right." The problem with such thinking is that it produces self-righteousness and condemnation. After all, self-righteousness is just the flip side of condemnation, only we feel good about how "right" we have been able to be. Evaluating ourselves according to a goodness/badness scale, we alternately feel good or bad about ourselves.

That is what we call *legalism*—the lie that says our relationship and attachment with God is based on our performance, that we must earn or maintain our standing with Him according to rules, codes and minimal expectations, that His welcome of and interest in us wanes with every wrong choice we make. Legalism squashes our heart and joy because it creates an unemotional, impersonal connection with God. Instead of being the apples of His eye, the children in whom He delights, the ones He calls by name unto future destiny, we end up as "anyones" and "everyones" who either make the grade or fail the test.

Indeed, when the issue of right and wrong becomes the primary concern, relationship with God, as well as with other people, gets subjected to how right or wrong we and others are. Legalism says relationship must wait until after evaluation. Depending on how well we have done on the test of the day (for example, how well we controlled our anger toward the kids), or how many spiritual reps (such as prayer, Bible reading, serving in Sunday school) we completed, we mark our standing and progress with God. It makes God's love and

> Loving forgiveness should be the single most prominent feature of our dealings with all other human beings.

acceptance conditional on our ability to be good and righteous.

The early church struggled with the issue of legalism, too. Because there is such a thing as right and wrong, sincere people like us will do our best to choose right over wrong. That is OK as long as we never let our choice of behavior become the basis for our standing with the Lord. He made His choice long ago to forgive all of our wrong choices so that He could have us with Him for eternity.

Read Galatians 5:4–6. The Law was a list of dos and don'ts. Circumcision was a physical acknowledgment that someone had received the list and that he was going to live according to it. Why, then, does circumcision not matter for believers in Christ?

_____

_____

What does matter for us and our spiritual life?

_____

_____

In an effort to live the way the Lord wants us to live, we can slip into a tyranny of trying to live up to His expectations—doing good and behaving well on our own strength. Though it is sincerely motivated, it is deadly to us—and to the other people whom we put under the same yoke of expectation. Living according to rules and regulations subjects us again to the very yoke from which Jesus set us free. That is deadly enough for our own relationship with the Lord, because we will perpetually come up short in our performance and mistakenly conclude that God would rather not have us around Him until we can live better and more righteously than we have managed thus far.

Additionally, legalistic thinking concludes that we should do what we can to help others get it right, too. The more *right* (spell that *m-a-t-u-r-e*) we become, religion promises, the better able we will be to see where other people are wrong. Everything ends up being a judgment—assessing how good or bad, how right or wrong other people are, and then sentencing them to some sort of imprisonment (a missed opportunity, lost relationship) or some sort of rewarding increase (ministry significance, closer relationship).

A UNIFORM STANDARD

All such judgments destroy relationship, coming between others and us. We judge other people as we judge ourselves—except we tend to accept our personal justifications for wrongdoing more so than we have patience with the sins of others. Being officer, judge, jury and warden in our own cases means that we tolerate far more in ourselves than we do in others. Or, at least, we rarely surprise ourselves with our own failures. Given our (internally) well-known tendencies and sinful past, we treat ourselves with a mixture of familiarity, disgust and pity, much like the town drunk is given a cell in which to sleep it off.

But when it comes to the really big stuff we do wrong, or when we visualize ourselves brought before the court of heaven, we realize we cannot fix our indiscretions as though they are parking violations in a small town where the clerk is an old school buddy. When our guilt is a foregone conclusion, and when a severe sentence stares us in the face, we drop all strategies for our defense and frantically put our hope in mercy. When we are really desperate, we seek forgiveness as the only means of salvation.

> We cannot have one attitude when we need forgiveness from others and the opposite attitude when others need it from us.

In financial terms, it's called *personal bankruptcy*—an acknowledged inability to satisfy the creditors, owing more than we have any possibility of repaying. Owing lots of money is very different than being owed lots of money. We have exactly opposite feelings in each instance. Jesus used that contrast to teach His disciples about how forgiveness works in the spiritual dimension.

He tells the story of a worker who owed his boss over ten million dollars, and who pleaded for more time in which to pay it off. (Read Matthew 18:23–35.) Instead of granting an extension on the loan, the boss wiped it off the books—completely. Shortly after this, the worker considered his new financial situation, realized a coworker owed him just under ten thousand dollars and demanded instant repayment.

All the other workers, who had been so amazed and happy for their friend when he had told them of the forgiven ten million, were shocked by his unforgiveness toward ten thousand. They informed the boss, who changed his earlier decision to eliminate the debt in order to match the worker's decision not to eliminate debt.

Jesus' point? We cannot have one attitude when we need forgiveness from others and the opposite attitude when others need it from us. That is why He teaches us to pray, "Forgive us as we forgive others" (Luke 11:4), and why He urges us to be merciful, just as God is merciful (Luke 6:36). Instead of allowing us to be thrown into debtors' prison, the Lord moved in after we declared

> Be merciful, just as your Father is merciful.
> —Luke 6:36

spiritual bankruptcy, and He paid off all our obligations. Based on what Jesus paid on the cross, the Father considers our debt paid in full. And we love that. "Thank God," we exclaim, "for forgiveness!" Without it, all would be lost.

CHOOSING TO FORGIVE

Forgiveness is one of the most significant action statements love ever makes. The compelling love of God sent His Son into the world as the means by which forgiveness was made possible for us all (John 3:16). He is a righteous, perfectly *right* God, but if the Lord had simply maintained His *rightness* and pointed out our *wrongness* without doing anything to forgive us, He would have spent eternity alone, without us. In a cosmos where there is a difference between right and wrong, between light and darkness, the two will always be opposite one another. They can never meet in agreement or join together.

That was the dilemma of God's love. That was the heartbreak of Adam's sin—introducing into God's creation the polar opposite of right. God knew from that point on that the wrong choices and doings of humanity would be a given element, a constant variable in the world. Having a choice between good and evil, we His people would often choose poorly. That left God with but one choice—forgive the sin or forget the relationship.

In our dealings with other people, we have the same choice. It doesn't work to have a relationship with someone *and* with their sin. We will relate to them either on the basis of who they are as a person *or* on the basis of what they have done to offend us. If not taken out of the picture, the wrong they did soon becomes the most prominent feature of who they are to us, and we inadvertently transfer our relationship from the person to the crime they have committed against us. Usually the transfer is unconscious on our part; we do not necessarily intend to cut off relationship with the person so that we can focus on the wrong done to us. But it happens.

Over the course of your life, you can see how offenses against you have locked up your relationship with various people. The more significant and painful the deeds or the remarks were, the more they overshadow your entire picture of those people. Indeed, those offenses upon which we dwell actually enlarge and become more consuming of all our thoughts. The little things that we overlook were not that painful or consequential, and that is why they slip unnoticed from our consciousness. But the big things—those jabbing, devastating words and actions that have crashed into our lives—loom in front of us and draw our thoughts to themselves with an incredible, almost irresistible magnetism.

For God so loved the world, that He gave His only begotten Son, that whoever believes in Him should not perish, but have eternal life.

—John 3:16

Like a giant black hole in space, the gravity of the transgressions against us sucks everything else into itself. Forgiveness is the only force powerful enough to counteract the offensive gravity and cause the black hole to collapse in on itself. Whereas our culture views forgiveness as a meek, though noble, afterthought to some terrible happening in your life, it is actually one of the most potent and impressive powers in all creation. It can lift victims above and beyond what was done to them, and it amazes their offenders.

God created the cosmos in such a way that love and forgiveness could always outweigh the heaviness of sin; mercy could always triumph over guilt. He did not want to surrender His loving intentions for us by allowing our sins to have the ultimate and determining influence in the cosmos. Forgiveness was His provision to assure that love could always have the final word.

Forgiveness is extraordinary and striking, and it leaves an unmistakably Godlike imprint on others. Because we live among people like ourselves who have been broken by sin, we will have many occasions on which to display this incredible characteristic of God to those around us. Intentionally and unintentionally, people will hurt us with their words and actions. They will disappoint us, betray us, oppose us, take us for granted, slander us and offend us. When the inevitable happens, what will we do? The Lord's hope for us is that we will choose to do what He chose to do—forgive.

FORGIVENESS IN ACTION

Until we understand what forgiveness is—and is not—it is very hard to decide whether or not we want to forgive others. In fact, it is probably our misunderstanding about what forgiveness entails that makes it harder to want to forgive someone. Forgiveness is a hard choice; it goes against every natural grain in our being. But the work of God's Spirit in us moves us steadily in that direction, miraculously and wondrously.

One of the lessons we have been learning is that our concept of most kingdom words is slightly off. God usually means something different than we do. Such is the case with forgiveness. Because it has been poorly defined—at least in practical terms—most of us struggle unnecessarily to answer the simple question, "What does it mean to forgive someone?" After choosing to forgive, we get confused by our residual feelings of hurt, and we wrongly conclude that we must not have really forgiven—or we wouldn't still ache inside.

Like real love, forgiveness is a choice of how to behave toward and relate to someone who has offended you. It is not a choice of how to feel as a result of what was done. Long before the throbbing in your fingers subsides, you can forgive the inattention of a friend who slammed the car door on them. Forgiving your friend will not reduce the swelling or the pain in your hand. Likewise, you can remain mad at your friend long after the pain disappears.

Forgiveness is not a feeling, nor is it necessarily tied to your feelings. It is a decision about what you want to have happen to someone who has hurt you. Do you want them to pay a penalty—of the same magnitude as your pain—or do you release them from the consequences they justly deserve?

> Forgiveness is a decision about what you want to have happen to someone who has hurt you.

Question: Sometimes the best way to understand the meaning of a spiritual term is to see it used in a nonreligious context, then transfer the word picture back into our spiritual vocabulary. Take the word *aphiemi, forgiveness* ("leaving or discharging something, cutting it loose"). This same word (shown in italics) is used in the following verses. Read the verses and try the exercise. Then explain in your own words what each verse tells you about what it means to forgive others' sins.

"And they immediately *left* the nets and followed Him" (Mark 1:18).

_____

_____

"But Jesus said, '*Let* her *alone*; why do you bother her? She has done a good deed to Me'" (Mark 14:6).

_____

_____

"And standing over her, He rebuked the fever, and it *left* her; and she immediately arose and waited on them" (Luke 4:39).

_____

_____

"He who had died came forth, bound hand and foot with wrappings; and his face was wrapped around with a cloth. Jesus said to them, 'Unbind him, and *let* him *go*'" (John 11:44).

_____

_____

"And a woman who has an unbelieving husband, and he consents to live with her, let her not *send* her husband away" (1 Cor. 7:13).

_____

_____

The New Testament term for *forgiveness* essentially means to separate yourself from something by: 1) sending it away—just as you throw away an unwanted credit card offer or shoot an arrow; or 2) leaving it behind—as you pass a slow-moving car or disconnect a caboose from a train. Simply put, forgiveness is the choice to separate a guilty person from the punishment their guilt deserves. Instead of saying, "Because of what you did, this is what is going to be done to you," forgiveness declares, "I discharge you from what you deserve to have happen to you; I release you to the Lord's keeping."

As much as all humans may protest their innocence, deep down we know we are guilty of mistreating, betraying and violating others. We know what punishment guilt deserves, so we try to convince everyone (especially ourselves) that we are not guilty. That is why forgiveness is so striking, why it stands out in such relief against the natural backdrop, why it marks us as Jesus' followers. Forgiveness bypasses people's denial; it grants them a peace-filled resolution they could not achieve by defending themselves.

> Forgiveness is the choice to separate a guilty person from the punishment their guilt deserves.

FORGIVENESS UNDEFINED

Because the natural world does not understand the nature of true forgiveness, it has come up with several forms of pseudo-forgiveness—ways of handling wrongs committed against us. But they do not work. They do not let us experience the total release God has in mind for us when we forgive those who have violated us. Forgiveness is profoundly spiritual, and God intends it to accomplish things in our lives, as well as in the lives of those who have offended us. What the world calls forgiveness is not what the Lord calls forgiveness. The world's perspective on forgiveness makes it small, unfulfilling and pathetic. The more we understand the majestic truth of forgiveness, the more we will want to do it as an act of love.

God is not trying to disadvantage His kids, but to advantage them. He does not want us to forgive so that we can be taken advantage of or endangered by others. He is not wanting us to prove something—such as we really are sincere Christians—by being willing to go through with a terrible experience. He wants us to forgive because it is so life giving and liberating for everyone involved.

WHAT FORGIVENESS IS NOT

The world has come up with counterfeits to true forgiveness, and those false concepts of forgiveness make it very hard for us to want to forgive. Our willingness to forgive other people the way that the Lord has forgiven us can be stymied from any one of several misconceptions about the nature of true forgiveness. The better you understand the difference between what God longs to have us extend to others and what our culture and fears offer to us in the name of forgiveness, the easier it will be to manifest this marvelous and life-giving spiritual characteristic. Here are some differences between true forgiveness and a few of the world's concepts about it:

Forgiveness is not the spiritual version of denial—claiming that something never occurred (or at least not that often), or that what the person did to you was "no big deal." It was a big deal, and that is why you are having such a hard time dealing with it. Trying to convince yourself that their offense was small only succeeds in making you feel petty for being pained by it.

Forgiveness is not saying what they did was OK or that you brought it on yourself or that you probably should not have been hurt by it in the first place. To say such things in the name of forgiveness only worsens matters because it introduces more confusion to an already bewildering turn of events by trying to put the blame on yourself. It won't add up, and you will end up feeling guilty for the hurt you feel.

Forgiveness is not justifying, excusing or explaining away an offense in an unhealthy, codependent "covering for" another person. By saying it was not their fault, you are left with a fatalistic sense of helplessness in an impersonal cosmos where "stuff" just happens; if you cannot blame people, you will bitterly or numbly blame fate ("That's life") or God ("Why didn't You keep it from happening?").

Forgiveness is not "getting beyond" the ache someone caused in your heart. Equating forgiveness with being over the pain created by what someone did to you adds insult to injury; you cannot dictate the level of pain you feel. (That's why we have aspirin for the body.) What makes forgiveness so impressive is the choice to forgive despite the pain that shreds your heart.

Forgiveness is not a willingness to keep entrusting yourself to an abusive, untrustworthy person who has hurt you. David kept away from his abuser, Saul, but chose not to take his own revenge when he could have. Trust is built up over time—and it is earned by what people do. Forgiveness is granted in spite of what they have done. Without seeing demonstrated change in their behavior, it is foolishness, not forgiveness, to put ourselves in the hands of those who have a pattern of violating us.

False notions about forgiveness tend to fall in one of two categories: 1) making you feel unsafe or 2) making you feel crazy.

Counterfeit forgiveness suggests that you must become (remain) vulnerable to repeated offenses.

"If you really forgive someone, you should be willing to forget the past, wipe the slate clean and not try to protect yourself against further abuse." That is a classic line used by (to name just a few) abusive husbands, unrepentant substance abusers and other individuals who want to put a legalistic load on the very people they have violated.

Forgiveness releases the violator from punishment; it does not put the violated person under bondage to remain vulnerable in the future. Jesus tells us to "turn the other cheek"—not as a command to keep being taken advantage of by the same person over and over—but as a command to not try balancing the scales of justice ("an eye for an eye") by seeking our own revenge (Matt. 5:38–39).

Pseudo-forgiveness leaves you with the impression that you should not be as hurt as you are by what was done to you.

"Can't you just forgive and forget and get past what happened? Why is it (still) such a big deal to you?" Once again, this puts the burden back onto the violated individuals and questions their integrity or their character, as though they are not trying hard enough to "be better" or were making too big a deal over such a small offense.

People who need your forgiveness deserve the execution of your judgment. They do not need your pardon unless they committed a crime against you. Anything that underrates the severity of the offense or tries to minimize its grievous aftermath in your life is not forgiveness.

SUPERNATURAL AFTERGLOW

Forgiveness is a complete "leaving behind" of the wrongs done against you by people. The hurt may remain; the consequences might still be in your life. But if you are still focused on the people who committed the wrongs, how bad they are and what they deserve to have happen to them ("I wish you could feel what it is like . . . "), you have not completely forgiven them.

This is where Scripture can be so helpful. When Jesus was being crucified, He spoke His forgiveness aloud. If you can repeat His words (aloud) while thinking about those who have wounded you, you can be assured that you have forgiven them. Jesus said, "Father, forgive them; for they do not know what they are doing" (Luke 23:34).

On the other hand, forgiveness is predicated on a full and final verdict of "Guilty," but it chooses to release the person from the punishment that should follow the verdict. Probably because we do not want to "judge" others, we resist an appropriate evaluation of what was done to us and try to make all sorts of excuses for why people did what they did. But you cannot forgive "innocent" people. That is like trying to solve a misprinted algebra equation in a high school textbook—you are left feeling there must be something wrong with you for not being able to solve it.

Forgiveness is unnatural. Our survival instincts and our sense of justice argue against it. We want our revenge—though we love to camouflage that raw passion in the language of fairness. Letting go of what happened to us feels like letting the person "get away with" what they did. And that doesn't seem right. We don't feel that we can be "done with" what they did to us until we get some guarantee that they will never do it again. We want things made right. We want to settle accounts for our ten thousand dollars in order to balance the books.

But the Lord says that wrongs cannot be made right or sensible in the limited arena of this world. In the final analysis, the only explanation for why people like us do what we do to violate others is found in the given reality of *wrong* as a choice in life and the fact that though God made people upright, we have "sought out many [evil] devices" (Eccles. 7:29). He, like us, wants things made right, so He has fashioned forgiveness, a most extraordinary and unnatural device for us to seek—and extend.

When forgiveness is granted—no matter by whom—it permanently rights a wrong and rustles the dusky dimness of the air we breathe with a shimmer of brightness in the likeness of the one true God.

> Forgiveness permanently rights a wrong and rustles the dusky dimness of the air we breathe with a shimmer of brightness in the likeness of the one true God.

LET'S TALK ABOUT IT

▲ How has your definition of a "truly spiritual" person changed as a result of reading this chapter?

_____

_____

▲ Why is loving people connected with loving God? Why do we have trouble loving unlovable people?

_____

_____

▲ Put into your own words why love is a choice of behaviors and not a feeling. Can you think of some practical ways you can begin to love others?

_____

_____

▲ What is the *new commandment?* In what way is it supposed to be the basis for everything we learn on our journey with the Lord?

_____

_____

▲ How would you define legalism? What is its telltale characteristic—on whom does it put the burden for sustaining relationship with God?

_____

_____

▲ Why does Jesus teach us to pray, "Forgive us as we forgive others"? Why does Jesus urge us to be merciful as God is merciful?

_____

_____

▲ True forgiveness is a choice of how to behave toward someone who has offended you. Forgiveness is a decision about what you want to happen to someone who has hurt you. Are there people whom you have not forgiven?

_____

_____

▲ What are some differences between true forgiveness and a few of the world's concepts about it? Which examples of false forgiveness have made you hesitate to forgive others?

_____

_____

▲ How is your thinking about forgiveness now different from what it was before reading this chapter?

_____

_____

YOUR TIME WITH GOD

Loving others Jesus' way involves doing things to and for them. Spiritual love is a choice of actions. It is how we deal with people, not how we feel toward them. Think of a few things God has done for you because of His love, and you will begin to get the idea of how fulfilling it is to love others.

Are there times you have mistreated, betrayed or violated others? Ask for their forgiveness after you forgive yourself. Ask God to begin a process of restoration in you. Perhaps the following prayer will help you to begin that process today:

I am thankful that You love me, Lord, and that I can be an expression of Your love to other people. Because of how You have loved me—and how You do love me—I want to learn better how to do the same with the people in my life. My love for others has its very foundation in Your love for me. With each kind word, with each loving thought, I am fulfilling a sacred trust to hold others in the light of Your love, reflecting what is true of You.

Your love is so powerful that it heals my hurt before it moves out from me as forgiveness toward others. Thank You, Father, for the compassion and understanding to forgive myself and to forgive others. I acknowledge Your presence within me and Your claim on my days. I want to radiate Your love, mercy and forgiveness to others.

Lord, I want to acknowledge how difficult it is sometimes to love and forgive people. Help me with places where I hurt and that are broken in me, both from the things I have done and those things that have been done to me. Heal those areas in my life. Lord, I do not want to hold others bound by not forgiving them. I willingly choose to release them because of their actions toward me.

Help me, God, to see daily opportunities in my life to show my love for others. Thank You that through my actions others can see the love You have for them. In Jesus' name, amen.

CHAPTER THIRTEEN

Being Recovered From Evil

A NYONE WHO HAS HAD A SERIOUS BOUT WITH FOOD POISONING CAN TELL YOU EXACTLY WHEN AND WHERE IT STRUCK—AND THEIR WELL-FOUNDED SUSPICIONS ABOUT WHICH FOOD CAUSED IT. The symptoms of food poisoning appear suddenly, unlike those of the flu. The gurgling, protesting stomach unmistakably announces that something is terribly, terribly wrong. While the body concentrates on ridding itself of the poisonous bacteria we unknowingly put into it, the rest of our life gets very small. We lie there like ship-wrecked sailors in the surf, waiting for the next wave of nausea (and worse) to toss our frail frame around. Our thoughts turn delirious—having once worried that we might die from the food poisoning, we begin to fear that we won't.

Everyone with food poisoning wishes they had never eaten the tainted food—no cream-topped desserts, no canned tomatoes, no beefy burgers are worth what follows if E. coli or salmonella organisms invade our bodies. *Why weren't we more careful in handling the leftovers or identifying the mushrooms? We should have cooked the meat longer.* The list of regrets gets repeated over and over as the one focal point of our tortured awareness. But there is no turning back the clock. Like tourists who accidentally boarded the wrong bus, we have to ride until it stops along its usual route.

Living through an assault of botulism is no one's idea of living. A living death can sometimes feel the same as a dying life. Some sicknesses lead to the end of people's lives on earth, but most sickness just makes earthly life more miserable. That is why we can say that sickness is a shade of death—just as lilac is of purple—because when our body is sick, something is *wrong* with the way it is working. *Death,* as the Bible defines it, is life *other than* how God intended it to be. Death in any form is the antithesis of God's way of life—it is antilife. Death degrades and violates and shrinks down everything that God has declared "very, very good" (Gen. 1:31). As a readout of evil, death's only interest is to vandalize and blight what is good.

In fact, one of the best ways to grasp the full implications of unrighteousness (evil) is simply to shorten it to *unrightness*—the

IN THIS CHAPTER YOU WILL LEARN . . .

▲ How evil and death distort God's intended order for all life.

▲ That you are comprised of body, soul and spirit.

▲ Why your body and soul are subject to affliction and assault by evil.

▲ About God's heart to recover and deliver you from every devilish bond.

▲ A balanced and hopeful perspective on the ministry of deliverance.

▲ How to walk in the freedom with which Jesus sets you free.

symptoms, the early cramping in the stomach, the "uh-oh-I've-got-a-very-bad-feeling that something is not right, and it's only going to get worse." Whereas the Lord and His righteousness want to increase and add to our lives—to bring more bounty, greater satisfaction, more joy—evil and unrighteousness want to do the opposite.

Since that first choice of our race to sin so very long ago, all people have been living out a life filled with numerous manifestations of evil. Relationships go wrong; people say and do miscalculated things that have terrible consequences in the lives of others. People suffer breakdowns and psycho/emotive disorders. Deathly things lead to loss—we lose our health, our business, our friends, our minds, our hope. Like an unpredictable tornado, evil and death have gathered their funnel clouds in the air and touched down at many points in our lives, leaving a swath of wreckage and confusion behind.

We are like people caught in a flood who have scrambled to the steeply sloping roof of our house to escape drowning in the rushing water. That roof is like the *world*—permanently angled and tilted dangerously toward the floodwaters. The *force of sin*, acting like gravity, relentlessly pulls us downward. Of course, our *flesh*—always wanting the easiest path of the least resistance—leans that direction anyway. Rounding out the picture of our lives here on the earth are the *evil spirited*—unseen forces that we don't think much about, like sudden blasts of wind knocking us off our feet.

Regardless of the form it takes, evil is toxic and destructive to human beings like a corrosive substance—a "corruption"—that erodes whom God designed us to be and that steals away the life He wants us to enjoy (2 Pet. 1:4).

Read Psalm 107:10–11. Why do people sometimes end up in miserable circumstances?

_____

_____

Read 2 Peter 2:19. If someone is constantly overcome by a sin, and it keeps getting worse and worse, what might have happened to him or her?

_____

_____

Read John 10:10. Put into your own words the three telltale indicators of satanic activity in people's lives.

_____

_____

It is no mere play on words to realize that life and death were never meant to go together. And it is no surprise to you to learn that various kinds of evil have impacted your life. In order to understand how evil can affect us so deeply and so permanently, we must learn a few facts about who and what we are. In other words, how did God intend us to be? Of what are we comprised?

BODY, SOUL AND SPIRIT

Though our natural language is ill-suited to adequately describe the components of our being as they were created by God to function, we can at least get a basic understanding of who we are in the Lord—and how we are assaulted by evil. In addition to your body, there are two other parts to who you are as an individual. You are made of "spirit and soul and body," and God wants them all guarded from loss or injury—"preserved complete" (1 Thess. 5:23). He longs to restore whatever ruin the forces of evil have already managed to cause in you. Deep in your innermost being, your "soul and spirit" connect to one another (Heb. 4:12).

Our bodies are rather obvious, and we do not need much additional understanding about them from a biblical point of view—other than to realize that all evil forces want to turn our flesh into an "instrument of unrighteousness" (Rom. 6:13). The other two aspects of our being, on the other hand, are less distinct and apparent to us. Even though they are used somewhat interchangeably both in the Scriptures and in our culture, the terms *soul* and *spirit* are not synonymous.

Your *soul* (*psyche* in Greek, from which we get our word *psych*ology) is essentially your consciousness—your mind, will, emotions and basic awareness in the natural world. The Greeks used the word for our "inner life" that moves us to live as we do—just as breathing animates a living body. Your *spirit* (*pneuma* in Greek, used in words like *pneum*onia) is a bit harder to define because it relates exclusively to the unseen, spiritual world where the Holy Spirit takes up His abode in your heart (Gal. 4:6). Whereas soul is like the air that people breathe, spirit is like wind that blows the air. The body is enlivened by the soul; the soul is animated by the spirit.

Unlike your liver and pancreas, neither your soul nor your spirit has an exact location in your body because they are not tangible parts of you. But like your internal organs, they (especially the soul) can become afflicted and unwell. *Sin*, ours and others', can leave deep scars across your soul. Broken edges from this derelict *world* can jab straight into even the most guarded places in your heart and mind. Your *flesh* can become so persistently demanding

And because you are sons, God has sent forth the Spirit of His Son into our hearts.
— Galatians 4:6

that you become captive to its addictions. Sometimes there are physiological or chemical reasons why *psych*ological disorders disrupt people's God-intended personality. But most often, the culprits for emotional and mental ailments—whether large or small—are those forces of burglary and ruin we are calling the *evil spirited*. They are like spiritual viruses and toxins that permeate the atmosphere of this life.

Just as our physical frame can come under attack from germs, toxins or injury, so too can the other, inner parts of our life. We have been made in God's image—intimately fashioned by Him personally. (Read Psalm 139:1–18.) We have, therefore, God-given and God-intended attributes that are designed to be part of His assignment and calling in our lives. Contrary to what our culture teaches us, we do not just happen to turn out the way we are purely as a result of natural heredity, the environment and chance.

Read the following verses. What do they tell you about when God formed His plans for your life? Do you think God fashioned you uniquely to fulfill His calling on your life? What would be the best way for the enemy to ruin or diminish your ability to fulfill God's intended desire for your life?

Jeremiah 1:5

_____

_____

Galatians 1:15

_____

_____

Jeremiah 29:11

_____

_____

> But by the grace of God I am what I am, and His grace toward me did not prove vain; but I labored even more than all of them, yet not I, but the grace of God with me.
> —1 Corinthians 15:10

We are what we (truly) are in our soul by the grace of God (1 Cor. 15:10). We are His masterpieces—poems He has rhymed and metered with precise beauty—and He fashioned us for accomplishing many good (as opposed to evil) works that He prepared, long ago, for us to participate in (Eph. 2:10). Since all evil sets itself in opposition to the will of God, evil forces will seek to defy and violate the Lord's plan for and work in your life. It is here, at the very core of your God-given personality, that the *evil spirited* mount their fiercest assault.

> For we are His workmanship, created in Christ Jesus for good works, which God prepared beforehand, that we should walk in them.
> —Ephesians 2:10

By erasing lines God has composed, or by rewriting the stanzas of our being, the *evil spirited* work to cripple our spiritual life and afflict our inner self with disorder, dismay and despair. The *evil spirited* supplant the beautifully lilting words of life and truth that were breathed by our Creator into our soul, and they try to replace them with choppy, guttural syllables without rhyme or meaning. Instead of being poems of rare beauty and distinction, we lose more and more of our words. They become disordered on the page, and we end up as cryptic, broken verses that are nearly impossible to understand—and that only faintly bear resemblance to the original poems composed by the Lord.

We know that the *evil spirited* are not the only death-dealing force to reckon with, but in combination with the tilted *world,* *sinful* temptations and the leaning of our own *flesh,* demonic forces do radically affect our lives—much more than most people choose to believe. We will see why and how the enemy of our soul wants to deflect attention away from the insidious assaults he mounts against God's children. But even more importantly, we will see how the Lord has made provision for us to resist those attacks and how to recover from any previous damage caused by them. Jesus offers us deliverance from the *evil spirited* and the unique nature of their attack on us.

BALANCED PERSPECTIVE

Because our Western culture argues so strenuously against anything in the spiritual dimension, and because some Christians become too mystical and sensational in their preoccupation with demonic influences, there is not much balanced teaching in the church at large about the deliverance Jesus wants us to have from the "rulers and authorities in heavenly places" (Eph. 3:10). The church tends to give them either too much or too little thought; Christians seem either afraid of or fanatical about the *evil spirited.*

Even though we are not supposed to be "ignorant of his [the devil's] schemes" (2 Cor. 2:11), the body of Christ has tended to relegate information about the *evil spirited* to the periphery of our doctrine. The lack of straightforward teaching on this subject has allowed all sorts of superstition and speculation to obscure the simple, powerful truth of Jesus' triumph on the cross—and what that can mean to each of us for personal freedom.

Interestingly, the Bible is fairly matter-of-fact about the *evil spirited*—not in terms of the hurt and harm they can bring, but more in the sense of what they are, what they do and how Jesus has already triumphed over them. Even the most cursory reading of the New Testament, especially the Gospels, reveals that the Lord cures spiritual ailments as frequently as physical illnesses. (Read Matthew 10:1; Luke 7:21; Acts 8:7.) Some physical infirmities are actually caused by demonic spirits. (Read Luke 13:11; Acts 19:12.)

▲ Jesus offers us
▲ deliverance from
▲ the *evil spirited*
▲ and the unique
▲ nature of their
▲ attack on us.

As we have been seeing over and over, there are several forces of evil against which we must contend as Christians, and no discussion of the *evil spirited* should ever remove from us the responsibility to resist the impulses of our own carnal nature. We must always consider ourselves "dead to [the desires of] sin but alive [responsive] to God" (Rom. 6:11). We must daily "crucify the flesh" (Gal. 5:24) and "make no provision" for its lusts in our life (Rom. 13:14). To glibly declare, "The devil made me do it," is to give ourselves too little responsibility and to give our enemy too much credit. In their zeal or in their foolishness, sincere Christians can blame too many of their conflicts on the unseen and not take enough personal responsibility for their own behavior.

Part of the reason that people get confused about which kind of evil is assaulting them is because all evil is bent on the same purpose and ultimately brings people to the same place—away from God's desire for them. The Bible tells us to "cleanse *ourselves* from all defilement of flesh and spirit" (2 Cor. 7:1, emphasis added), but it also indicates that most of our struggle will be against "spiritual forces" in the invisible realm (Eph. 6:12). Frankly, it is often difficult to identify and isolate a single culprit for the wreckage we find in our lives and in the lives of others.

So it behooves us to be gracious and merciful toward people who may become a bit overzealous in their focus on (or avoidance of) any of the forces of evil in the world. We do not need to make our case against any particular evil as though we are in a debate; we simply want to learn all the provision that Jesus has made available for us to use whenever we encounter any of its manifestations. Consequently, for the remaining portion of this chapter we will focus on the power of the Lord to deliver us from footholds of the *evil spirited* in the human soul. We do not want to speculate or become superstitious about the *evil spirited*, but to remain sanely spiritual and biblical in how we withstand or counter demonic influence in our life.

THE NATURE OF EVIL SPIRITS

What do we know from the Bible about the *evil spirited*? If we acknowledge that we do not know much with absolute certainty, we can at least say a few things about evil spirits themselves.

1. They are probably the fallen angels who were cast out of God's presence when He "threw them to the earth" because they joined Satan's rebellion against the Lord (Rev. 12:4, 7–9). As only a third of the heavenly hosts, they are but half in number compared to angelic beings who minister to us. (Read Hebrews 1:14.)

2. These fallen angels have been defeated twice already—once by Michael and his angels in heaven, and again when Jesus rose from the dead. (Read Matthew 12:40; Ephesians 1:20–21; 4:9–10.) Their eternal doom is already fixed; they are destined for defeat and torment "day and night forever and ever" (Rev. 20:10).

3. There is some sort of hierarchy within their ranks and different designations that indicate they can have varying influences over situations or people, ranging from some aspect of a person's soul to an entire nation. (Read Ephesians 6:12; Colossians 1:16; Daniel 10:13, 20; Mark 5:8–10.)

4. As false gods, their primary activity is to distort the truth of the true God—introducing religious heresies—"doctrines of demons" (1 Tim. 4:1), and afflicting and oppressing people. (Read Mark 1:23–26; 5:5, 15; Acts 16:16–18.) Thus they become false focal points (idols) of worship and servitude. (Read Deuteronomy 11:16; Psalm 106:36; Luke 16:13; 1 Thessalonians 1:9.)

5. They have no natural bodies, but some of them seem to find it intolerable to be without a physical body with which to manifest their essential trait (addiction, depression, self-hatred, fear). That is why the demons entreated Jesus, "Send us into the swine" (Mark 5:11–12). They want to be spiritually "connected" somehow to people. (Read Matthew 12:43–45.)

6. In whatever way they may adhere themselves to the soul—whether they are "in" people or just "pressing in on" them—they can be removed and dislodged in Jesus' name (Luke 11:18–20).

Read 2 Kings 6:11–17. Why do you think that people are more impressed with the reality and power of demonic forces than they are with angelic hosts and with the Holy Spirit? What does this imbalance tend to do to our view of the spirit world?

_____

_____

Read 1 John 4:3–4. Who is in you? In what way have evil spirits already been conquered?

_____

_____

Read Luke 4:36. Can any demonic power withstand the command of Jesus?

_____

Read Mark 16:17. Why is the name of Jesus so important for ridding people of demonic oppression?

_____

_____

Read Luke 9:1. From whom do we have the authority, capacity and privilege to deliver people from the *evil spirited*?

_____

DEMONIC ASSAULT

The *evil spirited* act like sudden blasts of wind to knock us off our feet, and they can afflict, pressure, propel and manipulate areas of the human soul to respond to their impulses. Just as a rapid heartbeat can be triggered by wayward impulses from our body—causing it to beat out of sync with its intended rhythm—so too can our soul be driven to move out of step with what God intended for it.

When any part of the human soul (thoughts, feelings, awareness, choices, memories, perceptions) becomes entangled by, constrained by or ravished by the *evil spirited*, people can be said to be in bondage. In a specific and particular part of their soul, they are not completely free to direct their own choices and follow the course of life they truly want to take. Some limited portion of their thinking or deciding or feeling is being exercised by a force beyond themselves. It is similar to a physical fixation; it is not impossible to withstand the addictive impulse, but it is certainly more difficult to resist than it would be if there were no addiction. Spiritual bondage (the generic term we will use for any kind of manipulation or oppression in the soul caused by the *evil spirited*) is like a soulish, instead of a physical, addiction.

The oppression that comes from the *evil spirited* never becomes so overwhelming to the human soul that a person loses complete jurisdiction over his or her being. People always retain at least some ability to come to Jesus no matter how repressive their captivity may be. (Read Mark 5:5–9.) Before you accepted Jesus as your Savior, your spirit was "dead," i.e., cut off from relationship with the Lord and cut off from the life He wanted for you (Eph. 2:1, 5). But since you opened your heart to receive the Holy Spirit, He has come, as the "pledge" of God's full inheritance, to dwell in your spirit (2 Cor. 1:21–22; 5:5). It may sound a bit strange to put it this way, but since then the Holy Spirit has *possessed* your spirit.

Therefore, a Christian can never be possessed by an evil spirit residing in his or her spirit. We may be oppressed, hassled and assaulted by the *evil spirited* just as much as we can be tempted by our *flesh*, the *force of sin* and the *world*. More importantly for us as believers in Jesus Christ, the Holy Spirit, who occupies our spirit, is always "at work" in us, "both to will and to work for His good pleasure" (Phil. 2:13).

Spiritual bondage can vary in degree just like any affliction of the body, but the more acute the oppression, the more able those forces are to impose their evil soulish attributes on a person's soul. Their evil will power begins to erode a person's will. Their "false" memories flood a person's recollection. Their personality traits scratch and scribble themselves like graffiti over someone's true self. In extreme cases, a person begins to see and hear things as a result of the demonic perceptions being pushed into that person's consciousness. Once again, it is important to remember that evil mostly manifests itself in depletion, brokenness, confusion, barrenness and misery—not in grotesque and frightening horrors as we see depicted by Hollywood.

Bound people do not rattle chairs or spew fire from their eyes—they live with inner brokenness and skewed perceptions. People who are constrained in their choices by evil spirits do not bite necks and vanish in darkness; instead, they loathe themselves for not being able to stop drinking or to quit frequenting adult bookstores. When the *evil spirited* ravish human beings, they do not empower those people with superhuman energies and magic; rather, they drain away the people's hope and strength and life. Instead of being majestic, created in the image of their heavenly Father, people end up pathetic, in the likeness of the spirits that assail them.

SOULISH SUSCEPTIBILITIES

How do people come into bondage to the *evil spirited*? Do they get ambushed or catch evil spirits the same way they catch a cold? Do some people just "come down" with the *evil spirited* the way that others end up with cancer or high blood pressure? Can we avoid being vexed and held against our will by the *evil spirited*?

These would not be simple questions to answer even if the subject matter was physical illnesses of the body. Doctors can trace some factors leading, in some cases, to adult-onset diabetes (diet, weight, heredity, stress) or high blood pressure (same list), but it is never a straightforward cause-effect equation. One type of cancer stems from too much sun; another (perhaps) from too much red

> ▲
> ▲ Spiritual bondage
> ▲ can vary in degree
> ▲ just like any
> ▲ affliction of the
> ▲ body.

meat; still other forms of cancer are associated with (it is too strong to say "are caused by") genetic disorder or chemical exposure. No one can predict who will be struck with appendicitis, and looking back over the life of a woman with Alzheimer's disease will not uncover the exact cause for her nearly erased self-awareness.

And when medical science speaks of stress, they are not able to quantify it or identify it as a microbial entity that invades your body. What is stressful to one person is not so to another. What science measures is what that stress is likely to do to the body. They cannot predict with any degree of accuracy who will be affected how. Nor can science measure pain, and yet doctors do their best to relieve people of it. Sometimes treating the symptoms of an illness completely misses the cause of those symptoms—like aspirin for the fever of strep throat—but we are happy to get some relief, nonetheless.

So it is with spiritual afflictions of the soul. No exact accounting is possible. The root cause of one person's bondage to fear might be the source of another person's partial captivity to a spirit of control. The horrific abuse suffered by one woman at the hands of her father may lead to a nearly overpowering hatred of men, whereas the same degree of violation done to her sister might make her susceptible to a demonically inspired, *more-than-normal* interest in sexual activity. Why does one brother's personality become nearly overwhelmed by pride, while another's does not? Suffice it to say that the causes of spiritual oppression are at least as difficult to pin down as are the causes of physical ailments. What plagues the body and the soul are not always easy to understand.

But having said that, there are some vulnerabilities that seem to make room for the *evil spirited* to gain a foothold in people's lives. We mustn't make too much of them or read them as rigid rules of thumb, but they can be helpful when it comes time for counseling, prayer and deliverance administered by believers to one another. This brief list should be amplified, modified and supplemented by leaders in your church with regard to your unique situation. Please do not become a self-styled, self-taught expert about a subject that is fraught with so much uncertainty. At the root of most deception is pride—thinking that we know best. Let's avoid that snare as we look for ways to help each other get free from the other snares of the *evil spirited.*

Soulish vulnerabilities to spiritual bondage—here are some of the possible times and ways in which the door to people's souls might have been left ajar, thus leaving them more assailable by evil. It may be when people:

1. Make intentional invitations to demonic forces—offering themselves in worship to evil powers in exchange for what

those powers give back, or asking to be used by evil powers (like worshiping Satan or swearing revenge "at all costs").

2. Utter binding vows or sworn curses—invoking the name of false gods or swearing never to express normal soulish emotions (like, "No one will ever make me cry again; I will never trust another leader").

3. Repeatedly disobey the Lord in order to secure their own future—continuing to do over and over what they know is wrong and daring God to do something about their repeated offenses (like being unforgiving, choosing bitterness or drinking immoderately).

4. Participate in prolonged contact with occult activity—getting involved in astrology, tarot cards and any other kind of divination, or being heavily involved in taking illicit drugs.

5. Suffer severe abuse or violation by people in authority—experiencing betrayal by those who were supposed to protect them or being used for the authority's selfish pleasure (like sexual abuse, manipulation in a cult).

6. Undergo life-threatening, traumatic episodes—being "shocked" by unexpected, scary events or going through harrowing chapters in life when one emotion dominated them or the people around (like school shootings and suicides, car accidents).

7. Go through life transitions and seasons of great change—experiencing puberty, midlife, retirement, pregnancy, the empty nest, or coming under tremendous stress through the loss of a job or spouse.

8. Inherit generational distortions, dominant (sinful) characteristics of parents or grandparents—being "genetically" predisposed to patterns of thought or behavior that are not just "learned" through observation.

Again, this list is brief and partial, and it cannot be the basis for "distinguishing of spirits" in your life or in anyone else's (1 Cor. 12:10). The goal for having such a list is not to worry about what might happen the next time you are pregnant, but to offer you a perspective on why your inner self has been somewhat out of sync since the birth of your child.

You do not have to be afraid of becoming bound by the *evil spirited* just because you are not yet able to walk in complete victory over a sin, but if you are unable to get the victory over a sinful habit after many weeks, it could be that there is more than your sin at work. The habit may be a manifestation of an evil spirit manipulating or hassling you.

> ▲ You do not have
> ▲ to be afraid of
> ▲ becoming bound
> ▲ by the *evil*
> ▲ *spirited.*

The Lord warns us not to learn the ways of false gods or "turn away and serve other gods" (Deut. 11:16; 20:18). If we do not actively "drive them out" of our land, they will become "snares" to us (Judg. 2:3). The practices of demons are not always grossly obvious. They are often just subtle distortions of the truth of the Lord, and that is why the people of God are warned against them. If the cultures surrounding Israel were dominated by false gods and demonic powers, it only makes sense that the culture surrounding the church and believers is permeated with similar spiritual evil. Therefore, what is culturally acceptable may still be devilish.

DEMONIC MANIFESTATIONS

If we cannot pinpoint the exact cause of evil oppression, can we, at least, spot its symptoms? Again, as is the case with medical science or psychology (the search for natural causes for personality disorders), spiritual discernment is not always clear-cut in its diagnosis of what ails someone. That is why the Lord gives His church the spiritual gift of discerning spirits, and why we are told to "test the spirits" (1 John 4:1).

As false gods, the *evil spirited* offer human beings three basic things—protection, provision and purpose. When our thoughts, emotions, choices or will power claim to be able to give us those three commodities, we ought to "think twice" about them.

Spiritual bondage in someone's life shows up in various ways. We cannot possibly cover all the manifestations in this chapter, nor is it possible to offer a foolproof test to differentiate between something demonic in someone's life and the "regular" wear and tear on the soul that comes from living. Nevertheless, if you can develop some discernment regarding the trademarks of spiritual oppression, that ability to "discern good and evil" will grow with practice (Heb. 5:14).

To begin with, the *evil spirited* that vex human beings are rarely bizarre or grotesque. Their primary ploy is not to frighten people but to prey upon them unnoticed like parasites. Thus, more than anything else, evil spirits affect and distort individuals' personalities—causing people to act or think in uncharacteristic ways. When people begin acting in a way that isn't like them, it may be a clue that spiritual forces are at work in addition to whatever else may be going on in their life.

Demonic footholds in the soul mostly show up in subtle ways, and of all the natural things you are familiar with, evil spirits feel the most like personality characteristics, emotions, dispositions, attitudes or prevailing atmospheres. That is why they so often go undetected—they mask themselves behind "stray thoughts" that "sound" like our own mind or emotions that "seem to come out of nowhere."

They are like subtle but strong suggestions, persistent points trying to be made, low-grade but definite feelings, unexplainable moods, stubborn states of mind, single, dominant personality traits.

Demonic beings can also manifest themselves in the guise of compulsions or obsessions—driving and harassing people with uncontrollable thoughts or intense, irresistible feelings and sensitivities. Hormones, stress and fleshiness can be very compelling in their own right, but ritualistic fixations, addictions and life-limiting coercions (phobias) are often indicators that a person is battling more than just flesh and blood. Likewise, when our minds are bombarded with negative, hopeless conclusions—propelling us toward despair with hateful, belittling remarks about ourselves or frantic, hopeless feelings about our future—it could be the litany of a demon we are hearing and not just normal insecurity.

Additionally, demonic presences that hover at the edges of people's souls can trouble and oppress them with unexplainable confusion or emptiness—engulfing people with mental and emotional blankness or entangling them with a profusion of racing thoughts and emotions. These are not just the anxious thoughts related to an upcoming responsibility or to the future, but a preoccupation and/or deadness of mind that virtually incapacitates someone from being able to live his or her life. The unstoppable stream of their consciousness floods all else and inundates every corner of their life with its preoccupation. They are "driven to distraction"— absolutely overwhelmed by thoughts or feelings that become their only reality.

> God has the keys to open all the prison doors behind which we have been trapped.

GOD'S HEART TO RECOVER US

Must we wait until we go to heaven before we can be recovered from what the *evil spirited* have done to us? Or can the Lord's kingdom come here and now on earth to deliver us from the ravages of the *evil spirited* and restore us to our rightful inheritance as unique creations of God?

Actually, that is the promise of salvation—not just an eternal rescue that begins *after* we leave this planet, but restoration and recovery that begin now: wholeness of body, soul and spirit. The Lord is a God of deliverances—rescues and recoveries—and He has the keys to open all the prison doors behind which we have been trapped (Ps. 68:20). He wants to give us restful peace in the midst of life's turmoil, bounty and blessing in the very presence of our

> God is to us a God of deliverances.
> —Psalm 68:20

enemies, gladness and joy as the overflowing reality even in desert places. He is very good at restoring our soul. (Read Psalm 23.)

The work of God in our lives cannot be properly understood unless we grasp His fundamental purpose—to deliver us and recover us from every kind of evil so that we can enjoy our life together with Him. Instead of letting the food poisoning run its course to deplete us, our Father in heaven desires to intervene with a cure. He offers us antidotes for every form of antilife. He isn't angry with us for being poisoned, like an exasperated mother trying to clean up after her teenaged sons. His wrath is reserved for "all ungodliness and unrighteousness," that infectious and ruinous virus that suppresses truth and leads us astray. (Read Romans 1:18; 2 Pet. 2:15.)

He wants to purge its poison from us (1 John 1:9). He wants to cure us and alleviate our misery. God wants to give us something for our stomach.

> If we confess our sins, He is faithful and righteous to forgive us our sins and to cleanse us from all unrighteousness.
> —1 John 1:9

If you have ever seen a young child in a hospital strapped down with restraints to keep him or her from tearing at the tubes coming from that little body, you understand how and why a father silently pleads to be able to change places with his six-year-old daughter. When her fevered eyes ask, "Why, Daddy?" he knows she cannot understand what is happening. And nothing matters to him except her recovery. He would do *anything* to make her well.

While the sickness or injury tries to steal her life away, her dad thinks about what might now become lost opportunities with her—flying kites and buying pretty dresses and having her seventh birthday party at the beach. His heart fills with images of her bouncy curls though the strands of her hair now lie matted to her head. Through the long hours of her fitful sleep when her little lips purse and her brow knits, her father can barely survive the emotion aroused by the contrast between what he sees on her pale, pasty face and the dimpled smile her face always wore before she got so sick. That is when he hates the evil of the wrongness that has intruded upon her life.

Exactly so does God hate the evil that has invaded the lives of His children. What breaks us breaks God's heart.

God cannot abide evil. Nothing evil comes close to Him because His righteousness is so complete and utter that evil must flee His presence. God "cannot be tempted" or fooled by evil (James 1:13). We, on the other hand, are tempted by or unknowingly consume "bad foods" that carry evil, like salmonella. When we eat toxic substances and start to feel bad, we say the food did not "agree with" us. Likewise, because we were made in the image of God and intended, as His offspring, to share His essential makeup, evil does not "agree with us." (Read Genesis 1:26–27; Acts 17:28; 2 Peter 1:4.) It always works bad things in us or through us.

God wants us to be holy—not like the Pharisees, so we can be members of a *holier-than-thou* club, but because He longs for us to experience the wholeness that accompanies holiness. The Lord does not want to turn us into little religious robots, all lined up and neatly groomed to parade uniformly through the earth. He isn't trying to cram us into a small life outlined by rules and regulations. He just wants us to be well—and to know which mushrooms are poisonous. So He teaches us to pray, "Deliver us from evil" (Matt. 6:13).

That is the essence of salvation. The Greek word for *salvation*, *sozo* [pronounced *sode'-zo*], means "make whole, make safe, heal, preserve, protect, deliver." Jesus came to "save that which was lost" (Matt. 18:11). He came not "to judge the world" and condemn people, but "that the world should be saved" (John 3:17; 12:47). Jesus is the "door" through which we enter a place of great safety and peace (John 10:9). He is the Rock of our salvation and the One who helps us know where and how to withstand the forces of evil (Matt. 7:24–25).

Question: The Hebrew word for *salvation* is *yeshuw'ah* [pronounced *yesh-oo'-ah*] from which the name *Jesus* (*Yesua*) is taken. It means "deliverance, aid, victory over, health, welfare." God, our Father, loves to be a Rock of salvation. Read the following verses; what do they tell you about the Lord and His rescue provisions for you? Deuteronomy 32:4

_____

_____

Psalm 18:2

_____

_____

Psalm 31:2

_____

_____

Psalm 62:6

_____

_____

Psalm 144:1

_____

_____

> Therefore everyone who hears these words of Mine, and acts upon them, may be compared to a wise man, who built his house upon the rock. And the rain descended, and the floods came, and the winds blew, and burst against that house; and yet it did not fall, for it had been founded upon the rock.
> —Matthew 7:24–25

He will swallow up death for all time. And the Lord God will wipe tears away from all faces, and He will remove the reproach of His people from all the earth; for the Lord has spoken.
—Isaiah 25:8

He shall wipe away every tear from their eyes; and there shall no longer be any death; there shall no longer be any mourning, or crying, or pain; the first things have passed away.
—Revelation 21:4

He Himself bore our sins in His body on the cross, that we might die to sin and live to righteousness; for by His wounds you were healed.
—1 Peter 2:24

The most significant aspect of our salvation is, of course, our eternal rescue from the power and consequences of sin and the *life-without-death* (in any of its manifestations) we will share with the Lord forever in heaven (Isa. 25:8; Rev. 21:4). In heaven the "former things" of loss, pain, sorrow, emptiness and oppression will no longer assail us. But they do now. And the things of death have laid waste our life like locust swarms stripping the vitality from our days.

PROMISED RECOVERY

When we battle an illness like food poisoning, we have much less strength and energy than normal. We don't want to do much—even fun, exciting things—because of how drained we feel. That is an obvious example of the ruinous, burglarizing effects of evil at work in our lives. As Savior and restorer, the Lord acts as our healer; He says, "I, the Lord, am your healer" (Exod. 15:26). Indeed, one of the benefits He offers His children is recovery from physical sickness for ourselves and, through us, for others. (Read Mark 16:18.) That provision, along with so many others (see the box below on Isaiah 53), was purchased for us when Jesus died upon the cross (1 Pet. 2:24).

ISAIAH 53

The most complete prophetic picture of Jesus' sacrificial death on the cross—why God offered His own Son and what was accomplished through Jesus' suffering—is found in Isaiah 53. It is very moving to read.

At the core of God's plan to save the world was the need to make Jesus like us in everything so He could be a truly representative sacrifice. The Father wanted Jesus to experience all the sorts of things we go through—to taste every flavor of death so He could free us from its power. (Read Hebrews 2:9–18.) That is why the cross is so central to every aspect of recovery and restoration in our lives.

Jesus was . . .	Like us . . .	So we could be . . .
Despised (v. 3)	Looked down on, made fun of, ridiculed, scorned	Loved, embraced and welcomed. (Read Psalm 22:24; Revelation 3:20.)
Forsaken (v. 3)	Rejected, left alone, abandoned, isolated, banished	Brought near to, accompanied by, never forsaken. (Read Deuteronomy 31:6–8; 2 Corinthians 4:9.)

Jesus was ...	Like us ...	So we could be ...
Burdened with sorrows (vv. 3–4)	Afflicted, pained, saddened, anguished, distressed, troubled	Relieved from our heavy loads, cares and weariness. (Read Isaiah 9:2–6; Matthew 11:28.)
Loaded down with grief (vv. 3–4)	Afflicted with chronic sickness of body and heart, worn out by sadness	Healed of our physical, mental and spiritual afflictions. (Read Jeremiah 33:6; 1 Peter 2:24.)
Wounded (v. 5)	Violated, defiled, stabbed (in the back), cut into	Restored, built up, renewed, repaired. (Read Jeremiah 24:6; Acts 20:32.)
Bruised (v. 5)	Broken, crushed, oppressed, smashed to pieces	Made whole and preserved in body, soul and spirit. (Read Isaiah 42:3–4; 1 Peter 5:10.)
Scourged (v. 5)	Whipped, lashed at a post, abused by force, unable to escape	Set free, liberated from self-loathing and eternal punishment. (Read Psalm 107:13–16, 39–41; John 8:36.)
Oppressed (v. 7)	Tyrannized, driven by outside forces, taxed, harassed, harried	Delivered from and given dominion over circumstances and evil spirits. (Read Psalm 9:9; 144:7–11; Acts 10:38.)
Afflicted (v. 7)	Humiliated, defiled, beaten down, mortified, depressed	Raised up, given double portion instead of shame, given joy for our mourning. (Read Isaiah 51:11; John 15:11.)
Put to grief (v. 10)	Worn out or weakened by sickness, sorrowed by protracted disease or pain	Renewed in strength and hope, sustained in body, soul and spirit. (Read Isaiah 40:29–31; 2 Thessalonians 3:3.)
Anguished of soul (v. 11)	Stressed deeply, sick from worry, ground down physically and mentally	Given peace (*shalom*), well-being, inner health, prosperity of heart, and rest. (Read Isaiah 55:12; Philippians 4:7.)

Prayer and laying on of hands in Jesus' name can heal every kind of sickness. (Read Jeremiah 30:17; Matthew 10:1; 14:14; Mark 3:10; Acts 5:16; James 5:16.) In fact, physical healing is one of the visible proofs that the kingdom and power of God is present—"the kingdom of God has come near to you" (Luke 10:9)—and that

Jesus has the authority to forgive people's sins. (Read Mark 2:1–12.) When sickness seeks to overpower us and to dominate our world, the restorative work of God's salvation can move in to liberate us from the bodily effects and symptoms of the ailment. He "sent His word" to heal us and pull us out of the pit of disease (Ps. 107:20).

Since the *evil spirited* always oppose God's purposes, they will resist and dispute and hinder what the Lord wants to do in and through people who have been thus preyed upon. That is why spiritual deliverance is one of the most significant promises of recovery given to God's children (Isaiah 61:1):

> *The Spirit of the Lord God is upon me because the Lord has anointed me to bring good news to the afflicted [depressed in soul or circumstance]; He has sent me to bind up the brokenhearted, to proclaim liberty to captives [captured exiles], and freedom to prisoners [yoked, bound].*

MINISTRY OF DELIVERANCE

There are so many manifestations of God's goodness and power, but the most significant of them are His love and grace that enable us to be forgiven for our sins. What should make us rejoice most is not that demons are subject to us in Jesus' name—which they are—but that His name has saved us from eternal death away from God. (Read Luke 10:17–20.) In commissioning His disciples, Jesus gave authority and instruction for ministering deliverance from evil spirits. (Read Matthew 10:8; Mark 3:14–15.) Obviously, then, demons are meant to be reckoned with in a believer's life, and it cannot be that Jesus gave us jurisdiction over something He would prefer that we avoided.

We have the prerogative and the responsibility to alleviate people from the cruel and debilitating loads that have been forced upon them by their enemies. As surely as God raised up deliverers (judges) in ancient Israel to free His people from the hands of their enemies, so He has raised us up with the same assignment. Whether their taskmasters are sinful or satanic, physical or spiritual, past or present, Jesus wants people free—and He kindly entrusts us with the hands-on work to bring about that freedom.

To bury our heads in the sand—hoping evil will pass us and others by—or to try insulating ourselves with a theology that keeps the *evil spirited* at bay—outside of our nation or our person—misses the main point. Jesus is our deliverer. He is our salvation from every manner of evil. But how He might lead us to pray for and to counsel with a family on the verge of financial ruin can vary with the spiritual realities behind where they are.

Jesus is our deliverer. He is our salvation from every manner of evil.

For instance, the money issue may be traced to neglecting to tithe, foolish spending sprees, an unforeseeable calamity that drained away a hefty savings account, a surprise mugging by mammon or a desire to get rich. Biblically, each of these is a possibility. Praying for a financial breakthrough without counseling the couple to tithe is incomplete ministry. So too is it incomplete to avoid the subject of their fleshly desire to get money or the possible involvement of the god of material confidence. All manner of evil feed off one another, but none are more opportunistic than demonic spirits.

Jesus was delivered into the hands of evil men, according to the predetermined plan of God, so that by "tasting death" He could deliver our race from death's tyranny (Heb. 2:14–15). The Lord promises deliverance and rescue for us.

Read Galatians 1:4. What is God's will and desire for us?

_____

_____

Read 2 Timothy 4:18. What gives God glory? On what basis does He stake His reputation?

_____

_____

Read 2 Corinthians 1:10. Why can we set our hope on the Lord?

_____

_____

Even though most deliverances from evil will be processes—worked out over a period of time—rather than instantaneous events, there will be times when God's miraculous intervention in our mental/emotional/spiritual condition brings complete freedom *in moments*. Instead of a *season* of deliverance, we experience a sudden rescue much like the deliverance that came to us when we first opened our hearts to receive Jesus as our Savior.

Such instantaneous deliverances, like sudden healings from bodily afflictions, are miracles. They happen as a result of the power of God, but the triggering event can be a "word" spoken to the bound person (Matt. 8:16); "Scripture" (Ps. 107:20); revelation of "truth" (John 8:32); a simple command (read Mark 5:8); "love" (1 John 4:18); "prayer and fasting" (Matt. 17:21) or simply as a sovereign work of the Holy Spirit who opens blind eyes.

> Since then the children share in flesh and blood, He Himself likewise also partook of the same, that through death He might render powerless him who had the power of death, that is, the devil; and might deliver those who through fear of death were subject to slavery all their lives.
> —Hebrews 2:14–15

DELIVERANCE HALLMARKS

Whether the freedom comes to us from the Lord *in a moment* or over the course of several weeks, what hallmarks does true, God-worked deliverance have? What are the unmistakable trademarks of genuine spiritual freedom? Although it is nearly impossible to generalize everyone's personal experience, when we have been "delivered from evil," we will usually experience, in the aftermath of the deliverance, several of the following:

1. **A sense of true choice about what we do, say or think**—In stark contrast to what it felt like before, we will have well-clarified options for thought and behavior. Wrong thoughts no longer have the power they once did to carry us away. Instead of being "driven" to say, do, think or have something, we will be faced with several small choices about whether or not we want to go down the wrong road.

2. **A sudden, surprising ability to move beyond former "stick points"**—Like the drone of a refrigerator that is most noticeable when it stops, the grip of what used to consume us just isn't there, and we notice its absence more than we noticed its presence. It is like awakening from a bad dream or jerking alert late at night while driving and realizing we cannot remember passing the previous three off-ramps.

3. **A hyper-vigilance and awareness of right and wrong**—Far more than just trying harder, we will have a deeper, more profound passion for getting things squared away in our life than we did prior to our deliverance. Rather than feeling cavalier about our sin, we become more desirous than ever of bringing every area of our life—not just ones connected with the wrong from which we have been delivered—into submission to righteousness.

4. **A sense that we have undeservedly been given a "new lease on life"**—We will feel strangely favored instead of condemned, much as the prodigal son felt. Though we deserve to be stripped of our birthright, we are, instead, treated like guests of honor. The sense of being covered and forgiven—when we should justly be punished—is so incredibly good that it gives us added incentive to shun the former patterns of bondage in our life.

5. **A deep conviction that we have been answered and led by God**—Unlike we felt before, we no longer feel all alone, crying out for the Lord's Word. We know this is His

answer in our time of need, and in the immediate aftermath of our deliverance, we will hear His voice more
clearly than we have in a long time. We will receive large
doses of confirmation about the course He wants us to
take and the things He wants us to do.

6. **A strengthened ability to resist temptation**—We will
experience an undeniable "calling out" from dark places.
Points and postures of shadow, gray zones and other areas
where we have not been living fully in the light will definitely feel "off-limits" to us. We will be aware of being
supported by the Lord and kept from succumbing to
temptation amid the very patterns that either led us into
bondage or that resulted from it.

7. **A restoration of our true personhood and spiritual
inheritance**—Patterns of life and thought that had been
supplanted by the bondage—personality and character traits
composed by the Lord as who we are—return to us rapidly
as though someone just removed a blanket that had been
covering them. Aspects of our ministry, spiritual authority
and personality recover as though they were never gone.

Although deliverance can either extricate us from circumstances
caused by evil spirits or free us from the grasp of those spirits themselves, the liberty we experience in deliverance brings us to a very
new place. It is like having the wind or current turn around and go
the opposite direction—advancing and aiding us, rather than
opposing us. That, in turn, increases our desire to celebrate and
praise God. Knowing that the Lord has turned our mourning into
dancing, our sorrow into joy, we will feel like shouting from the
rooftops, "Great is the Lord, and greatly to be praised!" We know it
was the Lord who accomplished this great deliverance for us by His
right hand and His mighty power. Somehow we just feel that everything that needs to be said is summarized in "Praise the Lord!"

"The angel of the LORD encamps around those who fear Him,
and rescues them" (Ps. 34:7). How grateful we are to the Lord who
is to us "a God of deliverances" and to whom "belong escapes from
death" (Ps. 68:20). One of the testimonies every believer can have
during the course of his or her journey with Him is that "He delivers and rescues and performs signs and wonders in heaven and on
earth," and He has also delivered me "from the power of the lions"
(Dan. 6:27).

LET'S TALK ABOUT IT

▲ Explain in your own words the difference between your soul and spirit.

_____

_____

▲ According to the chapter, is it possible for a believer in Jesus to be *possessed* by the *evil spirited*? Why not?

_____

_____

▲ As a result of reading this chapter, how have your thoughts changed regarding the nature of the *evil spirited*? Why do you think many people have doubts about their existence and uncertainty about their nature? How would you summarize what the Bible says about them?

_____

_____

YOUR TIME WITH GOD

Re-read the list regarding possible vulnerabilities to spiritual bondage. Are there points in your life that you may have been vulnerable to assault from the *evil spirited*? If so, you can ask the Lord to deliver you right now. Jesus loves to answer simple prayers for freedom. Depending on which of the vulnerabilities got quickened to your heart, pray a simple prayer like:

Lord, I acknowledge that I have made vows never to show emotions or cry again. I am sorry for doing this because I know that You created me to feel and to be free to express how I feel. I ask that You would break that vow, and I pray this in Jesus' name.

Lord, I ask that you would come and deliver me from the shock of_____ (fill in). I know my life has changed since then, and that I am less of who You want for me to be. I can see places where the evil spirited *want to rule over places and relationships that You intend to be good. Deliver me from these things and restore to me what has been lost. Remove the fear (or whatever dominant emotion/attitude you have felt try to hinder your normal responses to things) from me, in Jesus' name.*

Father, I can see in me the very same character traits that are in my (parents or grand parents)—the ones that have hurt and confused so many of us in the family. Thank You for my (parents) and for the righteous qualities they have passed on to me. But I ask that You would cut off any unrighteous root of the evil spirited *that has tormented and oppressed my family for generations. In Jesus' name.*

The chapter explains many possible manifestations of spiritual bondage in someone's life. One of these ways is in a single, dominant personality trait like: "That man is just so angry." "She just seems so resentful all the time." "They are just fearful about everything regarding their children." Is there a negative, but dominant trait in your life? Pray and ask Jesus to deliver you from the spiritual bondage of anger, resentment, fear, or _____. Ask the Lord to show you the situations where this manifests itself. Ask God to teach you how to respond differently in those times.

Look over the list from Isaiah 53. What stands out to you as an area of restoration of which you are in need?

_____

_____

Take a moment to thank Jesus for what He did so that you could be restored. For instance:

Jesus, I come to You in need of being renewed in strength and hope. Thank You that You were put to grief so that my hope can be renewed. I ask You to come into my heart and circumstances today and bring hope and strength to me.

The process of deliverance can begin with a simple acknowledgment and prayer to Jesus:

Lord, thank You that You want to see me made whole. I believe that You have the power to set me free. I recognize that there is a place in my soul in spiritual bondage to _____, and in Jesus' name I ask that You would set me free. Show me the ways to live in the freedom You offer, and teach me how to think and respond differently.

Jesus, I celebrate Your victory on the cross, which gave me forgiveness for my sins, healing for the bodily sicknesses that plague me and deliverance from evil. Thank You that You have inscribed my name in the Book of Life. Teach me how to walk in Your provision and authority. Give me good discernment for the sake of others—that I might follow Your example of healing any who are oppressed by the evil spirited. *In Jesus' name, amen.*

CHAPTER FOURTEEN

Being Part of the Whole

EVERYONE WANTS AN ANSWER TO THE QUESTION, "WHO AM I?" Some seek to know who they are in the context of the whole cosmos, as part of a grand quest for understanding the meaning of all things—and their relationship to that meaning. But most of us just want a simple handle on ourselves, to know what sort or people we are—whether we are outspoken or reserved, thoughtful or spontaneous, wise, fun-loving, fastidious, supportive or anything distinctive enough to have a word attached to us. In a sense, we want to know what we "look like," not physically, not externally—but on the inside in a way that shows up on the outside. We want to know what we are like and what, if anything, distinguishes us from everyone else.

When asking, "Who am I?", most of us are actually wondering if we matter: *Has there been, will there be a reason for me?* It isn't as though we insist on (or even hope for) being extraordinary or spectacular. We do not need to stand *above* the crowd—just as long as there is something that keeps us from being completely lost *within* the crowd. Though we are dwarfed and somewhat overcome by the vastness of the starry night sky, something profound stirs within us that challenges the lie that we have simply evolved as a versatile species, a remarkable organism. It is not our biology that fascinates and preoccupies us when we're in a staring contest with the cosmos, but our destiny and our identity.

That is not some carnal manifestation of human pride; it is a remnant of our creation. Wanting to be unique and to count for something is not the fantasy of self-importance. We were made in the image of the one and only God—the One who calls Himself, "I AM." Every human being—like all other beings—is capable of lapsing into arrogance and "think[ing] more highly of himself than he ought to think" (Rom. 12:3). However, what plagues most of us are not exalted opinions of ourselves, but the nagging doubts about our significance—do we have any at all, and if so, what, where, how?

The answer from God's heart is a resounding *yes*. He who "calls us by name," who counts the declining number of hairs on our head, who has "loved [us] with an everlasting love," says, "Yes, you do" (Isa. 43:1; Jer. 31:3; Luke 12:7). At this point in your journey with God, it should not be surprising to discover that the way in which the Lord answers the question of our significance on earth is a bit different than how the world tries to resolve it. As we will see, our identity is directly tied to our destiny in God and our connection to other of His children.

DESTINED FOR GREATNESS

We are not accidents. We were not spawned into the void of what the world was *before* God spoke to it. We were fashioned by our loving Father—chosen and selected according to the longings in His heart for exactly who and what we are. He created us with very particular design, not only for our inner being, but also for our purpose—to have relationship with Him and to have a fitting place in His grand purposes for the people of this planet. That is why we know we want more out of life than a company watch at our retirement party. We were made for more than continued existence.

God's whole agenda is to restore our beings into their original condition—by making us more like Jesus (Rom. 8:28–29)—and as we are being restored, to join Him in reestablishing His kingdom rule in all the earth. Hence, the more that we allow Him to do His work in us, the more we are capacitated to have His work on earth done through us. He wants us to be part of His whole plan for rescuing the people of the world from the death and evil that assail them.

Whether it is the "I got my own; you get your own" mentality, the self-sufficiency that prides itself on being able to handle life without anyone's help or the independence that removes people from close and caring proximity from one another, the culture in which we live teaches people to take care of themselves—with little thought of looking to the needs of others. The world tells us to preserve our life, to get everything we can for ourselves to assure our creature comfort and well-being. God tells us the exact opposite.

The life cycle of human beings is predictable and short; our brief lifetimes are fleeting moments in eternity. (Read Psalm 90:3–6.) Because of sin's devastating effects, none of us can escape life's labor, sorrow and physical death. These are the givens. So if we want our life to count for something, we must measure it in terms of what we can accomplish rather than of what we cannot avoid.

And we know that God causes all things to work together for good to those who love God, to those who are called according to His purpose. For whom He foreknew, He also predestined to become conformed to the image of His Son, that He might be the first-born among many brethren.

—Romans 8:28–29

The more we allow Him to do His work in us, the more we are capacitated to have His work on earth done through us.

Read the words of Moses, spoken near the end of his life, in Psalm 90:10, 12. True wisdom recognizes what about the length of our days on earth? And what about the sum total of those days?

_____

_____

Jesus teaches us how to overcome in life, not just by surviving a bit better and more happily than the rest of the world, but by participating in its re-invasion with His kingdom come. Meaning and significance will never be found by vainly attempting to conserve our life, but by purposefully thinking how to expend it.

We have a high calling from the Lord that makes us counterculture people. Jesus said, "Whoever wishes to save his life shall lose it; but whoever loses his life for My sake shall find it"—and find significance (Matt. 16:25). The instinct of self-preservation—wanting to protect, deliver, defend or do well to ourselves—is a good thing when it comes to escaping physical danger, but in the context of finding meaning and purpose for our inner lives, seeking to save ourselves is absolutely counterproductive. God designed us to save and serve others, not ourselves. We will never find our intrinsic value in isolation, independence or selfishness.

SERVING OTHERS

In God's eyes, of course, we already have huge value and significance. He is so taken with us that we do not need to do anything or be anything—other than ourselves—to bring pleasure to Him. But as our Father Creator, He wants us to have value and meaning in our own eyes—to see in ourselves what He sees in us. So, what's the plan? In what ways can we come to appreciate ourselves as He appreciates us?

First of all, we gain meaning by the part we play in the lives of others. Serving others is the primary mission God gives us in life. That was Jesus' assignment. Though His rightful position was next to His Father in heaven, He accepted the role offered to Him by God, to come to the earth as a servant for the sake of all of us. (Read Philippians 2:5–11.) His true identity was temporarily hidden beneath the servant garb—as ours will be when we serve others—but because He chose to humble Himself for the purpose of raising us up, God raised Him up and gave Him the name, as well as the position, above all others.

We see in Jesus' life a living out of one of the most basic kingdom principles regarding true identity and significance: The more we come *under* people to lift them up, the more significance we end up having. Servanthood is the secret to spiritual attainment. That is what Jesus meant when He said, "But the greatest among you shall be your servant" (Matt. 23:11). He was contrasting the world's notion of prominence and importance with what is the case in His kingdom, where our place in line is always counted from the rear.

Contrary to what some people imagine, Jesus was not telling us it is sinful or proud to aspire to greatness or to want to have our life count for something. Rather, He was explaining the true nature of significance in His kingdom—it can only be achieved by coming under others. In the world, leaders "lord over" (control, subjugate) their subordinates (Matt. 20:25–26). One of the ways people can tell how important someone is in an organization is to count how many individuals he or she is over.

> ▲ Servanthood is the
> ▲ secret to spiritual
> ▲ attainment.

Read Mark 10:43–45. Why is it tempting for us to have the exact opposite intention for our life than what Jesus had as His intention? What don't we like about serving others?

_____

_____

Read Luke 22:26–27. In what specific ways do you wait for other people to wait on you? Can you think of ways to wait on others in your church? At work?

_____

_____

In some churches the pastor is called the *minister.* You will also hear many Christians talk about *ministry* as a special, spiritual activity. Did you know that both expressions come from the Greek root word *diakonos* (*dee-ak'-on-os*), meaning "a servant, a waitress, an errand-runner"? _____

Not so in the kingdom . . . According to Jesus, spiritual value is measured more as it is in Olympic weightlifting than in corporate structuring—it is not how much you are over that counts, but how much (many) you have been able to get under and lift above your head. Our highest calling is to serve the purposes and people of God. There is no greater occupation or assignment than servanthood.

All real and lasting blessing—the sort that answers cosmic questions about our place in the universe and our meaning—comes by serving other people from a position that is lower than what we are accustomed to. "It is more blessed to give than to receive" (Acts 20:35). Even though this runs counter to what our natural thinking tells us, it is true. This explains why many Christians find their walk with the Lord somewhat flat and routine—they have not learned one of the greatest secrets to finding true fulfillment and meaning.

When done with others and with spiritual understanding for what is being accomplished in others' lives, as well as our own, serving fulfills our sense of destiny as almost nothing else can. Besides, helping care for others isn't necessarily some huge project or sacrifice. It is more like being a parent—you just do what you have to do because that is what you do as a parent. Sometimes you work in the garden without the kids even being aware of it. Sometimes you have a long and meaningful talk with them. Still, at other times, you just hang out with them and have fun.

What we do for others will change, corresponding to their needs and situation, but why we do what we do never changes. It's called *love*. We learned in chapters 3 and 12 that the Bible defines love in terms of "doing unto others." As we receive life, hope and instruction from the Lord, we are privileged to give the same to others. We give what we have been given. What an awesome calling, to help others come into their spiritual inheritance! In fact, as an expression of love, the degree to which we are involved "doing unto others" is the surest way to measure our true spiritual maturity.

Read John 21:15–17. Several times Jesus asked Peter, "Do you love Me?" Each time Peter replied, "Yes, of course I do. You know that I do, so why do You keep asking?" Read what Jesus said back to Peter. What was Jesus' point to Peter? How does that apply to you?

_____

_____

> ... knowing that from the Lord you will receive the reward of the inheritance. It is the Lord Christ whom you serve.
> — Colossians 3:24

Serving others is a way of serving Jesus (Col. 3:24). It is one of the few appropriate responses we can have to all that He has done for us. Like waiters and waitresses, we get assigned certain "stations" in a restaurant, and our primary responsibility is to serve the needs of anyone who sits at our tables. Ministry is hard work, but it is marvelously satisfying when God's power works through us to touch those people. And beyond the thrill of being used by the Lord, there is an additional benefit to us that ties back in with discovering who and what we are as unique creations.

SPECIALLY MADE PEOPLE

Although it is not the *only* way in which God intervenes in the world, His primary means for introducing rescue and blessing to people is through *other* people. Of course, God can and does step in supernaturally and sovereignly in the course of human history, but a close reading of the Bible reveals just how much He favors making use of His children to do His work on earth. He opts for us as His tools of choice because He loves people—each of us—and the entire focus of His work on earth centers on human beings—what He can do to them, but equally as satisfying to Him (and us), what He can do through them.

Creation was incomplete until God birthed Adam and Eve. Though God's judgment fell upon depraved mankind, He still chose to work through Noah to enable our race to survive the Flood. He raised Joseph to go before His people into Egypt to save them during the famine. In the same way, the Lord sent Moses—after teaching him it would not be by means of his natural upbringing, schooling or power—to deliver Israel from Egyptian captivity. Whether it is Joshua or the judges, Old Testament prophets or John the Baptist, God gifts His people with people. Most of the miracles in the Bible take place through the prayers, hands or words of men and women of God.

So we should not be surprised when we read Jesus' words about the "greater works" His disciples will do (John 14:12). The Lord who loves people like you and me loves to use us to do good to others. Just as Jesus "went about doing good, and healing all who were oppressed by the devil"(Acts 10:38), so are we intended by God to live our lives with high destiny and purpose, doing like-wise. "He who is least" in the kingdom of God has incredible min-istry potential (Matt. 11:11). The Holy Spirit works in our lives to make us vessels "useful to the Master" (2 Tim. 2:21)—not because of our own energies, but because of how He made us and how we cooperate with Him.

Read John 14:12. After telling His disciples they should believe in Him because they had observed the miracles He performed, Jesus switches the emphasis in His next statement. Instead of saying they would see even greater things in the future, Jesus tells His disciples (us) what? What implications does that have for your journey?

_____

_____

One of the most powerful messages contained in the Bible is that the Lord has uniquely crafted each of us, so that we corre-spond to an already existing, deep desire in His heart. When we were born, God did not have to learn to love us; He already did! The phenomenal and delightful variety we see evidenced among people bears testimony both to God's endless creativity _and_ to His loving "appetite" for each unique one of us. God is not just a lover of the human race; He loves each particular person.

The differences that we can see on the outside of people—their shapes and features—merely hint at the profound differences God has put in place beneath their physical appearances. Coming from the same set of parents, children may resemble one another physically, but they rarely are similar in the hundreds of aspects of their individual personalities. God composed our total being of many distinct components—like our conscience, our personality, our mental and physical talents and our emotional disposition.

MINISTRY-GIFT MIXES

In addition to these commonly perceived aspects of personhood, God also created each of us with another, little-known element of our being. An often overlooked development that happened hand in hand with the Resurrection was Jesus' gift-giving—when He elected to give people gifts, ministry gifts to His church. (Read Ephesians 4:7–13.) Throughout this chapter, we will refer to that part of us as our *ministry-gift mix*.

> Our *ministry-gift mix* is the combination of aptitudes, complexions, burdens and functions that make us apt for being special parts in the body of Christ and for accomplishing what He wants us to do in the kingdom of God.

Our *ministry-gift mix* is the combination of aptitudes, complexions, burdens and functions that make us apt for being special parts in the body of Christ and for accomplishing what He wants us to do in the kingdom of God. It gives a great deal of definition to how we function in life and in the kingdom of God.

Our *ministry-gift mix* is not what we do, but part of what we are. It is like a spice or a taste (flavor). Cinnamon does not do a job—instead, its inherent tang affects whatever it touches. Wherever cinnamon goes, whatever it may do, it will always have the qualities and characteristics of cinnamon. So it is with our *ministry-gift mix*. What we are is far more meaningful than what we do, or perhaps more precisely, what we are will *flavor* everything we may do.

Ministry-gift mixes are not the same as *spiritual gifts*, although there is some overlap and similarity between the two different types of spiritual enablements. *Spiritual gifts,* as we will see later in this chapter, are specific tools we are given in addition to our *ministry-gift mix*. *Spiritual gifts* are given by the Holy Spirit, whereas *ministry-gift mixes* come from Jesus. (Read 1 Corinthians 12:4–5.) *Spiritual gifts* are given to us *after* we receive the Lord and have the Holy Spirit inside of us. Our *ministry-gift mix* was woven into the very fabric of our soul while we were in the womb along with all the other bits of our "unformed" being (Ps. 139:16; Gal. 1:15).

Read Jeremiah 1:5 and see if you can identify the *ministry-gift mix* that God gave to Jeremiah.

_____

_____

Our *ministry-gift mix* is so much a part of our whole self that we sometimes have difficulty seeing it clearly at work in us. Though it is neither wise nor possible to pigeonhole ourselves or others into precisely defined *ministry-gift mix* categories, it is still useful and very illuminating to gain a basic understanding of each of the ministry gifts listed in the New Testament. (Read Romans 12; 1 Corinthians 12; Ephesians 4.) While it is enjoyable to learn about the various *ministry-gift mixes*, it can also be a bit puzzling because we see attributes and qualities of more than one ministry that resonate with who we are. Most likely, we are combinations of more than one *ministry-gift mix*.

The more we learn about our unique *ministry-gift mix* and how God intends us to function, the more fulfilled and effective we will be in life. A basic understanding of some of the qualities that set each of the *ministry-gift mixes* apart from one another enables us to better appreciate other people and their giftings—and function more effectively ourselves (according to God's design for us). As people, we do not all work the same.

PARTIAL REFLECTIONS OF GOD

Each of the *ministry-gift mixes* is an expression of God and His character. He is rich in mercy—hence, the *shower of mercy.* The Lord gives bountifully to us—hence, the ministry of the *giver.* Every one of the *ministry-gift mixes* has qualities that ought to be developing in every one of us. For instance, we are not all *teachers,* but all of us are encouraged to "teach one another" (Col. 3:16). Not all of us have the *ministry-gift mix* of the *helper,* but we are called to serve. Thus, the *ministry-gift mixes* are spiritual qualities of God's heart and of a mature believer's life.

The following brief descriptions of several distinct *ministry-gift mixes* will demonstrate just how radically unique we are and how marvelously God has created us. This is not meant to be a complete list. In some cases, newer, more descriptive names have been substituted for more traditional ministry titles.

▲ EXHORTERS find it easy to get close to people and their situations—usually by relating a similar personal experience—in order to help them move ahead or break through. Like expert mountain guides, *exhorters* can point out loose stones and shortcuts, and they make fabulous storytellers.

▲ TEACHERS see lessons to be taught in almost every situation; they want everyone to be secured and well grounded in truth. As tireless mentors, *teachers* take special delight when others gain a new or deeper awareness of truth.

Their organized touch brings simplicity and beauty to almost anything.

▲ SERVER-HELPERS derive the most satisfaction and fulfillment from being invisible, behind-the-scenes parts of a larger "team effort." Using their know-how, skills, time and talents, *server-helpers* undergird people and churches, relieving them of their burdens and workloads. They toil with eagerness and almost endless stamina.

▲ MERCY-SHOWERS see beyond people's sin and move toward their hurt with gracious sensitivity and compassion. Filled with great wisdom and strength, *mercy-showers* believe the best of others and want the best for them—regardless of what may have caused their present circumstances. They can reach those who are deep in pain or shame.

▲ APOSTLE-PIONEERS lay foundations of truth and understanding upon which others in the church build. As pioneers moving into spiritually uncharted or underdeveloped arenas, *apostles* rarely function conventionally or according to the status quo. Their trailblazing tendencies and their keen sense of direction inspire followers.

▲ GIVERS experience an almost irresistible desire to meet the physical and financial needs of anyone they meet. Compelled by cheerful generosity, *givers* invest in kingdom enterprises and facilitate others' vision. Having usually suffered several financial reversals, they have little worry about parting with more of their money voluntarily.

▲ EVANGELISTS continually "find themselves" in the middle of incredible opportunities to tell people about Jesus. And they do—with an eagerness to explain how people's life situations can be made so much better by the Lord. Not easily discouraged by roadblocks in life or in conversations, *evangelists* keep pressing ahead as carriers of the "good news."

▲ PROPHETS carry messages in their own hearts (like letter pouches) that come from the heart of God about His plans and purposes for people or churches. Wanting to counsel people according to God's revealed word, *prophets* are focused on one question: "What is God saying right now?" They act as excellent compasses in the woods.

▲ LEADER-CHAMPIONS rise up on behalf of people or causes with a combination of strength and initiative in order to establish lasting change for the better. Stepping up in support or defense of those in need, *leader-champions* assume responsibility for getting things done. They lead by taking care of anything that needs doing.

▲ PASTOR-TEACHERS seek out, gather and watch over other people with a strong desire to see each one of them flourish. Wanting to make sure everyone has whatever they need to grow, *pastor-teachers* "go over" the particulars of people's lives like someone finger-counting loose change in their pocket. They lead and feed their sheep.

God made us to work best in a certain manner and mode. While most of us focus on living according to His plans for our behavior (for example, not lying, not being resentful), we often neglect His plans for our *ministry-gift mix*. A foot is designed to do more than merely resist the temptation to kick someone; its purpose is far more meaningful—to support the body in standing and to carry it throughout the day.

Over the course of our journey, we become increasingly aware of God's calling on our life and His selection of us for a particular role. God does not regret calling and gifting us—"the gifts and the calling of God are irrevocable"—even if we choose not to respond carefully to our divinely created composition and capacity to fill a significant part in His kingdom (Rom. 11:29). Fruitfulness in our spiritual and natural life increases dramatically when we focus on living according to how we were designed.

Once you understand the importance of God's pre-selection of your role within His larger plan, you will see examples of it throughout the scriptures.

> ▲
> ▲ God made us to
> ▲ work best in a
> ▲ certain manner
> ▲ and mode.
> ▲

Read Acts 9:15; 10 and Galatians 2:1–9. Even before Paul was saved, he was called to the Gentiles. Was Paul's ministry to the Gentiles his own idea?

_____

Read 1 Timothy 2:7. Who appointed Paul?

_____

Read 2 Timothy 4:5. What was Timothy's particular calling?

_____

SPIRITUAL GIFTS

Our remarkableness, and that of those around us, gets even more exciting when we come to understand another of the ways in which the Lord lavishes us with gifts. Not only did He craft us in the womb before we were born into this world, but He adds to whom He has already made us. When we are "born again" in the spiritual dimension, we can be endowed with what the Bible calls *spiritual gifts.*

Spiritual gifts are not natural talents, skills or aptitudes. They have nothing to do with our personalities, vocational choices, training or native intelligence. The fact that we have talents, jobs and skills is not in question—believers and unbelievers alike have such qualities as part of their God-fashioned being. One person has an eye for detail and is able to remember what a friend was wearing when the two of them went to dinner three years ago. Another individual is incredibly good at translating the most difficult concepts into easily understandable terms.

These are wonderful attributes, but they are not *spiritual giftings* in the sense described in the Bible. God is marvelously creative in how He composes our person in the womb. Just as He "sends rain on the righteous and the unrighteous" regardless of their lifestyle, so He is indiscriminate in fashioning every person with qualities and talents suitable for the offspring of the Most High (Matt. 5:45). Nevertheless, what we call natural abilities, capabilities, skills or talents are not the same as the *gifts* of the Spirit.

Without the Holy Spirit, a person cannot have or exercise a *spiritual gift*—just as no one can truly say, "Jesus is my Lord" except through the agency of the Spirit (1 Cor. 12:3–4, 8). Each *spiritual gift* is a supernatural empowerment given by the Holy Spirit, like a special tool in our hands, to accomplish something that natural talent or know-how could not do. They are "grace gifts" [*charis* (grace) + *ma* (miraculous faculties)]. Remember our definition of grace from chapter 4—something is done for you that you could never do on your own, and as a result of what is done for you, you end up in a much better position. *Spiritual gifts* are grace (couldn't-do-on-our-own) gifts (things-given-to-us-that-we-didn't-have-before).

Beyond the ultimate goal to glorify Jesus, *spiritual gifts* are given primarily to accomplish three specific purposes. *Spiritual gifts* themselves are not marks of maturity. How those gifts get used and how they are manifested in wisdom, grace and good order—that is what displays our maturity.

Read each of the following verses. The three main purposes for *spiritual gifts* are:

1. To confirm the truth of the Word of God, to bear witness to the Good News. (Read 1 Corinthians 2:4–5; Hebrews 2:4.)

> Each *spiritual gift* is a supernatural empowerment given by the Holy Spirit, like a special tool in our hands, to accomplish something that natural talent or know-how could not do.

2. To build up members of the body of Christ, to encourage and mature fellow believers. (Read Romans 1:11; 1 Corinthians 14:3–4, 26.)

3. To serve others with instruction, direction, healing and counsel. (Read 1 Timothy 1:18; 1 Peter 4:10.)

There is no hard and fast rule for receiving a *spiritual gift*. It can happen sovereignly and suddenly in your life. Or a *spiritual gift* can emerge in your life slowly; over time you become more aware of its existence, and you become better versed in how it works in ministry situations. But most of the time, at least from what we read in the Bible, *spiritual gifts* are bestowed on you the same way in which the baptism in the Holy Spirit is usually administered—by the laying on of hands.

One of the most exciting privileges of spiritual leadership is to be able to pray for the impartation of *spiritual gifts,* as directed by the Spirit, to those individuals who receive covering and care from those leaders. As your pastors or leaders pray for you, the *spiritual gift* will often be identified in an accompanying "prophetic utterance" (1 Tim. 4:14).

We do not know how many *spiritual gifts* one can receive, but we are told to "earnestly desire" them—to really ask God for them (1 Cor. 12:31; 14:1). Which gifts we end up with, then, is a result both of God's plan and our desire. Neither do we know for certain if the list of *spiritual gifts* in 1 Corinthians 12:8–10 is inclusive and exhaustive. Because there are so many ways in which *spiritual gifts* operate, we will only define the *spiritual gifts* in general terms and give the essential characteristic of each. (Read 1 Corinthians 12:6.)

1. **Word of wisdom**—reveals the plans and purposes of God for individuals or groups. It makes sense out of several things happening in someone's life by disclosing what God is doing at a deeper level. By alerting individuals to the "spiritual season" they are in, or where they are on the map of God's dealings with them, a *word of wisdom* orients people to better cooperate with what He is up to in them and through them.

2. **Word of knowledge**—brings to light facts about people, their past or their present (physical condition or life situation). The one giving the word could not know the detail about a person's life; it is usually very specific in what it identifies, like an illness or an unfulfilled ministry dream. The whole point for God disclosing the detail is so He can answer the need or resolve the problem in a miraculous display of His intervening power.

> For to one is given the word of wisdom through the Spirit, and to another the word of knowledge according to the same Spirit; to another faith by the same Spirit, and to another gifts of healing by the one Spirit, and to another the effecting of miracles, and to another prophecy, and to another the distinguishing of spirits, to another various kinds of tongues, and to another the interpretation of tongues.
> —1 Corinthians 12:8–10

3. **Gift of faith**—enables people to hold on to what the Lord has promised to do for them even though things do not look very promising. More than just faith—the decision to believe God's words that every believer is supposed to exercise—the *gift of faith* acts like an irrepressible buoy that rides above the water no matter how large the waves. The spiritual *gift of faith* creates an atmosphere of expectation, an eager anticipation about what God will surely do soon.

4. **Gifts of healing**—bring about a dramatic reversal to any condition of the body, mind or heart that has been afflicted by evil or sickness. As with the *gift of faith*, think of this spiritual gift as a more concentrated form of the healing virtue that is available to every believer through prayer. One of its attributes seems to be the way in which it not only recovers someone from affliction to health, but also makes them even healthier than normal in their mind or body.

5. **Effecting of miracles**—creates a steady flow of supernatural signs and wonders to be marveled at by all who witness them. Though every believer should expect the Lord's miraculous intervention, the Lord will use those with this spiritual gift much more frequently and more significantly to introduce His transforming touch to people. Many of the well-known evangelists who conduct large crusades with many miracles have this gifting.

6. **Gift of prophecy**—communicates the heart of God for people in such a way that there is no doubt where they stand with Him and what He is setting Himself to do. Although there can be a predictive element to prophecy, it more often discloses secrets of people's hearts and/or the hidden things in God's heart for them. We can all prophesy, but the *gift of prophecy* seems to be some additional capacity with prophetic insight for people. (Read 1 Corinthians 14:24, 31.)

7. **Distinguishing of spirits**—enables the identification of which of the *evil spirited* is oppressing people or their situations. Because the forces of evil can disguise themselves, and because people who appear to be spiritually OK are not necessarily so, God gifts some in the church to be able to spot evil for what it is. (Read 2 Corinthians 11:14–15.) All of us are to "test the spirits" (1 John 4:1), but this spiritual gift discerns, in a more heightened fashion, what is resisting God's plan and how to counteract that resistance.

8. **Kinds of tongues (languages)**—gives extraordinary facility in (unlearned, unknown to the person speaking) languages with which to communicate the Good News, to give praise to God, to pray to the Lord (and to prophesy to people), so that the people can hear it in their native tongue. This spiritual gift is not just the prayer language that we receive when we are filled with the Spirit, but an additional, more public declaration of God's words to people who need to hear them.

9. **Interpretation of tongues (languages)**—translates any message spoken in an unknown language so that everyone present can benefit from the message. Whether the unknown tongue is simply a prayer language used in devotion or the spiritual *gift of tongues* operating prophetically, this spiritual gift enables everyone to be blessed by what is said because they can hear it put in their own language, though not usually a word for word rendering.

PARTS OF A WHOLE BODY

God has placed each of us in the body, just as He desires and according to His master plan for reaching the world (1 Cor. 12:18). Like members of a championship football team, let us celebrate the uniqueness of those around us and how they complement our own *ministry-gift mix* and our *spiritual gifts*. God has designed different people differently (in order to serve various functions in life), just as He composed the human body. Eyes do not act like ears. (Read 1 Corinthians 12:12–27.) Just as our bodies have different parts and organs, so too does the body of Christ.

Not only does the Lord want us to be part of what He is doing in the whole earth, but He also wants us to be part of His whole family on earth, called the church, laboring alongside other believers. As individual and particular parts of the body, we are designed to do (and not do) certain things. That degree of God-ordained specialization only makes sense if we are connected to other Christians whose uniqueness complements and supplements ours.

It is one thing for us to learn how to function as unique ministry parts. Unfortunately, that is where many Christians stop. They do not realize that God designed us to discover the wonder of who and what we are by belonging to something bigger than we are and by exploring our connection to others.

But now God has placed the members, each one of them, in the body, just as He desired.
—1 Corinthians 12:18

Read the following verses and put into your own words what they mean for your connection with other Christians.
1 Corinthians 12:21

_____

_____

1 Corinthians 12:24

_____

_____

2 Corinthians 8:14

_____

_____

The Scriptures make it clear that the reason we should be "zealous for *spiritual gifts*" is to edify the rest of the church (1 Cor. 14:12). While our *ministry-gift mixes* and *spiritual gifts* give us extra ability to witness to unsaved people, they are mostly spoken of in the Bible in relationship to the church. That is why, for the remainder of this chapter, we will focus on the church—what it is, how it works and why it is so important for you to become part of a local group of believers.

God chooses to accomplish much of His purposes on earth through His special designs for each of us. We should never forget, however, that He is also always at work to reshape and restore us in the process of our journey with Him. We minister to others while getting worked on by the Lord. Remembering this dual purpose will help us make more sense out of why God wants each of us to be part of a group of believers where we live.

The two primary passages that deal with *ministry gift-mixes* and *spiritual gifts* both do so in the context of church. (Read 1 Corinthians 12–14; Ephesians 4.) In both cases Paul explains the way things are supposed to work in church.

Take time to read 1 Corinthians 12–14 and Ephesians 4, but look at the specific verses that follow to get a feel for what Paul is saying:
1 Corinthians 12:7—What is the main purpose for our ministry uniqueness?

_____

_____

_____

1 Corinthians 14:5—On what basis are spiritual giftings rated—how impressive they seem when delivered, or the extent to which they edify the [local] church? On what basis should people in ministry be evaluated?

_____

_____

1 Corinthians 14:26—When is it that spiritual giftings seem to manifest themselves most? Does it seem like ministry should be more or less connected to a fellowship of believers?

_____

_____

Ephesians 4:11–12—These *ministry-gift mixes* are supposed to equip whom for what?

_____

_____

Ephesians 4:16—If everyone is functioning properly in their spiritual giftings, what will be happening to your church?

_____

_____

THE LOCAL CHURCH

Anywhere "two or three have are gathered in My [Jesus'] name," He is in our midst (Matt. 18:20). As temples of the Holy Spirit, we are always in the presence of the Lord, and He promised to be with us always—"even to the end of the age" (Matt. 28:20; 1 Cor. 6:19). So why does the Lord set us in a body of believers? Why should we bother being a part of a local church?

▲▲▲▲▲▲▲▲▲▲▲▲▲▲▲▲▲▲▲▲▲▲▲▲▲▲▲▲▲▲▲▲▲▲▲▲▲▲
God's plan for joining us together as believers
enables us to reproduce in others
the life that we have been given.
▲▲▲▲▲▲▲▲▲▲▲▲▲▲▲▲▲▲▲▲▲▲▲▲▲▲▲▲▲▲▲▲▲▲▲▲▲▲

To begin with, let's remember that the Lord's ways for us are designed to give us an advantage for life, not to take advantage of us. God's plan for joining us together as believers enables us to reproduce in others the life that we have been given. God "makes a home for the lonely" (Ps. 68:6), and He urges us to assemble together more and more, rather than less and less (Heb. 10:24–25). That is because there is special strength when we congregate with

Let us consider how to stimulate one another to love and good deeds, not forsaking our own assembling together.
—Hebrews 10:24–25

That they may all be one; even as Thou, Father, art in Me, and I in Thee, that they also may be in Us; that the world may believe that Thou didst send Me.
— John 17:21

other believers—a strength that comes from unity and spiritual communion. Jesus wanted His disciples through the ages to be one with each other and with Him (John 17:21).

HOW DO YOU KNOW WHEN YOU HAVE FOUND THE "RIGHT" CHURCH?

There is no such thing as a perfect church. Every church has its strengths and weaknesses, and all of them have problems. No one church is best for everyone, and that is part of why there are so many styles, varieties and denominational groups of churches. Depending on the doctrinal bent and leadership style of the main leader, churches will emphasize slightly different issues; no two churches will agree on everything. (Sounds like people, doesn't it?)

But given all the options of what church looks or sounds or feels like, how do you find where the Lord wants you to fellowship? Here are some helpful thoughts:

1. Ask for and expect the Lord to lead you. He does have a home in mind for you—a place of worship where you can grow spiritually and where you can contribute meaningfully.

2. Look for churches where Jesus is openly worshiped and celebrated. His name should be praised and called upon frequently, and each time you visit, you should hear Him proclaimed as the Savior, the Son of God.

3. Watch to see what gets studied and quoted: Is the Bible trusted as the Word of God for all generations? If any person or book is given an equal or greater weight of authority than God's Word, keep looking for a church.

4. Listen to the "voice" of the principal leader (pastor); does it speak to you personally and regularly seem to address the very issues or questions that have been on your heart? The teaching should resonate with your "daily" life.

5. Lastly, do you like going to this church? Do you leave feeling encouraged and built up? Do you look forward to what God will do in your life the next time you gather with the rest of the church? If not, keep looking.

By this all men will know that you are My disciples, if you have love for one another.
— John 13:35

Church is the perfect setting for us to experience and to offer the love that Jesus said would characterize His followers (John 13:35). The Lord Himself actively teaches us to "love one another" (1 Thess. 4:9), and that is not always an easy lesson for us to learn. If you do not have much ongoing contact with other believers—week after week—you can be fooled into thinking you are loving others (because you have little frustration or problem with any of them). But until you spend meaningful time with others, you do not really have much occasion to love them *in spite of* what they do.

Regular fellowship becomes a proving ground for love and forgiveness between Christians. Let's face it; following God is much easier when we are not being jostled by fellow travelers on the journey. We learned earlier that impurities in our own soul are the main culprits when it comes to why it is hard for us to love others (1 Pet. 1:22). Being with other Christians regularly will bring impurities to the surface of our heart. How sad that some believers imagine all the trouble with people in church is with the people in church. Some Christians are like kids with slivers in their hands—God asks them to hold still so He can get at the slivers with a pair of tweezers, but they keep pulling away and squirming around, hopping from church to church, getting more and more infected by the very stuff that could be extracted in fellowship. God uses church to increase our love and to refine us.

EFFICIENT INCUBATOR

The whole point of *church* is to make Jesus more meaningful and significant in people's lives. Church is helping those who already know Him become more like Him and introducing Him to people who aren't yet aware of His love for them. Church is an ongoing setting God places you in so that you can personally receive from and give to others. Feelings of guilt and rejection cripple ministry. Church provides a sense of belonging. Being accepted by a group and being honestly accountable to them will defeat most lies in your life.

> Since you have in obedience to the truth purified your souls for a sincere love of the brethren, fervently love one another from the heart.
> —1 Peter 1:22

> The whole point of *church* is to make Jesus more meaningful and significant in people's lives.

CHURCH AS AN INVITATION

Local churches extend an invitation with five parts to it. When looking for a church home, you should see to what extent a body of believers invites you to:

Receive mending and nurturing—to be valued for who you are, loved for who you are, recovered from where you have been and challenged to keep growing in the Lord.

Belong to a family—to be welcomed into a context of loving relationships between individual people who are part of something bigger than themselves, but still cherished as unique children of God.

Embrace a vision—to be told what God's particular assignment is for that church and how you personally—with your giftings—can add to the fulfillment of it as a truly contributing part.

Become a discipling disciple—to be shown how you can join the line of spiritual succession among believers, learning from mentors, then passing along what you learn to others.

Serve as a partner—to be mobilized for the sake of others, expending yourself and your resources in a way that gets you under people, not just sitting alongside them while you watch a few others perform.

The local church is the most effective environment for growing Christians in their walk with Jesus and for growing Christlike qualities in them. What they see modeled in the lives of older believers, as well as all the testimonies they hear, speeds up the process of maturity. When the whole church is assembled to receive instruction and teaching, one message gets transmitted to everyone at once, instead of needing to be repeated over and over. Of course, most of what the Lord teaches you will come as a result of your personal Bible reading and through informal conversations with other believers.

But in church you get exposed to perspectives and understandings God has already taught to your spiritual leaders. God is not interested in having each of us reinvent the spiritual wheel. He places ministries and people in each church to train and mend the people to be better able to minister to still others (Eph. 4:11–12). One-on-one discipleship is more effective than large-group teaching for getting at the specific issues of our lives, but such discipleship is even more effective within the context of an entire group of people who are being led in the same direction and being taught similar truths. People who walk with us closely over time, and who really get to know us, are very helpful in keeping us on track with the Lord.

The local church is much more than a building or a Sunday morning worship service. It is a vital part of the whole growth and development process in your spiritual life. Every church is unique. God gives each church a special collection of people and purposes. God has always dealt with people both *directly* and *indirectly* through His dealings with whole groups. Church provides additional confirmation, direction and instruction in your personal search for His will for your life. Not only can you be part of *church*, but you can also watch God add others to you.

The early church knew the importance of devoting themselves to prayer, teaching *and fellowship*. Church is the proving grounds for your spirituality. Church is more than the sum of its parts. Not only can you share in the larger joy and accomplishments of the whole congregation, but even the individual part you play has

> And He gave some as apostles, and some as prophets, and some as evangelists, and some as pastors and teachers, for the equipping of the saints for the work of service, to the building up of the body of Christ.
> —Ephesians 4:11–12

more significance than it would on its own. You will be encouraged not just by conversions, but by the transformations you witness in other people through the months and years together.

VALUE ADDED TO US

You and I cannot be well known to all the world; that is reserved for a very few, and almost none of them will be believers in Christ. What impresses God cannot impress the world. What impresses the world does not impress God. But within our local congregations, we can become well known and well loved. That is God's intent for us and for church. By our own example and by paying attention to what the Lord is teaching us, we can have a huge part in affecting the eternity of people around us (1 Tim. 4:16). Nothing has more meaning for our lives than that.

Read Philippians 2:17. At the end of Paul's life, his claim to fame is having been expended for others. Why does that give him such satisfaction?

_____

_____

Read John 10:17. What did Jesus mean by saying this? From what you have learned, what kind of life do we enjoy after laying down our life for others?

_____

_____

To make a difference in the lives of other people will cost us immeasurably—lots and lots of "labor" and agony (Col. 1:29). But the value it gives to our lives is even more boundless. That is why Paul says how gratified he was to be "poured out" and spent on behalf of his friends whom he had mentored (2 Tim. 4:6). He understood that there is no greater love than to willingly "lay down [our] life" for other people (John 15:13), and there is no truer way to follow Jesus' example in spending our life for what really counts (1 John 3:16). Jesus poured out His lifeblood as a sacrificial lamb, a servant scorned by the world, and because He did, we have an example to follow (Mark 14:24).

The whole reason the Lord has designed and gifted us as He has is so that we can be equipped for every good work for the sake of others. Nothing we can do—good or otherwise—will change the inestimable value He already places on us—we cannot add to the meaningfulness we already have in His life. Nothing of serving, attending church or ministering to others with our spiritual giftings

> Pay close attention to yourself and to your teaching; persevere in these things; for as you do this you will insure salvation both for yourself and for those who hear you.
> —1 Timothy 4:16

> We know love by this, that He laid down His life for us; and we ought to lay down our lives for the bretheren.
> —1 John 3:16

> And He said to them, "This is My blood of the covenant, which is poured out for many."
> —Mark 14:24

will increase our standing in His eyes. He has always looked upon us with unparalleled favor and grace.

But if you long to understand yourself better and to appreciate your value and meaning to the Lord, there is no better way than through serving a group of people with your unique combination of giftings. Being an effective, working, serving part of a local church will revolutionize how you see yourself. Once again, we see that all God asks us to do is really for our sakes, not His. That is the wonder of love.

> If you long to understand yourself better, there is no better way than through serving a group of people with your unique combination of giftings.

LET'S TALK ABOUT IT

▲ We are made in the image of God—the One who calls Himself "I AM." As a result of reading this chapter, how has your thinking changed as to the purpose for which God has designed and gifted you?

_____

_____

▲ What is our highest calling? Are there mottoes, phrases or principles you were either raised with or cherish that do not line up with the way the Bible instructs us to live in terms of serving or looking to the needs of others?

_____

_____

▲ Often it takes others to help show us really who we are and what attributes and qualities are unique to us. With a friend, look over the list of *ministry-gift mixes.* Talk about them together. What do you think are the one or two *ministry-gift mixes* that most describe who you are?

_____

_____

▲ What are the three main purposes of *spiritual gifts?* What *spiritual gift* do you think you have? Why?

_____

_____

YOUR TIME WITH GOD

For some people, belonging to a local church can bring feelings of fear or uneasiness. Why does God want us to be part of a local church? Are there specific reasons you may have for not wanting to participate in a local church? Take a moment to ask the Lord to answer any questions you have or speak to any places of fear or hurt in your life.

The Bible instructs us to ask God to give us *spiritual gifts*. Take a moment to pray a simple prayer like:

> *Lord, thank You that You are the giver of all good things. I thank You that You want to give me spiritual gifts to use as tools to help other people know You more. I ask that You would give me more of Your gifts and that You would teach me more fully how to use them.*
>
> *Show me, Lord, where I have sought from You only for my sake, and not for others. As You gift me, give me the attitude of a servant so that I can be more like Jesus. In His name, amen.*

Since He also wants us to have as much meaningful connection as possible with a group of believers, why not thank Him for your church? If you are not in a church, ask Him to lead you to the one He has in mind for you.

> *Lord, thank You for Your body here on earth. I praise You for the way You designed all of us to connect to each other, and I especially want to bless You for how You have blessed me with my church. Thank You for my leaders who care for me and for my fellow Christians. Alert me to ways I can serve them more.*

Or:

> *Father, I trust You and Your plan for me. You have said it is not good for us to be alone, and You intentionally made me to be connected to other Christians—for their sake, but also for mine. Lord, remove from me any fears or pride that keep me disconnected from the rest of the body. Set me where and how You think best. In Jesus' name, amen.*

Having Stories to Tell

HAVE YOU EVER TOTALLY SURPRISED YOURSELF BY KNOWING THE ANSWER TO A TRIVIA QUESTION? Some obscure fact about distant geography, the original title of an old band's first hit, the year in which a country won its only World Cup or the name of the nearest galaxy? Have you ever helped a young man fix the tie he is wearing for the first time in his life, or worked out an algebra problem for one of your kids? Have you ever told a friend about a great place to shop for clothes or given someone the name of the fragrance you were wearing? Have you ever been a bit shocked to realize that people took you seriously and actually acted on your advice?

If so, you have a sense for how God is going to use you throughout the rest of your life.

One of the most continual sources of amazement on your journey with the Lord will be the ways in which He involves and utilizes you—how He arranges for you to be right there at the perfect moment to say or do something that profoundly impacts another person. You will find yourself sharing simple things that create extraordinary changes. A small, heartfelt prayer for a coworker's housing need, the words of empathy spoken to neighbors in the midst of their teen's brush with the law, the natural telling of stories about Jesus' involvement in your own life—upon such unadorned doings the kingdom of God advances into one life after another.

Most of us are fairly intimidated by the prospect of ministry—doing something spiritual to or for others. Our minds race with disqualifying thoughts of how unworthy, how unprepared, how unknowledgeable or how hypocritical we are. Even our admiration for how God uses spiritual leaders can create a subtle suggestion for why we should not try to minister ourselves: "Oh, I wish so-and-so was here; she (he) would know what to do." *What do I know?* we think to ourselves. *I'm not doing that well myself, so how can I help anyone else?*

The reluctance to open our mouth or our life in Jesus' name can also come from plain old fear—we truly do not want to say or do the "wrong thing" and thereby ruin someone's life. We do not want the pressure of people looking to us as though we know what we're doing (when we don't). What could be worse than finding ourselves on stage, going completely blank on our lines in front of everyone. Blurting out trivia answers while sitting comfortably at home watching a TV game show is fun; being a contestant on the spot in the studio moments before the cameras roll is a bit more nerve-wracking. Any normal person will be assailed with thoughts of sur-render—*What do I know? I can't think of anything. What if I get asked a question I don't know? What do I know? What am I doing here? Oh no, Oh no . . .*

▲▲

The Holy Spirit will be like a secret radio piece in our ear, giving us the answers to all the questions.

▲▲

That is one of the reasons why Jesus tells us not to worry ahead of time what we should say or what we have to know (Matt. 10:19). The Holy Spirit will be like a secret radio piece in our ear, giving us the answers to all the questions; He'll tell us what to say and do. It will be our little secret—when everyone wonders how we knew to say what we said, we will know that we didn't. He did.

GRACE AGAIN

It's that grace theme again. God not needing us to do what needs doing; us not being able to do it on our own. God offering to do through us and for us; us saying yes or no to His invitation. We were saved by grace, and He wants us to live and help others live by that same grace. God is like a husband who buys an anniversary present weeks in advance, but who is so thrilled with the gift and how much he knows his wife is going to enjoy it that he cannot wait until the actual date of their anniversary to give it to her. Our Father has invited us to an incredible eternity where we will rule and reign with Him, but He does not want to wait until then to anoint us as His regents and agents. (Read Matthew 19:29; 2 Timothy 2:12.)

In fact, Jesus already held a service to deputize you (in proxy) for ministry, and He has spoken over you empowering words that authorize you to be in situations that you think you have no busi-ness being in:

> *And Jesus came up and spoke to them, saying, "All authority has been given to Me in heaven and on earth. Go therefore and make disciples of all the nations, baptizing them in the name of the Father and the Son and the Holy Spirit, teaching them to observe all that I commanded you; and lo, I am with you always, even to the end of the age."*
>
> —MATTHEW 28:18–20

But when they deliver you up, do not become anxious about how or what you will speak; for it shall be given you in that hour what you are to speak.
—Matthew 10:19

In other words, He says He has everything you are going to need. We are like friends who get asked to go fishing, and our only thought is that we have never gone fishing in our life and do not own any tackle. When we try to disqualify ourselves on that basis, our friend says, "Oh, I knew that. But I've got plenty of extra stuff; you won't need anything. I'll teach you how to fish . . . and I'll even bait your hook for you."

What's the best way to fish alongside your kind friend, who happens to be an expert fisherman, when you have never fished before? Do what he tells you and imitate his technique. It's simple and easy unless you feel that you should know more about fishing without asking, or you go off to try fishing by yourself, or you decide ahead of time (even before you cast your line in the water) that you won't catch anything anyway.

And suppose after several trips with you alone, your friend invites another person along; what's the best way to help this fishing novice become as good of a fisherman as you are? Repeat what your friend told you and continue to imitate his technique so that your new friend can imitate it as well. That is the sum total of ministry.

TEACH WHAT TAUGHT

Jesus simply says, "Teach others what I have taught you."

He does not say, "Teach everyone everything they are ever going to have to know about everything in My kingdom. And by the way, this is actually a test to see how well you have paid attention and how much you know as a result of all the time I have invested in training you." The curriculum we have to offer other people is very simple; it all comes from the truth of God's Word, of course, but the particulars and the order in which we are to share them with people do not follow a prescribed outline that everyone (except you) knows. Your commission is to tell the people around you what the Lord has done for you and what He has shown you. That is why He says we will be His "witnesses" (Acts 1:8; 2 Tim. 2:2).

Though there are "expert witnesses" in some trials, they are people who have no firsthand, personal knowledge of the events; their expertise is about other matters—such as ballistics. In the kingdom of God, eyewitnesses are the expert witnesses. You may not know all the stuff that others know, but you do know what you "have seen and heard" (1 John 1:3). Even if you cannot recall all that you have ever seen or heard in the Lord's dealings with you, when the opportunity arises or when a situation triggers your memory, you will be fully capable of giving your testimony and presenting the evidence from your life about what Jesus has done.

> Jesus simply says, "Teach others what I have taught you."

Not everyone will believe or want to hear your deposition or your eyewitness account of what you "have seen and heard" (Acts 22:15, 18). But many will. For the sake of the few, we tell the many. This incredible relationship with the Lord—based on His love, forgiveness, grace and kindness—is available to all people. We have been entrusted with the most fabulous "secret," the stunning and spectacular news of God's unquenchable affection for our neighbors and friends. He is not laying on us a heavy yoke of duty when He invites us to tell people what He has done for us. Rather, as we have been learning all along, He welcomes us to participate in things that will bring us indescribable joy (Acts 4:20).

▲▲

Jesus will teach you how to fish in the lives of people; all you have to do is follow His lead, His instructions and His technique of love-casting.

▲▲

Jesus will teach you how to fish in the lives of people; all you have to do is follow His lead, His instructions and His technique of love-casting (Mark 1:17). When you witness the life change in your friends, the rescue brought to your coworkers, the transformation of someone's mental or emotional condition, the total and absolute forgiveness of people's sins—you will have tasted the rarest delicacy on earth, the finest food imported from heaven—God's kingdom come; God's will being done . . .

My mouth shall tell of Thy righteousness, and of Thy salvation all day long; for I do not know the sum of them. I will come with the mighty deeds of the Lord GOD; I will make mention of Thy righteousness, Thine alone.

O God, Thou hast taught me from my youth; and I still declare Thy wondrous deeds. And even when I am old and gray, O God, do not forsake me, until I declare Thy strength to this generation, Thy power to all who are to come.

For Thy righteousness, O God, reaches to the heavens, Thou who hast done great things; O God, who is like Thee?

—PSALM 71:15–19

We cannot stop speaking what we have seen and heard.
—Acts 4:20

Follow Me, and I will make you become fishers of men.
—Mark 1:17